HARDPRESS.NET
HOME OF HARD-TO-FIND BOOKS

Essays by a Society of Gentlemen, at Exeter
by Hugh Downman

Address:
HardPress
8345 NW 66TH ST #2561
MIAMI FL 33166-2626
USA
Email: info@hardpress.net

54 ed. by K.

To be returned

ESSAYS, &c.

ings ein Sfini

H. Downman.

ESSAYS,

BY A

SOCIETY of GENTLEMEN,

AT

EXETER.

—— Sermone opus eſt modo triſti, ſæpe jocoſo,
Defendente vicem modo Rhetoris atque Poetæ
Interdum Urbani. ——

HORAT.

PRINTED BY AND FOR TREWMAN AND SON.

LONDON:
SOLD BY CADELL AND DAVIES, STRAND;
ROBINSONS, PATERNOSTER-ROW; AND
ROBSON, NEW BOND-STREET.

The Society to which Mr. Isaac Disraeli belonged published its first volume in 1796, under the title of "Essays by a Society of Gentlemen at Exeter." The "Advertisement" relates that the "Essays were read at the stated meetings of a society, originally united by private friendship;" that should the volume meet with approbation another would follow; and that "the names of the authors have been concealed; they would add no importance to truth, no acuteness to investigation—they would neither sanction error, nor enliven insipidity." The opening "Address to the Society" was delivered by its first President on the 28th June, 1792, and thus begins:—"I congratulate you on the establishment of a Society, which promises to be not only a source of entertainment, but of advantage. Being at least *lovers* of literature having *some* taste for the arts, *some* acquaintance with the sciences, it was natural that we should wish to meet together. It was natural to suppose that at such a meeting we should experience a conversation different from that of more promiscuous assemblies; a conversation in which wit might be joined with hilarity, learning with humour, information with decent gaiety; while properly trained, our minds would be subservient to that bond of politeness which consecrates the intercourse of scholars and gentlemen. A conversation, in which every individual might join without restraint, where arrogance would not with a loud voice usurp the prerogative of speech, nor vanity produce its long roll of tedious egotisms; where all would know when to speak, and when to be silent; a disclosure of sentiment, from which captiousness would be banished, where intentions would be understood; and neither a jest, nor a difference of opinion, wound the bosom of pride, or provoke the retort of anger. Such, or resembling these, were, I imagine, the ideas we formed to ourselves at the origin of this meeting, neither have we, nor is it likely that we shall be disappointed." This must, indeed, have been a model society of scholars and gentlemen. It appears that the members did not hold dry, formal meetings, but "a dinner, and the consequent enlivening glass," contributed to the success of their symposiums. They combined with "the feast of reason and the flow of soul," the severer delights of written essays, poetry, science, and criticism alike being pressed into the service of their agreeable réunions.

ADVERTISEMENT.

THESE Essays were read at the stated meetings of a society, originally united by private friendship. When a number of papers had accumulated, it was supposed, that a selection from them would not be uninteresting; and, as in a miscellaneous publication, no advantage could be attained by arrangement, the order, in which each member read an essay, has been adopted.

Should this volume meet with approbation, another will probably follow, at no great distance. The names of the authors have been concealed: they would add no importance to truth, no acuteness to investigation—they would neither sanction error, nor enliven insipidity.

EXETER, 21st July, 1796.

CONTENTS.

[vii]

CONTENTS.

ADDRESS to the SOCIETY.

READ JUNE 28th, 1792.

GENTLEMEN,

I CONGRATULATE you on the Eſtabliſhment of a Society, which promiſes to be not only a ſource of entertainment, but of advantage. Being at leaſt *lovers* of literature, having *ſome* taſte for the arts, *ſome* acquaintance with the ſciences, it was natural that we ſhould wiſh to meet together. It was natural to ſuppoſe that at ſuch a meeting we ſhould experience a converſation different from that of more promiſcuous aſſemblies; a converſation, in which wit might be joined with hilarity, learning with humour, information with decent gaiety; while properly trained, our minds would be ſubſervient to that bond of politeneſs which conſecrates the intercourſe of

B   ſcholars

scholars and gentlemen. A converfation, in which every individual might join without reftraint, where arrogance would not with a loud voice ufurp the prerogative of fpeech, nor vanity produce it's long roll of tedious egotifms; where all would know when to fpeak, and when to be filent; a difclofure of fentiment, from which captioufnefs would be banifhed, where intentions would be under-ftood; and neither a jeft, nor a difference of opinion, wound the bofom of pride, or pro-voke the retort of anger.

Such, or refembling thefe, were, I ima-gine, the ideas we formed to ourfelves at the origin of this MEETING, neither have we, nor is it likely that we fhall be difappointed.

Objections to it have, I underftand, arifen from the fecond part of our inftitution, by which we are not only expected to commu-nicate our thoughts in converfation, but in writing. Yet fo perfectly is each Member at liberty in the choice of his fubject, language, and form of compofition; to decline writing altogether, or having written, to withdraw his manufcript, that the chains are merely fhadowy and ideal.

The

The advantage, however, of writing is obvious. All men do not converfe with equal facility and pleafure; neither is the mode of our affembling, at leaft during a portion of the time, calculated for exertions of the mind which may be called ftrictly literary, or fcientific. A dinner, and the confequent enlivening glafs, point out the application of the few fhort hours allotted us, to other purpofes. To that mental relaxation which feverer ftudies demand; to that opennefs of heart which generates the ϵπϵα πϵροϵντα, flying in fucceffion from friend to friend : not to circumftantial narrations and details, and the production of arguments, uninterefting perhaps to the company in general, and unconvincing, from preffure of time, or inaccuracy of ftatement, to either of the antagonifts. But the man whofe thoughts do not flow fo readily in converfation, may by an effay in writing prove that he poffeffes both wit and humour; and ingenuity may produce it's arguments at leifure on any fubject not interdicted by our rules.

Permit me to congratulate you once more, on the diffufion of knowledge, which has enabled us to form a meeting of the liberal

nature

nature which our's promifes to affume. To enter on the general benefits attending this diffufion is not my intention ; it might lead to difputed points which ought to be avoided. But fo far perhaps I may deliver my opinion, that the extenfion of knowledge beyond certain limits is forbidden by that ftate of fociety to which it owes it's very exiftence ;—that where it is diffufed to a certain degree, it carries alfo it's correfpondent bleffings ; and that no ill effects are to be feared, except in the part where it's ftreams mingle with thofe of ignorance, when they may become the abundant fourcc both of private and political mifchief. Hence may originate fraud, chicanery, and that reftlefs turbulence of fpirit which murmurs at, and endeavours to fubvert the gentleft and beft conftituted authority.

Ingenuas didiciffe fideliter artes
Emollit mores, nec finit effe feros.

This diftich conveys an undoubted truth. But a particular emphafis is to be laid on the word *fideliter*, which admits of various degrees.

With refpect to *ourfelves*, though we may not perhaps think our original ftock of learning, or the fubfequent cultivation of our minds,

minds, adequate to our prefent wifhes, we fhould be loath to confefs, however we may fail in the minutiæ, or in certain branches, that we had not that general acquaintance with polite literature, which produces the effect mentioned by the poet ; and that we did not feel ourfelves better men, and better citizens.

At the inftitution of a fociety like ours, it may not be deemed improper to fay a few words on literary focieties in general.——When Bacon had declared war againft opinion, and fet philofophy on it's true bafis, that of invef-tigating facts, and drawing conclufions from them, it was plain to fee that an affociation of intellects was to be formed ; from a con-fcioufnefs that the multiplicity of facts re-quired, could not be the production of one, but of many. This drew the learned into a clofer union, and gave rife to literary repub-lics, in which the fpirit of rivalry was fubju-gated, envy deprefsed, yet a full latitude af-forded to virtuous emulation. The folitary tyranny and pride of learning was annihi-lated, and that ferocity of manners, which difgraced a Scioppius, a Luther, and even a Milton.——Hence is derived that modeft and

B 3   amiable

amiable fcepticifm, which fubmits every hypothefis to it's proper teft, and banifhes all
appearances of dogmatic vanity. In every art
and fcience proofs are required, not affer-
tions, or conjectures. Even the enquiries of
Locke were conducted, not by an affumption
of principles, but by really examining every
exifting operation of the human mind.——Thus
was the world emancipated from a flavifh de-
pendance on authority, and a diftant profpect
of truth and certaihty unfolded to our view.

Since the eftablifhment of the Royal Society, many others have been inftituted in
various parts of Europe; with thefe you are
doubtlefs well acquainted. They are, generally fpeaking, fubfervient to the interefts of
philofophy and learning; to thofe arts the
cultivation of which diftinguifhes polifhed
nations, and which are ufeful to human life;
or to thofe objects of tafte which agreeably
amufe, and abftract the mind from low cares,
and pleafures merely fenfual.——Befides the
more public and well-known academies,
many private literary meetings have exifted,
which have given birth to publications of various kinds.

Though

Though ingenious difcuffions on philofophy or the arts will be liftened to with pleafure, it is the fenfe of this fociety that it's
members fhould prefer polite literature and
criticifm : and while it interdicts no fpecies
of compofition in any language, no fubjects
but merely profeffional ones, perfonal fatire,
and thofe involving religious or political controverfy, wifhes them to turn their thoughts
to profe rather than to verfe.

Yet fuch are the charms of *real poetry*; fo
many and various are the elegancies which
may be conveyed in verfe, either in our own
or the dead languages, that I fhould be very
forry if any member withheld, from the fociety, compofitions of that kind, which, if he
pleafes, he is at liberty to withdraw, and
which voluntarily communicated will certainly
be confidered as a mark of attention.

To fay the members fhould prefer polite
literature and criticifm, is a feeming inaccuracy ; for the former, generally fpeaking, includes the latter. Yet as criticifm is employed in making obfervations on previous
fubjects, it may appear to be rather an adjunct than a principal ; a fcyon fprung from
the ftock of learning and genius ; their child,

not

not their co-equal ; and can only affimilate with its parents, when poffeffing fo much of their fpirit and liberality as to cenfure with candour, and praife with impartiality.

Having the honour of being your firft Pre-fident, I was unwilling to enter on that office in filence, though well aware how much more ably fome of you might have treated the fub-ject, and inftead of an imperfect fketch, de-livered an elegant and finifhed compofition. You will however, I truft, fuffer my good intentions to plead my excufe ; for though my deficiencies in other refpects may be con-fpicuous, I fhall yield to none in zeal and good wifhes for the fociety, and as far as lies in my power fhall endeavour to contribute to it's profperity and permanency.

LINES

L I N E S

Read at the Second Meeting of the Society.

———— *Sociali fœdere menfa.*

MILTON.

A THEME invites—a rugged word the theme,
That ne'er was heard by the Caftalian ftream :
Unclaffical, unmufical, unmeet
Ears charmed with Attic eloquence to greet.
A word, which echoed mid Parnaffus' fhades,
Had ftartled in their haunts the Aonian maids ;
And grated difcord on the fweeteft ftring
That deck'd the Lyre of their harmonious king.

   And yet the word this focial group endears ;—
They'll lend, if not their pleafed, their partial ears,
Whilft I thro' many a difficulty rub
To trace the birth, the progrefs of a CLUB.

Or,

Or, if you choose a less Vandalic name,
Call it SOCIETY—my theme's the same.

    The social passion is our noblest quality;
Nay, the first mark we gave of rationality.
For when, like beasts 'mid the wild forest, man,
A sullen, solitary savage ran;
A generous few, of more exalted mind,
By mutual converse brightened, and refined.
Some secret cave this club primordial knew,
Whence laws arose, and civil compact grew.
(For rules they framed, and articles they drew.)
At length resolved a brutal race to tame,
Who claimed, but ill deserved a brother's name,
They met, debated, then with one consent
Elected NIMROD their first President.
The great Symposiarch struck mankind with awe,
And made the vanquished world obey *Club-law*.

    Not, that when envy, hate, or interest binds
In some pursuit men's else-discordant minds,
The secret *junto* can with justice claim,
O CLUB! thy honest, and untainted name.

No *club* is theirs, but bafe *affociation*,

Who meet to plan the downfal of a nation.

The Roman band, which Cæfar doomed to die,

Call not a *club*, but bold *confpiracy*.

The Scythian dames, colleagued mankind to drub,

Was a moft foul *cabal*, but not a *club*.

When thieves affociate, or Banditti join,

Theirs is a *gang*, no *club*, nor theme of mine.

That concourfe to a different purpofe tends ;

To feftive, friendly, or inftructive ends.

To fpecify them more there's little need ;

All here concentrate—therefore I'll proceed.

 What time the Britons, truft fage Blackmore's lore,

Stripped naked Picts of vefts they never wore,

When good king Arthur reigned in ancient days,

(Long live his name adorned with laureled praife !)

A band of knights, the guardians of his throne,

Infpired with fouls congenial to his own,

To love, to loyalty, and honor ftable,

Proclaimed themfelves the *Club of the Round Table :*

For there in circling joy the moments flew ;

Envy, nor proud pre-eminence they knew.

When

When war's shrill tempest echoed thro' the land,
Around the king they took their honor'd stand :
The signal given, each couched his beam-like spear,
And scattered havoc thro' the ranks of war.
Brothers in arms—in peace : still side by side
They crowned the board with mirth,—they conquered,
  or they died.

 The well-earned honors of this friendly band
Increasing flew to many a distant land :
And oft the 𝔱𝔞𝔣𝔢𝔩 𝔯𝔬𝔫𝔡𝔢 inspired the strain
Of northern scald, or bard of bold Almaine :
Nor Italy denied her polished lays ;
And France, not then degenerate, sung it's praise.

 Our Saxon fathers, once this land's disgrace,
A godless, letterless and lawless race,
Quitting the carnage of the murderous field,
Obeyed the milder statutes of the *Guild*.
The social intercourse and converse gay
Wore, like collision, each rough point away.
The members met in the convivial hall,
And laughed and quaffed, and "merry beards wagged all."

       Hence

Hence *Chambers, Corporations* took their birth :
Still to live well is their great aim on earth.
And furely if good living merits praife,
Vaft is their worth who live well all their days !
Live, faid I ? to their Being's no ceffation :
Immortal clubs fhould be their appellation.
No member drops, but one his place fupplies ;
" They fall fucceffive, and fucceffive rife."
Thus ftreams, tho' changing ftill their waters flow,
Or to themfelves, or names no period know.
Hail favored race ! while death all elfe devours,
A *legal immortality* is yours !

   The Greek Sympofium claims my wandering lays,
The pride of Greece in her triumphant days.
Athens ! thy turrets to my view afcend,
Thy temples fwell, thy porticos extend.
Sages and heroes of exalted mind,
By wifdom tutored, and by tafte refined,
Life's cares forgotten, croud the feftive room,
And mid their laurel wreaths the rofes bloom.
" The feaft of reafon and the flow of foul"
Deck the gay board, and crown the fparkling bowl.

Mirth

Mirth fmiles, whilft wit the friendly jeft infpires,
Nor Virtue frowns, nor Decency retires.

   Hark ! Plato reafons, and his accents flow
Soft as Hyblæan fweets, or fleecy fnow.
Now Sophocles the tragic fcene difplays,
And Rapture liftens to his lofty lays.
See Xenophon, by " both Minervas crowned,"
And Clineas' beauteous fon in arms renowned ;
Yet not more dreadful in the bloody fray,
Than mild and pleafing in the feftive day.
On Socrates they look, an honored name,
" His country's brighteft glory and its fhame !"
His moral precepts fink into the mind,
And thofe who fought but mirth, inftruction find.

   Be ours to emulate the Attic feaft ;
Let wit to wine afford its higheft zeft :
Wit free from cenfure, mirth of malice void,
And learning not by pedantry alloy'd.

   Nor from thofe other clubs withdraw your praife,
They yield inftruction to more polifhed days.
Like Nimrod's noble band in times of yore,
Or Arthur's nobler knights who graced this fhore,

A

A focial phalanx, be it ours to fhare
(Should lettered foes affail with goofe-quill fpear)
The toils and dangers of a paper war.

Nor on your Saxon fires contemptuous fmile;
Theirs was the honeft heart that knew no guile.

Let us from them, what kingdoms cannot buy,
Adopt, the precious gem, SINCERITY.

No counterfeit can pleafe—that jewel gone,
Words bear no price—French pafte and Briftol ftone.

C. R. I.

A

A

VINDICATION

OF THE

CHARACTER OF *PINDAR*,

By a Tranflation of the Two Odes which have occafioned his being accufed
of mercenary Behaviour ;

AND REMARKS ON THEM.

PINDAR is certainly to us an obfcure
writer, not fo much from his language, or
any defect in the arrangement of his own
thoughts, as from a want of our knowing the
perfons, cuftoms, incidents, and mythological
circumftances to which he often alludes.
Many of them would in vain be fought for in
other Grecian writers, tho doubtlefs all were
well underftood by his contemporaries. No
really obfcure author could have gained fuch
celebrity. Tho his tranfitions are at times
feemingly abrupt, all of them, where we are
acquainted

acquainted with the particulars above mentioned, are intelligible, and we acknowledge
their propriety. We may therefore reafonably believe, that in paffages, the fenfe of
which is lefs apparent, we have only to blame
the lapfe of time, which has deftroyed the
clue to guide us in our refearches.

But, befides thefe caufes, men unendowed
with that penetration and enthufiafm which
ought to attend a commentator on Pindar,
have hazarded their conjectures, and delivered obfervations, which inftead of eluci-
dating the text, have ferved only to propagate
error. Thefe were the Scholiafts, who lived
at too diftant a period after their original, to
clear up the difficulties, which, at the time
he wrote, did not exift. Not only his poetical works, but his character hath in fome
degree fuffered from their ftupidity, and the
repetition of their *fabulæ aniles.* The mind
of man is exceedingly ductile, and an opinion however falfe, when once ftarted, and
circulated, it is not eafy to refute. The
truth perhaps is not enquired into—we give
credit and fubmit to the delufion.

On perufing Tafker's tranflation of the Ele-
venth Pythian Ode, and Weft's of the Second
Ifthmian,

Ifthmian, with their notes, what Englifh reader would not conclude that Pindar owned his writing for hire, and vindicated his previoufly bargaining for the price of his compofitions ? The charge was derived from the Scholiafts, and appears to have warped their minds to the fame opinion. Yet thefe odes not only demonftrate quite the contrary; but that Pindar treated the idea with contempt.

When Mr. Weft relates a tale from the Scholiaft on the Fifth Nemean Ode, who fays, Pindar afked three drachmas for it, a price fomewhat under two fhillings, and obferves that probably there is an error in the fum; he might with greater juftice have noticed the abfurdity of the ftory, which is indeed too ridiculous to be believed : as if the natural beginning of that ode could not have entered Pindar's mind, without a caufe fo idle and incredible.* For, according to

---

* Fixed on it's bafe, unknown to other lands,
  The ftatue of the Sculptor ftands,
     I form not one of thefe ;
  In every veffel, from Ægina's fhore
  Sail forth my Ode ! thy theme to pour
     Throughout the liftening world—brave Pytheas' praife :
  Who in the Nemean games, around
  His forehead the Pancratic wreathe hath bound.

the

the Scholiaſt, Pytheas at firſt refuſed the price aſked by Pindar, thinking it better to purchaſe a ſtatue, but afterwards changed his opinion. Yet this weak traditionary legend has perhaps contributed to pervert the language, and diſtort the ſentiment in theſe odes to a meaning never intended, a meaning which Pindar himſelf cautiouſly endeavoured to obviate.

That he received preſents, and valuable ones, from thoſe whom he celebrated, is very probable. That he might be envied on this account, and that his detractors might accuſe him of being mercenary, is likewiſe probable. But that he would have deſpiſed himſelf had he meanly bargained for a price, will appear an evident truth to thoſe who read without prejudice, follow the natural train of ſentiment, and compare the different parts of the compoſitions with each other.

The error concerning the tendency of the ſecond Iſthmian Ode was of old date, for the Scholiaſt tells us " Calliſtratus thought that Pindar not having received a ſufficient reward from Xenocrates on account of his parſimony, addreſſed his ſon Thraſybulus, and compoſed the verſes for him inſtead of his father. That

C 2   all

all which is inferted about money is a kind
of complaint; as if he was defirous, the fon
fhould give him a reward equal to his defert."

The Scholiaft as well as Calliftratus was
furely not only blind to the beauty of the firft
ftanzas, and mifapprehended the Poet's intention, but could not have read the third
antiftrophe, which fhews that Xenocrates was
generous even to profufion. Befides, as all that
relates to him is in the paft tenfe, it is likely
that he was dead before the ode was written.

The love of country; the praifes of friendfhip, hofpitality, truth, wifdom; the enthufiaftic defire of fame; a deteftation of riches
if improperly ufed; contentment derived
from the beft fources, rectitude of conduct,
and integrity of manners; are the themes on
which Pindar delights to dwell. He is not
only the fublimeft, but the moft moral Poet
of antiquity. It is impoffible to read his odes
without a confcioufnefs that the writer warmly
felt every amiable, as well as exalted emotion
of the human mind. And I have no doubt
that his encomiums owed their luftre, in the
eyes of his countrymen, not more to the fuperiority of his numbers, than to the intrinfic
excellence of his character.

THE

THE

ELEVENTH PYTHIAN ODE.

To THRASYDÆUS, a THEBAN YOUTH,

Victorious in the FOOT-RACE.

ARGUMENT.

PINDAR, after an invocation to the God-
deffes of Thebes, having mentioned the victory of Thrafydæus in the country of Phocis,
where Pylades once reigned ; digreffes to the
ftory of Oreftes.   From this digreffion he
takes an opportunity of vindicating his own
character, and afferting his independence.
He then returns to his fubject, notices his
Hero's victory, and thofe of his anceftors ;
concluding with his opinion of riches, and
the praife of a happy mediocrity.

STROPHE

ODE.

STROPHE I.

Daughters of Cadmus ! Semele ! to whom
Was given to fhare the Olympian dome !
Fair Ino ! by the Nereid train
Hail'd a bright Sifter of their liquid reign !
    To where the ftreams of Melia flow
Oh ! haften with the imperial Dame
Who bore Alcides, genuine Heir of fame !
To where the golden tripods fhine
Within the fanctuary divine,
    Moft dear to Phœbus, bender of the bow !

ANTISTROPHE I.

By him Ifmenian named ; the place
His true prophetic anfwers grace.
    Offspring of Harmony ! e'en now
      Affembled Heroine Forms draw near,
Hither your native band they call,
    Attentive to their ardent vow
      The folemn invocation hear !
That when the incipient fhades of evening fall,

                              Your

Your tuneful voices you may raife
To facred Themis, Pytho's praife,
And, where no falfhood takes its birth,
Delphi, aufpicious center of the earth.

EPODE I.

Seven-gated Thebes your favours thus fhall blefs,
And Cirrha's games your wonted care confefs,
   In which, reluming his paternal fires,
     Young Thrafydæus to the altar bore (1)
Renown's confpicuous meed,
   The third rich trophy added to his Sire's : (2)
Inwreathed with conqueft on the fertile plains
     Govern'd by Pylades of yore,
Whofe hofpitably-kind domains
Embraced Oreftes of Laconian feed.

STROPHE II.

Whom, while his mighty Father bled
   By Clytemneftra's direful hand,
His prudent Nurfe, Arfinoe, led
   Far from the gloomy fcene, and treacherous land.

                       What

What time the Woman of relentlefs mind,
 Caffandra, daughter of the Dardan King,
To Acheron's infernal fhades confign'd,
 Deftined with Agamemnon's Ghoft to wing
Her flight, and feek the dreary flood,
(3) Forced by the keen-edged brafs, diftain'd with royal blood.

ANTISTROPHE II.

Her thoughts did Vengeance thus provoke,
 Becaufe befide Euripus' wave,
Her Iphigenia yielding to the ftroke,
 Far from her country found an early grave?
Or, like the wanton Heifer fired,
 Becaufe in foreign bed her foul defired
Nocturnal, guilty joys to fhare?
 Detefted deed, e'en of the youthful fair (4)
Bound by the holy nuptial tye,
 Nor could fuch crimes abhorr'd in mute oblivion lye.

EPODE II.

Officious is the tongue of fame,
Arraigning multitudes divulged her fhame;

For

For Envy ſtings with ſurer force
The offending Great ; in humbler courſe
The Lowly act their deeds impure,
The Sin is, like themſelves, obſcure.
Thus, after all his labours paſt,
 To proud Amyclæ now return'd,
The Son of Atreus breathed his laſt,
 While Greece her Chief of Heroes mourn'd.

STROPHE III.

And with him fell, to ſavage hands betray'd
The beauteous, and prophetic Maid,
In vain for Helen's cauſe he fought,
And ſpoils of glorious victory brought,
Snatch'd from the effeminate and baſe,
When blazing fires inwrapp'd Troy's hated race.
But while the rays of early morn
 Beam'd on his graceful head,
To aged Strophius' friendly manſion borne,
 And at the feet of high Parnaſſus bred,
Oreſtes flouriſh'd ; ere in fated time
The avenging ſword his Mother's crime

        Amply

Amply rewarded : while infteep'd in gore
Ægyftus prefs'd the ground, her luftful Paramour.

ANTISTROPHE III.

Surely my feet excurfive ftray,
  Leaving the certain path behind,
Illuded by a third deceptive way : (5)
  Or fome impetuous wind
Hath driven me from my deftined port,
As the light bark, of furious ftorms, the fport.
Thine is the deed, Enthufiaft Mufe ! (6)
Nor I thy myftic power refufe.
Wert thou impell'd by fordid gain,
For filver hire to pour thy vocal ftrain,
Not thus the devious verfe fhould flow,
  Each interwoven theme fhould tend
  With added praife my Heroes to commend,
With added wreathes to grace each favour'd brow.

EPODE III.

To dignify the Sire's exalted name,
Tranfcendent in the Pythic game ;

Or

(7) Or Thrafydæus ; while around his head
 Frefh-won, refplendent glories fpread—
 Now matchlefs in unwearied force,
  Inftinct with victory the chariots roll,
 And in Olympia's highly-honour'd courfe
  Beaming triumphant light their fteeds attain the goal.

STROPHE IV.

 Now ftripp'd, on Pytho's facred ground,
 As fwift they fcour the maze around,
 Their fpeed the Grecian throng with envy fpies,
 With fhame their vanquifh'd Rivals cede the prize.—
(8) Yet, I contemn not wealth which Heaven beftows,
 And venerate the fountain whence it flows !
 But every paffion of my mind
  To what unblamed I might acquire,
 Was ever from my youth confined,
(9) Tó the poffeffion of the tuneful lyre.
 And when the moderate ftation I furvey'd,
  Of every civil good, the beft,
  That competence with peace was bleft,
 In lafting beams of happinefs array'd,

I could not but lament the fate
Of Princely power, and Regal ſtate.

ANTISTROPHE IV.

The virtues of inferior life
No torturing, ſecret ſting contain ;
　If e'er renounced for envious ſtrife,
Man ſuffers voluntary pain.
　Who, with tranquillity his Friend,
Hath reach'd the height of bliſs below,
Deſtined no pride or inſolence to know,
　He, when this mortal life ſhall end,
May ſcorn the horrid gloom of death,
Serenely bright reſign his breath,
Leaving his race, the ſweeteſt gift of fame,
The inheritance of his unſpotted name.

EPODE IV.

This gift Iölaus bade his ſons to ſhare,
Iphicles' illuſtrious Heir ;
This honourable boon divine
The Brothers of celeſtial line,

Caſtor,

Caſtor, for arduous deeds renowned,
And Pollux with each royal virtue crowned,
Who to Therapne's ſhades retreat, (10)
Or ſeek by turns Olympus' lofty ſeat.

THE

SECOND ISTHMIAN ODE.

To THRASYBULUS,

On occasion of a Victory obtained in the CHARIOT RACE by his
Father XENOCRATES of AGRIGENTUM.

ARGUMENT.

PINDAR having praised the ancient Poets,
who sung as inspired by Love, without pros-
tituting their talents for gain ; mentions with
scorn the saying of an Argive, " Money makes
the Man," who himself experienced the loss
of money and friends together——pays a compliment to Thrasybulus, whose mind was
better informed ; and plainly, tho briefly, in-
sinuates that he sings the actions of Xenocrates
not for hire, but because they were illustrious and deserved it. He celebrates these
actions ; then having praised him for his virtues and hospitality ; encourages his son not

to

to conceal them, nor his ode, through fear
of exciting envy: for his ode, he tells him,
was not intended to be confined to one place,
but to make known the merits of his Father
to the world. And this he bids Nicafippus,
his meffenger, recommend to Thrafybulus
his hoft, or rather in my opinion, and as I
have tranflated it, Gueft.

ODE.

STROPHE I.

Whoe'er in days of old
The Mufes' car O Thrafybulus·! prefs'd,
   (The Mufes wreathed with radiant gold
Who all their fervid hearts poffefs'd)
Moved on; and from the eager lyre
Darted the ftrains of amorous defire;
Strains, on which nectared fweetnefs hung;
Praifing the beautiful and young,
The plants by high-throned Venus graced,
And fruit of ripening bloom, delicious to the tafte.

ANTI-

ANTISTROPHE I.

The Mufe from fordid lucre free,

Afk'd then no mercenary fee.

Unbribed her lip, nor tinged with filver hue,

   Difdaining Flattery's honey-breathing throng,

Terpfichore, to virtue only true,

   Poured no luxurious, foftly-foothing fong.

EPODE.

How changed! She now the Argive's maxim loves,

And his the teft of merit fhe approves ;

" Wealth, wealth alone is man complete."

He fpoke, and with his gold, beheld his friends retreat. (11)

(12)But thine is Wifdom's better part—

   Nor actions mean, to fame unknown,

Am I compell'd with panegyric art

   In fabulous and purchafed verfe to crown.

I fing confpicuous deeds,

The Ifthmian triumph, and victorious fteeds.

The triumph, Neptune's favourite care,

   Who gave Xenocrates to bind

   The wreathe with Doric Parfley twined

                                Around

Around his flowing hair :
The chariot and tranfcendent man to adorn,
Of Agrigentum's eyes the rifing morn.

STROPHE II.

On whom in Crifa's game
Wide-ruling Phœbus fhed unrivall'd fame.
Nor, where with beauty all *her own* array'd,
   In gorgeous *Athens* he exalted ftands,
   Mock'd he the Driver's irritating hands,
Well-pleafed his car-directing fkill to aid,
When with nice fway, or loofing every rein,
He wing'd the panting Courfers o'er the plain.

ANTISTROPHE II.

Him too the Heralds of the facred rite,
   Priefts of Saturnian and Elean Jove,
Confcious applauded ; as with warm delight
   His friendfhip they recall'd, and generous love.
(13)Hailing Nicomachus with grateful mind,
   For him, the complicated found
   Of inftrument and voice they pour'd around ;
For him, on victory's golden lap reclined,

D

In

In their peculiar feat, the green abode,
Sacred to Heaven's great Sire, Olympia's Guardian God.

EPODE II.

Where mingled with immortal praife
   Ænefidamus' Sons have often come ; (14)
   Nor is to thee unknown the lofty dome
(15)O Thrafybulus ! nor the enchanting lays
   Of choral harmony, divinely fweet,
   Nor fongs to thrill the foul, which rapturous Bards repeat.

STROPHE III.

For rock, nor difficult accefs, appears
To him, who from the *Mufes* bears
Their honours to the heroic few
To whom poetic gifts are due.
Urge on who lift with vigorous might
The Difcus in it's rapid flight !
Xenocrates hath paft their fartheft goal
In every gentler virtue of the foul.

ANTI.

ANTISTROPHE III.

When in the public haunts he ſtood
Revering crouds his face with tranſport view'd.
Studious to nurſe the generous ſteed,
To cultivate the games by Greece decreed,
  With ſolemn rites adored
 For each ethereal Power to ſpread
The hallow'd feaſt ; no furious gale
  E'er tempted him with anxious dread
  Around his hoſpitable board
To furl the expanded ſail :
 But in the Summer's calmer day
To Phaſis, rich with golden ore,
 When Winter reign'd with bluſtering ſway,
He ſteer'd his courſe to Nilus' fertile ſhore.

EPODE III.

 Oh ! let not then his Son in ſilence hide,
(Becaufe pernicious thoughts infeſt
And hang round Envy's venom'd breaſt)
 But publiſh'd with decorous pride
 The untainted virtues of his Sire reſound !

Nor let these hymns oblivious sleep,
Unchain'd by me, and form'd to keep
   No stationary bound.
This, Nicasippus, fail not to commend
To my accustomed Guest, and ever-valued Friend.

NOTES.

NOTES.

(1) THO Pauw in his notes on Pindar, P. 240, ftiles Thrafydæus and his Father *Cives*, and *Privati*, it does not appear, that in antiquity of family, or extenfive poffeffions, they might not have equalled any inhabitants of Thebes.

(2) Pindar's fubject was the praife of Thrafydæus; he mentions his victory, and two victories of his anceftors. Thefe he ought to have proceeded to celebrate, had he not digreffed on the ftory of Oreftes. The connection is flight; but he chofe to expatiate; and when he returns to his fubject, makes a fine ufe of the digreffion in the third antiftrophe. There may however be more propriety in it than hath generally been imagined, if we confider that Pindar's odes were religious as well as laudatory; that Agamemnon and Oreftes were deified heroes, and perhaps had temples in Phocis.

(3) Agamemnon was killed by Clytemneftra with a facrificing ax; in that early

period,

period, inftruments in general were made of brafs.

(4) This fhould have occafioned no diffi-culty to a tranflator. Lay a ftrefs on ναις, and the fenfe is plain. "Adultery is a de-teftable crime when the paffions are moft ftrong, even in *young* wives, how much worfe then in Clytemneftra who had been *fo long* married!"

(5) As if a traveller in a place where three roads meet, fhould take that which would lead him out of his way; or a fhip be forced from its track by a ftorm; fo Pindar fays was his digreffion.

(6) Μοισα το δε τεον. Ει μισθω
συνεθευ παρεχειν
φωναν υπαργυρον, αλλοτ' αλλα χρη ταρασσεμεν,
η πατρι Πυθιονικω
το γε νυν, η Θρασυδαιω &c.

The common literal tranflation is, Mufa! hoc quidem tuum eft. Si mercede pacta es præbere vocem argento-conductam, aliàs alia oportet commifcere, aut Patri Py-thionico nunc, aut Thrafydæo, &c.

Benedict's paraphrafe, or tranflation of the Greek Scholiaft on this paffage, is as follows: "At vero O Mufa, fiquidem reverâ operam
tuam

tuam ut victorem Thrasydæum laudes, pacta mercede locasti, debes nunc encomio tota incumbens modo hoc, modo illud ei inferere, vel in Patris Thrasydæi Pythiorum victoris, vel in ipsius Thrasydæi laudem."

I should paraphrase it in this manner:—O Musa, hæc tua est digressio. Si autem mercede pacta es, aliter scribendum est, non liberè ut tibi placet, de Agamemnone, vel Oreste, vel quovis alio subjecto; sed nunc hoc, nunc illud inferere de Thrasydæi Patre, vel ipso Thrasydæo.

Allowing this to be the real and natural meaning, Pindar not only disclaims any bargain for a reward, but introduces the praise of his heroes in an oblique manner, with much greater delicacy and beauty, than if the panegyric had been more plain and direct.

Mr. Banister, who, after I had written on this subject, published translations of some of the odes of Pindar, and of the XI. Pyth. among the number, sanctions likewise the common error.

ANTISTROPHE III.

" But in digreſſive ſtrain I widely ſtray
  Far from the glorious ſubject of my ſong,
Through unfrequented paths I take my way
  By ſome new object borne along,
      Driven by every riſing gale ;
      Thus o'er the ſwelling ſurges ſail
Ships, their oars and pilots loſt.
  But come, O Muſe ! thy art divine
Muſt guide me from the dangerous coaſt,
  And bid in poliſh'd numbers ſhine
The honours of his race and name,
  Whoſe generous temper will reward our pains ;
  Then raiſe the voice, and ſwell the raptur'd ſtrains,
To fill the records of immortal fame."

Baniſter's Tranſlation of Pindar, p. 83.

Here the obnoxious paſſage is delicately expreſſed. The language of Mr. T. is more
exceptionable.

ANTI-

ANTISTROPHE III.

" But oh ! my Friends, where does my fancy ftray ?
Bewildered in the three-fold way :
Full of the mufe-infpiring God
From the right path thy devious feet have trod ;
Thus when oppofing winds conflicting roar,
The bark is driven wide from it's expected fhore.
O Mufe, return ! thy champion's praife rehearfe
In the *filver-purchafed verfe* ;
For thy Pythian-victor's fire,
And Thrafydæus' felf, fing thou *the fong of hire.*"

Tafker's Tranflation of Pindar, p. 74.

So convinced is Pauw of the injury done to Pindar's character, that he arbitrarily alters the text. Notæ in Pind. P. 240.

" Mufa Pindari non erat venalis, et hæc ipfa in medio civitatis gaudio civis cantabat civibus, privatus privatis : Tales enim Thrafydæus et Pater : Peffimi Grammatici, qui ubique Pindari φιλαργυριαν crepant, peffime ου in ιι mutarunt. Apparet etiam ex cohærentia loci, quæ fic optima : nam poft ου μισθω τυ συνηθιυ, appofitiffime fequitur nunc αλλ' αλλα χρη ταρασσωμιν." He inferts ου inftead of ιι and τω before

before συνεθευ, while for αλλοτ' αλλα he reads αλλ'
αλλα.

Heyne, in his edition of 'Pindar, thus remarks on the criticifm of Pauw.

" Etfi quam turpe illâ ætate habitum fuerit
mercenariam victori celebrando operam præbere, ignoro ; probo tamen in Pauwii emen-
datione illud, quod improbam Grammatico-
rum fraudem detexit, labem avaritiæ Pindaro
ubique inurentium. *Sed interpolatione receptæ
lectionis rem confici nolim.*"

If my interpretation be a juft one, the fenfe
is not only clear, but the common reading
hath more propriety and elegance than Pauw's
emendation.

In his Additamenta, P. 101, Heyne likewife
propofes an alteration for the fake of the meter, which as it does not greatly change the
fenfe, I have no objection to. He reads τε
συνεθευ, and for αλλοτ' αλλα puts αλλα σε. His explanation of the paffage is not, in my opinion,
admiffible.

" Si pacta effes Mufa carmen (fi vocem
venalem mercede locaffes) nil impediret quo-
minus modo hâc, modo illâ digreffione ute-
reris; at nunc in honorem Thrafydæi, ejufq.
patris, hymnum condis, qui felicitate et gloriâ
                                            florent,

florent, adeoq. materiem carmini præbent
fatis amplam." He proceeds, " Omiffum erit
e more poetarum μαλλον, αλλα μαλλον, η, *aliena
potius,* quam quæ in honorem patris P. dicta
funt. Sufpiceris tamen in η latere μη pro αλλα
μη πατρι Π. *non autem cum celebrandus fit pater
victoris et victor ipfe :* qui proprias laudes fup-
peditant."

This latter part of Heynes' remarks is very
forced. I do not fee the juftice of fuch an
interpretation, even fuppofing we read μη.
Neither does it appear how a perfon bribed to
celebrate the praifes of a man fhould be permitted to digrefs rather than one who was not
bribed. Nor how his digreffion was excufed,
by faying he had ample materials for his ode
without it. Nor how it would become him
to treat of other fubjects in preference to the
honour of his patron who had paid for the
encomiums. Befides, would not Pindar have
condemned himfelf, if immediately after fo
long a digreffion he had written, " O Mufe,
if thou wert hired, there would be no impe-
diment to thy making digreffions ?" Whereas
the fact was, that his digreffing, as he pleafed,
fhewed clearly that he was a free agent, un-
purchafed, and therefore could model his
compofitions

compositions in any manner moſt agreeable to himſelf.

(7) Pindar now alludes to the victories of his heroes; for tho I have ſaid "tranſ_cendent in the Pythic game," this is only a circumlocution for the epithet πυθιονικαν. Theſe victories were the late Pythian one of Thraſydæus, the chariot-race at Olympia, and the foot-race of his Father in the Pythian games. The plural number is only uſed poetically.

(8) We muſt keep in our minds the idea of " ει μισθω συνεθευ," which is uppermoſt in the poet's thoughts, when after the few, but ex_preſſive lines appropriated to his heroes, and as it were caſually introduced, he goes on with θεοθεν τραιμαν καλων &ε.

If my Muſe is hired (ſays Pindar) ſhe ought to dwell on the glorious actions of Thraſydæus and his anceſtors; on the Olympian, and Pythian victories. I ſhould value riches indeed proceeding from the gods (not acquired by baſe means) wiſhing through my life only for what it was lawful to obtain."

(9) This

(9) This verfe is not warranted by the original, tho the fentiment may be fairly deduced from it.

All that Pindar fays of a middle ftation refers to himfelf, and his own opinion, naturally confequent from what precedes; to fhew his content, and abhorrence of acquiring money by difhonourable actions.

(10) Therapne was a vale in Laconia where Caftor and Pollux were born; and a temple was confecrated to them in that place. The Englifh language would fcarcely bear the Greek quantity of Iolāus, and Iphīcles in this ftanza.

(11) Mr. Weft confiders " the beginning of this ode as containing a fort of apology for the poet's taking money for his compofitions. He likewifes excufes his conduct, as the perfons celebrated came from countries very remote, and no way related to Thebes, Pindar's birth-place; fo that he could have no manner of concern in their victories, and confequently no inducement either public or private to write on fuch fubjects without being rewarded for his trouble." Is fame then nothing? the " virum volitare per ora" which Pindar appears to be fo fond of? If he fpread
the

the reputation of thefe people through Greece,
was not his own diffufed with theirs? Befides
every Greek had an intereft in the games,
and a victory obtained in them was confidered
as the height of human felicity. Mr. W. too
fays " the fame beftowed by Pindar on thefe
perfons could not be very great, fince it cannot be fuppofed that he had a perfonal knowledge of moft of them, and muft have learned
particulars attending their circumftances, genealogies, &c. from themfelves, their friends,
or countrymen." But perhaps people, and
efpecially thofe in fuperior ftation, who regu-
larly attended the games from father to fon,
were better known than he imagines. As to
the value of Pindar's praifes, Horace efti-
mates an ode from him above the worth of an
hundred ftatues. Voluntary prefents might
have been given to Pindar, but there is a wide
difference between receiving them, and either
afking for money, or previoufly bargaining for
a particular fum. The thought of acting in
fuch a manner Pindar certainly defpifed.
Pauw in a note on the firft antiftrophe of this
ode exclaims with much enegy, " Nonne
calumniatores funt peffimi, qui optimo &
generofiffimo vati φιλοκερδιαν fordidam exprobare
audent :

audent; hæcce legentes contra inimicos vitio
ifto inquinatos data opera haud dubie fcripta?"

(12) ισοι γαρ ων σοφος.   ωκ αγνωτ' ανδω,
Ισθμιαι ιπποισι νικαν, &c.

Sed enim es Sapiens.   Non ignota cano,
(Cano) Ifthmiam equis victoriam, &c.

Pindar's ideas here are rapid; and he requires a paraphrafe.   I have given that in
my tranflation, which feems to me naturally
to arife from the mode of expreffion, as well
as to agree perfectly with the liberality of the
preceding fentiments.

· WhyHeyne fhould render χρηματα χρηματ'Ανηρ,

Pecunias! Pecunias! Heus Homo!——
or, ωκ αγνωτ' ανδω, nec ignaro cano, I fee no
good reafon.   The firft is plainly the faying
of the Argive, and is beft, and moft intelli-
gibly rendered in the common manner.   The
latter is an inelegant tautology.   "But you
are wife, I fing not to one who is ignorant."

The fame words are thus paraphrafed by
Benedict in his edition.

" Quo autem hæc tendant, fcilicet ad mer-
cedis petitionem, lubens dicerem, nifi tibi
Sapienti verbum fat effet."   What a contradiction to all which goes before!   What a
forced conftruction!   While a pitiful archnefs
and·

and cunning is afcribed to Pindar, totally
different from the whole tenor and genius of
his poetry, and which would have difgraced
the meaneft writer.

The " εσσι γαρ ων σοφος" was the ftumbling
block. For in another note Benedict fays,
" Attamen ejufmodi funt Poetæ verba, ut
laudes perfonæ potius tractare, quam merce-
dem exigere videatur : *quanquam verbum Sapienti fat eft.* This is a fneer which affects not
the author, but the critic.

Pauw propofes altering the text in this paffage likewife. P. 345. He places a full ftop
after εκ αγρωτ' αειδω, and inftead of Ισθμιαν ιπποισι
νικαν, reads Ισθμια δ'ιπποισι νικα. His words afford a curious fpecimen of his contempt for
others, and the opinion he entertains of his
own fagacity.

" Εσσι γαρ ων σοφος, εκ αγρωτ' αειδω] Hæc pef-
fimè copulantur cum fequentibus : Diftin-
guendum eft τελεως poft αειδω : et hæc cum
emphafi Thrafybulo dicit, cui non ignota
erat Mufa illa venalis, ut fic acrius adverfa-
rios, et eorum fordes infectaretur : Nihil
apertius, aut convenientius : Vide tamen quid
boni interpretes, quorum me miferet pudet-
que. Mox novo plane fpiritu ad rem accedit,
et

et animo exultante canit, Ισθμιαν ιπποισι νικαν, Ταν Ξενοκρατει Ποσειδαων &c. Et in his error est scripturæ, quem olfacere possunt omnes, qui nares modo admovent propius paulo: Scribe, et scribe ocyus, Ισθμια δ' ιπποισι νικα, Ταν Ξενοκρατει Ποσειδαων &c. *Isthmia est victoria currulis, quam ego celebro, quam præbuit Neptunus Xenocrati!* Locus est elegans, & vere Pindaricus."

As I do not agree with Pauw in this opinion, nor see the necessity of altering the words, or adopting his punctuation, let us once more paraphrase the passage.

Sed enim Tu sapiens longe aliter cogitas; non ad pecuniam, sed Viros ipsos spectas. Neque ego obscura, aut in angulo latentia, cano facta, uti Vates lucri cupidus, cujus laudes ab illis qui non famam merentur, argento sunt emptæ; sed clàrissima, omnibusque nota, viz. Isthmiam victoriam, &c.

Pauw's observation, " Hæc cum emphasi Thrasybulo dicit, cui non ignota erat Musa illa venalis," ascribes the same kind of archness to Pindar, which I noticed in the remark of Benedict. *" You understand me; you know the man I allude to."* Surely this is neither elegant nor Pindaric. With the spirit of

E   Lyric

Lyric poetry, the author in general terms reprobates the venality of modern bards.

(13) The victories here ascribed to Xenocrates are the Isthmian, Pythian, Athenian, and Olympic. Nicomachus was the driver of his chariots when the Athenian and Olympic prizes were won.

(14) Ænesidamus was the father of Theron and Xenocrates.

(15) Thrasybulus (as appears by this sentence) had been in Greece, and attended the games, perhaps repeatedly, if not a victor himself; at these times it is not improbable that he might have visited Pindar. See likewise the VI. Pythian ode.

(16) Mr. W. in his translation of this Antistrophe leaves out all reference to *Phasis* and the *Nile*, and says the original is so obscure, that the learned will pardon him, if he has not hit on the right meaning. The metaphor, it must be confessed, is a violent one, as are many of Pindar's. Xenocrates' table is a well-furnished vessel: it's sails are spread both in fair and stormy weather, i. e. in good or evil fortune. And as a real ship made it's voyage for the riches of Phasis in summer, to Egypt in winter, so in prosperity or adversity

fity Xenocrates fpared not his treafure, nor relaxed his hofpitality.

(17) It is manifeft that this Ode was a free-will offering from Pindar to Thrafybulus. That he was afraid he might conceal it from modefty, or fome prudential reafon. Thrafybulus did not covet it. What would a candid mind fuppofe Pindar's motive to be? A return, perhaps, of favours received from the father, a tribute of gratitude to his memory, and of friendfhip to the fon.

T. V.

SOME

SOME REMARKS

ON THE

EARLY POPULATION of EUROPE,

And particularly of ITALY.

" Salve, magna Parens frugum, Saturnia tellus
" Magna Virûm : tibi res antiquæ laudis & artis
" Ingredior, fanctos aufus recludere fontes."

Georgic. *Lib.* 11, *v.* 173, &c.

To the claffical Reader no objects are fo interefting, no profpect fo inviting, as the remains of thofe ages, whofe heroic exploits have engaged his early attention, and captivated his youthful fancy, as thofe regions, which have produced heroes, and been the fcenes of their actions. Curiofity, however, fcarcely contented with the relations of hiftorians, or with the mutilated fragments which time has fpared, is eager to learn the
origin

origin of thefe heroes, and to trace their progrefs from foils, that gave birth to beings
feemingly fuperior to the human race.   If, in
the former cafe, we only afcertain imperfect
veftiges, in the latter our knowledge is ftill
more deficient ;   and tho' rude æras, when
even the annalift was fcarcely known, muft
foon be buried in oblivion, or leave only the
little which memory or tradition preferves ;
yet that little will be exaggerated by vanity,
will be obfcured by invention, and increafed
to a difproportioned magnitude by haughty
fucceffors.   Rome, the greateft fingle object
in the old world, the moft interefting fcene
to the fcholar, the antiquary, and the philofopher, has fuffered from each caufe.   Our
knowledge of a remote æra, neceffarily imperfect in its outline, has been filled up by
the captivating, but faithlefs colours of the
flattering hiftorian, and we have admired a
fictitious picture with the enthufiafm, which
the fubfequent glory of the Roman empire
excited, and which the heroic actions of its
fons had long fupported.   The remains of
Rome are fplendid enough to countenance
the moft romantic ideas of what the capital of
the world has been, and the trophies which

have

have furvived the defolation of barbarous conquerors, and the more fatal effects of fourteen centuries, fupport whatever can be faid
of her power, her opulence, and her fpirit.
Thefe remains have been often illuftrated;
and various circumftances have induced me
to prefer examining its ftate during the earlier periods, by which I may amufe an hour
agreeably, and furnifh an entertaining, probably an inftructive and interefting fubject of
converfation.

With the ORIGINAL INHABITANTS of every
country, we are little acquainted. They were,
it may be fuppofed, hunters, while prey
abounded; and afterwards lived on the fruits
which the earth fpontaneoufly produced.
They were probably rude, uncultivated, cruel,
and incapable of recording the progrefs of
fucceffive years, or the events that diftinguifhed them; of their own origin, they certainly knew nothing. Various tribes have
been found, in this uncultivated ftate, and
the defcriptions of the new Zealanders, their
perfidy, their cunning, and their cruelty, are
almoft copies of what we read of the Læftri-
gons and the Cyclops. In the hiftory of every
nation of the old world, there is a race, of
whofe

whofe origin nothing can be known. They are the Αυτόχθονες of the Grecians ; the Pifmires, according to one Grecian fable ; the ftones thrown by an imaginary Deucalion and Pyrrha, according to another. Thofe who have looked at hiftory with a penetrating eye, and extenfive views, have found the earth once covered with men, whom culture had fcarcely enlightened, whom civilization never refined. They excavated the rocks to procure protection from the elements ; their limited wants were fatisfied with the rudeft covering, and with the fimpleft fare ; the fweet acorn afforded them food, the fimple rill their drink. The poets, glancing at this condition, and finding the wants of this race few, and eafily fupplied, gave their age the name of Golden, and raifed beings who were really little fuperior to brutes, by their encomiums, to a race fcarcely inferior to their deities. Some of the moft beautiful verfes of Ovid, are defcriptive of this ftate ; and he is fo enamoured with the images, that he repeats them within fourteen lines. The concluding ones, a part of the repetition, are fingularly elegant and highly poetical.

" Ver

" Ver erat æternum, placidique tepentibus Auris

" Mulcebant Zephyri natos fine femine Flores.

" Mox etiam fruges Tellus inarata ferebat :

" Nec renovatus ager gravidis canebat ariftis,

" Flumina jam Lactis, jam flumina Nectaris ibant,

" Flavaque de viridi ftillabant ilice mella."

If we call in the affiftance of philofophy, and argue that, in fimilar fituations, men are probably not very different, the fafcinating picture will difappear ; and, in its ftead, we fhall find the rude, cruel, uncultivated favage. The picture of the Cyclops, in Homer, may have been a faithful copy : the gigantic and cruel Læftrygons were probably of this early race, and the numerous labours of the multifarious Hercules, feem to have been only the conquefts of more civilized hords, led by able chieftains, over thefe favage monfters. At a later æra, the conquefts of the Grecian Thefeus were evidently fimilar. Their dens in part remain. The caves of Ifpica in Sicily, about fifty miles from Syracufe, have been attentively examined by De Non. They are excavations of the rudeft kind ; and the modes

modes which the inhabitants feem to have employed for fecurity, appear to have been the contrivance of a race, without arts, without proper tools; in fhort, without every affiftance but inftinct. Mr. Bruce is inclined to fink Thebes, with its hundred gates, to hordes of favages inhabiting the excavations of a hundred hills, and fupports his opinion by the prefent names of the mountains, beeban el meluke, the ports or the gates of the kings. In the colder climates, thefe caverns are fecured with greater art, and there is little doubt, but the Druids' houfes are the remains of the habitations of our anceftors. This mode of life may have been alfo the origin of the word Αυτοκθονες, as the Arcadian cuftom of living in the cavities of the mountains gave their defcendants, and even their colonies, according to Diodorus, the appellation of Αβοριγιναι. The idea we affix to Aborigines is very different; but the term equivalent to it, among the Greeks, was εγχωριοι. Excavations at leaft, in the mountains of different countries, ftill exift; and as fimilar habitations have been fometimes neceffary, they were, probably, at a remoter æra, not uncommon.

This

This race yielded to the flow but fteady oppofition of a more enlightened nation, emerg-
ing from the fhores of the Euxine. Their remains are ftill to be found in the Celts, and
the Cumri, if Celtic is more than an appel-
lative from the drefs ftill preferved in the
Caledonian petticoat, the Keltie. In this I
agree with the ingenious Mr. Pinkerton ; but
cannot allow that the Celtic race merits the
fevere reproaches which he has, with fuch
great profufion, fcattered. They were inferior to their conquerors ; but that they were
incapable of becoming their equals by cultivation, has not been proved.

To this new race we muft look for the more
immediate fource of the population of Italy,
and indeed almoft the whole of Europe. They
impofed on the conquered nations their arts
and their language, receiving only in return,
like the Englifh in America, the Weft India
and the Friendly Iflands, the primitive appellatives, and a few terms of more immediate
neceffity, or more frequent ufe. The names
of mountains and of rivers are of this kind ;
and when we find Pelafgi fo nearly refemble
Pel-Lafg, an elevated chain of mountains,
defcriptive of the triangular region contained
by

by the Danube, the Hellefpont, the Ægean fea, and the Adriatic, the firft and original feat of the Ionians ; when we recollect that Thel, a valley, and Sala, the river of a valley, is a ftriking defcription of the vale of Theffaly, watered by the Peneus, we can fcarcely avoid confidering them as primitive names. Again: Ath-is is an elevated country ; Locris or Locria, is a mountainous country ; Rumon, Servius tells us, was the old name of the Tyber, to be traced from the Celtic name for river, which we difcover in Rha, Rho, Rhu, Rhiu, Rhei, Rhine, and Rhrone, the radices of the of the Greek ῥέω and ῥόος. The old Celtic word Ock, a river, is to be traced through many degrees of longitude. It is found in Ockfakow, the city on the river ; and in Ock-enton, in this county, the town on the rivers ; for as it has the Saxon adjunct, we may readily allow it the anomaly of the Saxon plural. The river has been ftiled the Ockment, but the town is fingularly fituated between two rivers, and therefore picturefquely defcribed by the title of THE TOWN ON THE RIVERS ; as Tiverton, in the neighbourhood of the fords of the Ex, and the Lowman was, with equal propriety, called Twa-ford-ton. Pendennis

caftle

caftle is found in Cornwall; and in Cilicia, as
Governor Pownal informs us : indeed, from
Penmainmar to the Appennines, the old original Celtic word Pen, a head, metaphorically
the top of a mountain, occurs in the names
of hills, or towns on hills, in every region.
On the Alps, a temple was erected to the
Pennine Deity, the God of the Hills, evidently
Apollo, the original Deity of the Celts, by
his diftinguifhing mark, the Eye; and the
neighbouring hills were ftiled the Graian
Alps, not from the Grecian Hercules, but
from the Celtic appellation of Phœbus, viz.
Grian. It is curious to obferve with what
care Mr. Whitaker has endeavoured to prove
Pennine, to be Poenine, and to connect the
Graian Alps with the Grecian incurfions, at
a period, when the appellation of γραιοι did
not exift.

A mong the primitive appellatives, the word
Fire is fingularly confpicuous. The Grecian
word πῦρ, according to Plato, is Phrygian
and barbarous, but the Phrygians were a
Celtic race, and the word is retained in all
the modern languages, not from the Greek,
but from the common Radix in the Celtic :

n

π and φ are convertable confonants, and the force of the Grecian upfilon is equivalent to the Englifh y. The pronunciation of the word which means Fire, is nearly the fame in all the languages of Europe; in the German Fuer, and the Swedifh, Fir. In the fame way an author of no inconfiderable learning, Mr. Lemon, has traced all the modern languages to the Greek; his great fupport confifts in thofe original words, derived from the common Radix, and his ingenuity has fupplied the reft. The Radix of Alps, which is ftill to be met with in the Celtic, fignifies a high mountain; and I very lately met, in a northern author, with the expreffion of " an Alp of ice."

An ingenious gentleman, who thinks with great force and originality, and with whom many of us have lately had an opportunity of converfing, Governor Pownal, without any particular reference to the prefent fyftem, has fuggefted fome fingular obfervations on the early language, of which we ftill find numerous traces.*‧ He could not avoid feeing the progreffive advances of thefe colonies from the fouth-weft; and indeed Stillingfleet, in his 'Origines Sacræ,' long fince pointed them out.

* Effay on the Study of Antiquities,

As

As the ſtrangers then were ſuperior in their knowledge, and the arts they poſſeſſed, to thoſe whom they viſited, the latter ſuppoſed them to be endowed with ſupernatural powers, and called them gods : the Mexicans did the ſame, and every rude race is conquered under the conviction of ſome ſuperiority in their more civilized opponents.   They brought with them a new language, and the language of the gods and men was conſequently different.   This is not, he obſerves, ſuppoſition only : Homer diſtinctly mentions the difference ; and, from his account, the probability of the ſyſtem muſt be appreciated. Briareus, he tells us, was by men called Ægeon ; but Eigeon, in the Cumraig, ſigniﬁes the ocean, whoſe interſected bays may have given the idea of an hundred hands, or at leaſt an appropriated term for the officer, ſuppoſed to have ſuperſeded Neptune. Again: Xanthus, he ſays, was called by men Scamander ; and Commendwr * ſigniﬁes, in the Cumraig, a winding river; and with the Welſh prefix ys, we have very nearly the Celtic appellation, which Homer called that

* The w in Welſh has the force of the double o.

of

of men. Aftyanax, Plato tells us, is fyno-
nymous to Hector; but we know that Aftyanax is the protector of the city ασυ αναξ, and
Ach-Twr, in the Celtic, has the fame meaning. Bri-amwn is, in the Welfh, the chief
defender; the etymon probably of πριαμνω the
old orthography of προαμνω to protect, and of
Priam, the king of Troy. Paris, in the
Hellenic language, is ftiled Alexander, an
appelative of the fame meaning; and in the
Welfh, I am informed, the prounciation of
Priam is Priaf or Parif—perhaps an inftance
or two more, from the fame author, may not
be uninterefting.

Troy Troia is, in its Celtic appellation,
Tre-oim the fettlements of the Oïm, an
eaftern race, improperly confounded with the
Tartars. Aια or Ey means country, and is
the root of γαια, and many other appellatives;
Troja, therefore, is Trè-o-ia. Hium has almoft
conftantly the epithet facrum : it is the
Ηλ-Όον, the temple of the facred Oon. The
oracle of Dodona was eftablifhed by the inha-
bitants of Epirus, and Duwdewin is, in the
Welfh, "God's oracle." It's priefts were
Selloi;

Selloi*; but Sellwr, in Welſh, is one that ſeeth things at a diſtance—the origin of Seer.

In our inveſtigation then, of the ſource of the inhabitants of Italy, we muſt examine thoſe nations, which, from the eaſtern coaſts, preſſed on the Italian Celts, of whom our knowledge is very inconſiderable; for, if the ſource of every tribe cannot be traced, there is not the ſlighteſt reaſon to conclude that any of the Aborigines remained even at the period, when the earlieſt records commenced. There are none, whoſe names are recorded, that have the ſlighteſt pretenſions to this honour, except, perhaps, the Umbrians, and an obſcure race, the Hirpiæ. It flattered the vanity of the Romans to be thought the deſcendants of Æneas. The ten years ſiege of Troy had raiſed even the vanquiſhed nation to a high rank, in the ſcale of heroes, and the ſacred character, as well as the filial piety of Æneas, rendered it an object of importance in their eyes, that he ſhould be conſidered as the founder of the empire. Virgil was too dexterous in his courtly adulation, to omit the opportunity of flattering Auguſtus with this

* Hom. Il. XVI. v. 234 Sophocl. Trachin. v. 1175.

origin,

origin, and the wily Halicarnaffan has written the early hiftory of the Romans with a perfpicuity and precifion, which even an eye witnefs of the events could fcarcely have attained. This will appear more remarkable, when we reflect, that no part of the Roman hiftory was committed to writing till the 6th century from the building of Rome, at leaft 900 years from the building of Alba, and fcarcely two monuments furvived the deftruction of the city by the Gauls, in the 4th century ab urbe conditâ. There is a difference in the chronological computation, which at once deftroys the circumftantial narrative of Dionyfius and the merit of Virgil as a chronologift. This refpects the duration of the Albanian kingdom, for fome authors calculate its extent at 300, while others fuppofe that it lafted 400 years. In no inftance, however, is this period afcertained by the rudeft annals, or the fmalleft pretence even to traditional information, but by the epoch of the deftruction of Troy: the names of the kings, as well as the duration of their refpective reigns, are adapted, with a ftudied accuracy, to this preconceived period. The founding appellations, therefore, in the 6th book of the Æneid, Procas, Capys,

F   Numitor

Numitor, are scarcely of more importance to
the chronologist, than fortemque Gyan, fortemque Cloanthum are to the poetical reader.
Herodotus informs us, that 400 years probably intervened from the destruction of Troy
to the building of Rome. It was fixed at 300
years by Virgil, in the opinion of our countryman Spence, in consequence of the pre-
deliction for the sacred number 3. Thus he
supposed 3 years to have elapsed from the
destruction of Troy to Æneas landing in Italy;
30 to the building of Alba; and 300 to the
building of Rome. This fancy, however,
was unworthy of the poet, tho' it is evident,
that it has influenced other authors: Trogus,
the prototype of Justin, followed the same
computation.

If the interval is uncertain, the other ques-
tions are equally disputable. Dionysius traces,
as we have seen, the Romans from Æneas, and
gives many reasons for concluding, that he certainly reached the shores of Italy with his vanquished Trojans. In different authors, the
wanderings of Æneas are differently described; and this variation proves only that
the object of his voyages was imperfectly
known; not that they had no existence, a

supposition,

fuppofition, which Cluverius and Bochart have ftrenuoufly fupported. It may appear furprifing, that he extended his voyage to the extremity of the Adriatic, again to coaft round Italy and Sicily. But, at that time, navigation, except among the Phœnicians, was very imperfect: the longeft voyages were performed by keeping the coaft always in fight, and following the direction of the fhores. That hardy experienced race often croffed the feas, while their neighbours feared to leave the coafts. The navigation of the Adriatic, however, was fo dangerous, as to juftify the timidity and caution of Æneas; and later experience has fhown, that, in his voyages, he followed the current, which, with fhips like his, to have oppofed would have been dangerous, and to have flighted, imprudent. The general voice of antiquity fupports, in this refpect, the teftimony of Dionyfius; and we have only the divine authority of Homer and Neptune in oppofition. The language of Homer, if his infpiration be admitted, is however equivocal.

Νῦν δὲ δὴ Αἰνείαο βίη Τρώεσσιν' ἀνάξει,
Καὶ παῖδες παίδων, τοί κεν μετόπισθε γένωνται.

A

A flight reflection muft fuggeft, that the prophecy is not inconfiftent with the reign of Æneas over the Trojans in Italy; nor does the prophet imply that his kingdom fhould be on the-fhores of Afia, while Afcanius reigned at Rome. It is not furprifing that, in thofe times, when communication between even neighbouring nations was difficult and interrupted, that the tranfactions of Italy fhould have been little known in the Ægean fea. If the expedition of prince Madoc had been real, 600 years would have elapfed before the deftination of his colony was known. Had the fhips of Columbus been loft, he might have reigned in Hifpaniola for ages, before Spain would have known the exiftence of his defcendants. But the queftion will recur—Did Æneas reign in Troy, or on that part of the weftern coaft of Afia, where Troy ftood? Hiftory, and even tradition, have not fupported the affirmative, and the prophecies of Neptune muft, of courfe, lofe their credit.

I muft not, however, pafs over thefe celebrated lines fo curforily: they have occafioned no inconfiderable difficulties, and the firft grammarians and hiftorians have laboured

boured in this field. It is well known, that Strabo confidered them as decifive, in oppofition to the idea of Æneas' eftablifhing a kingdom in Italy.* Others have eluded the difficulty by fuggefting that Πάντοσιν fhould be fubftituted for Τρωσσιν. This conjecture is not only violent but arbitrary : it is cutting the knot, that may be untied, nor does the credit of Neptune require fuch an equivocal fupport. To the opinion of Strabo we muft oppofe his own opinion in his XIIth book ; and indeed the general confent of antiquity, the teftimony of Plutarch, of Juftus Solinus : even the authors, which Ryck † has collected with a different defign, fhow that tradition has handed down no very obfcure memorials of Æneas's having carried a colony of Trojans into Italy. We may therefore fafely confider them as fome of the very early inhabitants of that delightful country. Who the inhabitants of the coaft of Afia, where Troy ftood were, we fhall foon have occafion to fhow.

---

* Lib. XIII. p. 606.   C. 906 A. Ed. Almel.

† See his differtation on the firft Colonies of Italy, and the arrival of Æneas, publifhed at the end of Holftenius' notes on Stephanus of Byzantium.

When

When Æneas arrived on the fhores of Italy, he found it inhabited by various nations. The chief of thefe, every confiderable tribe, came feemingly to the fupport of Turnus, himfelf confeffedly of Grecian origin, to oppofe the new prefumptuous invader. I feize this idea with more eagernefs, to purfue the enquiry under the aufpices of Virgil, and relieve the dark difquifitions of antiquity by the pleafing harmony of the moft polifhed poet. Never were annals delivered in a more fafcinating drefs, and if Virgil did not truft his trifling traditional records, his prophetic fpirit is at leaft as infallible as Homer's.

Mezentius, the firft of the allies, comes from the Tyrrhenian fhores, of an Etrurian race. Aventinus follows, the fon of Hercules. Catillus and Coras, twin brothers of Tybernus, were of an Argive race, a circumftance which Homer confirms,

" Argeo pofitum Colono Tibur."

The founder of Prænefte is faid to have been the grandfon of Ulyffes, and to thefe Virgil feems to join the Gabini, the Hernici, the inhabitants of Amafenus and Anienes, as fubjects of the fame monarch. Gabii was, indeed, a fingular city ; and the circumftance of

its

its being lately difcovered, after being hidden for ages, by afhes and lava, and having tortured the inveftigations, and the conjectures of antiquaries, may juftify me in fpeaking at a greater length on the fubject.

Gabii of the Volfcians, is fuppofed to have been built by Galactus and Bius, two Grecians, who found no proper afylum in Sicily, and confequently led a colony into Italy. This, at leaft, is the narrative of Solinus, and is confirmed by Plutarch, who tells us, that Romulus acquired fome Grecian literature there. The inhabitants were confeffedly Grecian, and their tutelar deity was the Argive Juno. Virgil feems to have avoided, with peculiar caution, the term city, fince in V. 773, of the 6th Æneid, he mentions it as one that will be built by the Albanian kings; yet thofe who ' cultivated the plains of Juno of Gabii,' muft have had a fixed refidence. The robber, the hunter, the nomadic fhepherds, had feldom a place of reft ; but, in Italy, fociety had advanced far beyond thefe æras. Perhaps, in the firft inftance, the fcattered habitations of the early fettlers might have been alluded to ; in the fecond, the city as founded by the kings of Alba.

" HI

" Hi tibi Nomentum, & GABIOS urbemque Fidenam:

" Hi Collatinas imponent montibus Arces."

The ſtratagem employed by Tarquin to reduce
it is well known.   Sectus thus deſcribes it in
the following characteriſtic lines.   I need not
apologize to you for copying from Lucius
Junius Brutus.

" Could I by ſly impoſture, hope to win

" This Ardea, as I did the town of Gabii,

" I would again ſubmit my back to the ſcourge,

" And, from my father's cruelty a ſuppliant,

" Intreat the gulled inhabitants ;——nor wait

" His hint, by cutting down the talleſt poppies,

" In the preſence of the meſſenger, I ſent him,

" To ſlay their leaders."———

Gabii ſeems to have been built between the
æra of the foundation of Alba and of Rome ;
and its power muſt have been conſiderable,
ſince Tarquin was obliged to adopt the artifice juſt mentioned, to gain poſſeſſion of the
city.   In the time of Dionyſius it ſtill exiſted,
and his evidence may at leaſt be admitted re-
ſpecting

fpecting the objects which he faw. In his
hiftory of Tarquin, he obferves " Νυν μεν ωκ ετι
συνοκυμενη πασα, πλην οσα μερη παιδοχευεται την οδον. Τοτε
δη πολυανθρωπος κι ει τις αλλη μεγαλη."[*] Horace and
Propertius mention its deferted ftate, which
Lucan attributes to cruel wars, and inteftine
commotions. From thefe accounts, we cannot expect to make any confiderable difcoveries among the new-found ruins of Gabii.
In the beft days of the Roman empire, it was
deferted and in ruins; and its remains do not
promife any thing rich, elegant, or curious.
The difcovery will however clear up the difficulties which have been felt refpecting the
fituation of Gabii, a circumftance of little import, though it has engaged much attention.
The Halicarnaffan exprefsly tells us, that it
was 100 ftadia from the city, in the road to
Prænefte. Lloyd has given a fomewhat different account; but I need not enlarge on
the fubject : the Campo Gabio ftill remains,
and the ruins of the city have been difcovered.

The forces, which Meffapus brought, were
from Etruria, a country, whofe inhabitants,

* Lib. iv. LIII. P. 242 Edit. Hudfon.

as will be afterwards explained, very certainly came from Greece, the fource of the little fcience and literature, which Italy firft received. Yet critics have arraigned Virgil for bringing the people of Etruria under the banners of Meffapus, whom every hiftorian has placed in Illyria. It is however highly probable, that Meffapus, if not a colonift, was a rover or a pirate, the conftant occupations of the Illyrians in thofe days, and the opinion is particularly fupported by the fable of his be‑ing the fon of Neptune. Some fecret hif‑tory probably influenced the poet, for this chief alone leads his forces in regular or‑der, and arranges their fteps by modulated founds. Servius fuppofes, that a compliment was intended for Ennius, who boafted of de‑riving his origin from the Illyrian ; others, that he alludes only to the fefcennine verfes, as Fefcennia was one of the cities, that furnifhed troops to compofe the Etrurian, or the Illy‑rian army. But though the Etrurians in fu‑ture ages were Arcadians, yet it muft be ad‑mitted on the authority of Herodotus, that a Lydian colony was eftablifhed in Etruria, long before Ænotrius brought the Pelafgi from Pe‑loponefus. The arguments of Dionyfius Ha‑licarnaffus, licarnaſſus, who thought the Lydians Αυτοχθονες have been examined by the learned Cumberland, and it would be to copy from him, if I was to engage in the queſtion. The memory of the Lydian origin was retained in the time of Virgil and Horace, and accounted highly honourable. There is no evidence that this colony was ever eſtabliſhed in Greece, and to admit that ſome wanderers may have come in a very remote æra immediately from Aſia, will not materially influence the future argument, in which the Etrurians are ſuppoſed to be chiefly derived from Peloponeſus. It is indifferent whether they came from the parent ſtock, or from a colony at firſt derived from a nation ſimilar in its cuſtoms, its manners, or its language.

The Sabines were other Auxiliaries of Turnus, and formerly inhabited the city Cures or Quires, from whence the Romans, at a future period, were called Quirites. The ſituation of Cures, the Sabine capital, has become the ſubject of curioſity, as it was that of Horace's farm, and has occaſioned an ingenious eſſay by M. Capmartin de Chaupy, entitled " Decouverte de la Maiſon de Campagne d'Horace." It was not, as Cluverius

has

has fuppofed, in the place called Vefcovio, but a little below, on the left fide of the river Corefe, on the fpot now called Monte Maggiore. Virgil extends the Sabine confines farther than the accounts of other antiquaries fupport him. The whole race, it is faid, migrated from Peloponnefus; but, in tracing the fubject to its fource, I fufpect we muft look farther for their orign. That the Sabines were a peculiar race is univerfally admitted; they were noble, generous, warlike, patient, abftemious, and chafte. They preferved this character with little alteration for many centuries, in an age when licentioufnefs was not only venial, but fafhionable, and have been commended for fimilar virtues by almoft every antient author. The teftimony of Livy and Cicero is clear and decifive. Virgil's examples of chaftity are drawn from the Sabines: they have difarmed Juvenal of his fatyrical arrow; and Horace, in his villa among the virtuous inhabitants of this diftrict, is never weary of emulating their good qualities. Statius, Martial, and Silius Italicus add their more feeble acclamations to the general praife. The character of the Sabines appears to be the chief reafon for fuppofing them to have

migrated

migrated from Sparta ; but this is infufficient,
unlefs we fuppofe Sparta to have monopo-
polized the virtues of the Pagan world.   To
omit the trifling obfervations of fome etymo-
logifts, who derive the name of Sabine ἀπο
το σεϐεσθαι ; of an early Italian race, with a modern Greek appellation, we may obferve Silius Italicus and the hiftorian quoted by Dionyfius, fuppofe the name to have been taken
from Sancus or Saba; the former their tutelar deity, the latter a popular chief; or, as
fome have fuppofed, the fon of Sancus, or
Sangus.   I have purfued this fubject in various authors farther than it would be ufeful or
interefting to follow the enquiry at prefent.
The refult is, that Sangus, the tutelar deity of
the Sabines, either by the complaifant hierar-
chy of Rome, or in confequence of the union,
after the conclufion of the Sabine war, was
admitted in the rank of the tutelar gods,
with their early deity Fidius, fo commonly
called on in the terms medius fidius in the
latter æras, and with another deity, called
Semon.   They were all confidered as names
of the one god, and evidently borrowed from
the ideas of their original race.   The race of
the Sabæans extended from the Perfian to the
Arabian

Arabian gulf. The firſt nation diſtinguiſhed by this appellation, was ſituated on the Perſian ſea, the offspring of Chus, and the whole nation was afterwards ſtiled Scythian; the ſame which gave inhabitants to Aſia, to Greece, and the reſt of Europe. Scythian was their Celtic appellation; and is only Chuthes, with the Celtic præfix ys. Whether the tribe, which was afterwards diſtinguiſhed by the name of Sabine, had before fixed in Peloponneſus is uncertain; it is robable they had not, for their primitive manners came, ſeemingly uncorrupted, to Italy, together with their tutelar deity Sangus, that is San-chus. San or Zan is the name of the ſun, the ſacred fire, emblematic of the deity: in other words the god of Chus. Semon, in the ſame way, is the Sem-On—the Holy One, the ſacred word, which for ages meant the deity, and preſerved, though over looked, in the ſacred ſcriptures. Fidius was probably only the Roman title of Sangus, by whom the Romans ſwore to preſerve inviolate their treaty with the Sabines, from fides, a very old Roman word; but etymology is not my objeɛt, nor ought I without ſome apology alieni meſſi falcem inſerere. That the three
deities

deities mentioned were the fame, we have the authority of Ovid. The paſſage has uſually been curtailed; and for this reaſon only, I ſhall tranſcribe the whole.

> " Quærebam Nonas Sanco, Fidione referrem,
>
> " An tibi, Semo Pater ? Tunc mihi *Sancus* ait
>
> " Cuicumque ex iſtis dederis, *ego munus habebo*
>
> " *Nomina terna* fero, ſic voluere Cures."

Cures, in this paſſage, means the Romans, for it is oppoſed in the context to Sabini. Some authors have ſuppoſed the Sabines to have been deſcendants of the Umbri and to have been of Gallic origin, but without any real foundation. Their veneration for the early ſpring, which may have been attributed to the adoration of Belen's fires on the firſt of May, is an eaſtern cuſtom, and, at one time, ſeems to have prevailed through the whole of Aſia. It is ſtill retained (Aſiatic Reſearches, v. 4,) in India. The Abioi, from whence Sabioi, and Sabini may be eaſily derived, were a race of ſingular mildneſs, probity, virtue, and benevolence, in the north-eaſt of Aſia.

Whether

Whether, therefore, the Sabines came immediately from Greece, or were of the same race, which supplied Greece with its most learned and enlightened inhabitants, is of little consequence : they were certainly very nearly connected. Were the English colony at Jamaica to people another island, the new colonists would not be distinguishable at a future distant æra from Englishmen

Halesus, a descendant of Agamemnon, leads the Osci and Arunci, which sufficiently points out their orign. Æbalus, the son of Telon and Sebethis, has a Grecian name, and a fabulous origin. The Marrubian priest practices the arts of Medea ; and the whole description of Hippolytus is decidedly Grecian, in every part. Turnus, himself of Argive race, leads a band of Argives, with their allies, from the same shores. Of these the Sicani alone are doubtful, for Sicily was the alternate prey of the most powerful pyrates, and the most successful robbers. Neither history nor tradition, however, support the opinion, originally derived from the name, that any of the Sicilian colonists came from the banks of the Sicoris, a river of Spain. The idea of Bochart is more probable, that the term Sicani is merely local from the plural
Sikenin,

Sikenin, of the Syrian Saken, the neareft fide of Sicily to Phœnicia. The language and meaning of Diodorus fupport the fame opinion. Ταύτης δε της χωρας τα μεν προς ἑω κεκλιμενα μερη κατωκην Σικελοι, τα δε προς δυσμας Σικανοι. If thefe antagonifts be removed, the Sicani will prove to be certainly Grecians, for it has never been pretended, that any other nation has the flighteft claim to the honour or difgrace of having feized this fertile ifland; and indeed the whole tenor of hiftory, forming fo confpicuous a part of the Grecian mythology, leads to the fame conclufion. The Tyrrhenians are a later colony from the fame iflands. Their language, their hiftory, and their reputed anceftors, Hercules and Omphale, fupport, without any contradiction, this origin.

Among the various races, for there is no clue to guide us in the inveftigation of the inhabitants of particular diftricts or cities, I find little reafon for believing any of the Italian nations to have been of a Celtic origin, except the Umbri, the Hirpiæ, and the inhabitants of Abella, Avellia or Nola, for each term has been admitted in different editions of Virgil. The former inhabited the gloomy fhades of the Appennines, feemingly driven to thefe

G   dreary

dreary regions by the fuccefsful invaders. They have had no hiftorians, and appear to have been too defpicable to obtain the notice of their neighbours. The little information, that can be obtained on this fubject, is from the incidental accounts of hiftorians, collected often from more antient authors. Thus Solinus, in his Polyhiftoricon, cap. 8, from Bocchus; Ifidore, in his Origines, l. 9, cap. 2; the Scoliaft on Lycophron Alex ad v. 1360; Marc. Anthony, as recorded by Servius in Æneid lib. xii. confider the Umbri as a Gaulifh or Celtic race. Another Celtic tribe remained at a much later æra, among the Sabines, the Hirpiæ, by fome authors confounded with the Hirpini, whofe origin, whofe cuftoms, and whofe habitations, were different and diftant. The Sabines have been confounded with the Umbri, probably on account of the Hirpiæ, but as the latter preferved, and were diftinguifhed for peculiar cuftoms, it is not probable that thefe were the fame with the tribes of the furrounding nation. The prayer of Aruns, in Virgil, is fingularly characteriftic, and leads us to the origin of this race.

" Summe

" Summe Deûm fancti cuftos Soractis Apollo,

" Quem *primi* colimus, cui *pineus ardor acervo*

" Pafcitur, et medium, freti pietate, per Ignem

" Cultores multâ premimus veftigia prunâ :

" Da Pater ————"

The addrefs of peculiar diftinction to Apollo, the chief deity of the Celts ; burning the fir; the religious rite (cultores, freti pietate,) ftill preferved, or preferved not long fince in the weft of Ireland, where the common people ufed fuperftitioufly to leap through St. John's fires, and account it a mark of the protection of the deity, to efcape unhurt, point out a religious inftitution purely Celtic. Silius Italicus alludes to the fame rites :

" Tum Soracte fatum, præftantem Corpore & Armis

" Aquanum nofcens, *patrio* cui ritus in *Arvo*

" Dum pius Arcitenens incenfis gaudet Acervis

" Exta ter innocuos latè portare per ignes;

" Sic in Apollinea femper veftigia prunâ

" Inviolata teras ; victorque vaporis, ad Aras

" Dona ferenato referas Solennia Phœbo."

In

In the time of Pliny, the Hirpiæ were reduced to a few families, but they retained
their antient fuperftition : they worfhipped
Apollo, on their Acervi, as the Irifh celebrate
the rites of Belen on their carns, and were
confidered by the Romans as a race of fuperior
fanctity. On this account, they enjoyed various immunities. Solinus, copying probably
from Pliny, gives a fimilar account. Strabo,
though accurate in defcribing their fituation,
calls them Hirpini, a name derived, he fays,
απο τε ηγησαμένε λύκε της αποικίας : Ιρπον γὰρ κάλεσιν οι
Σαννίται τον λύκον. It is evident that, in this paffage Strabo confiders λυκος to mean Lupus ;
and, in this fenfe, he is copied by Feftus :
but λυκος * is the old Grecian word for Sol,
from a Celtic root, and the origin of the Latin
Lux *Lucis*—Can it be doubted then, but that
this was the real meaning of the original name,
perverted by their Sabine neighbours ?

It may be of importance to add, that fome
villages, apparently Celtic, ftill remain in the
mountainous parts of Italy. Dr. Symonds,†
in his lectures laft year, mentioned a fact,

* Macrobii Saturnalia, lib i. cap. 17.
† Profeffor of Modern Hiftory at Cambridge.

which

which has escaped the notice of modern travellers. In the mountains near Barano, (probably Baranio, in the district of Verona,) are seven
villages inhabited, as is said, in the only account of the observation that I have seen,§ by
the descendants of the Cimbri, who invaded
Italy in the time of Marius, and twelve others
within ten miles of Verona.　They still speak
the Cimbrian language, and conversed easily
with the king of Denmark, who saw them in
his visit to that country, about sixty years
since, so similar was their language to the
Danish.　As it is not probable that they retain
any records of the invasion, the very learned
professor perhaps thought his supposition the
most probable; yet, perhaps, it may appear
equally reasonable to believe, that they are the
remains of the Umbri, that race which yielded
to the invaders, and retired to a gloomy, but
secure retreat, in the Apennines.　Future
travellers may, perhaps, attend to them more
accurately, and elucidate their origin.

That the inhabitants of Abella were of Celtic
origin, is doubtful; the only foundation for the
opinion, is their use of the Cateia in the teutonic

§ Gentleman's Magazine for November 1794.

　　　　　　　　　　manner.

manner. The word is said to be Celtic, in an author, who has not attained the reputation of accuracy, but whose work I have not been able to procure, M. Bullet, in his Celtic Dictionary.

The Trojans I have already said, were a Grecian colony. Within the reach of tradition, Dardanus led his Cretan followers to the shores of the Hellespont, a situation pointed out by its commanding, at the entrance of the Euxine, almost all the commerce of these rude ages. Perhaps I may have occasion to revert to this subject, in examining the successive changes, and the different routes, which trade, and the various mercantile objects have experienced. At present, the advantages of its situation are sufficiently demonstrated from Alexander having chosen this spot for an Emporium, and Constantine having transferred the seat of the Roman empire to its neighbourhood, for the same reasons.

These various historical facts, though I have endeavoured to enliven them by digressions, and divest them of their ruder dress, may, I fear, have appeared tedious. The deduction from them is, that the Romans were originally derived from Grecian colonies, and ultimately
mately

mately from Afia, from tribes probably inhabiting the countries bounded by the Mediterranean, the Nile, the Euphrates, and the Red
Sea; for thofe Grecians who came from
Egypt, feem to have had the fame original.
This opinion will have an additional fupport,
when we reflect, that the language of Rome
certainly originated in Greece, and is, in
reality, the antient Greek, varied according
to countries, of the firft colonifts; fometimes
exhibiting traces of the Æolic, more frequently of the Doric dialect. This fubject, however,
requires particular examination.

As Troy was a colony from Crete, it is not
furprifing that the language fhould be the
fame. Ulyffes, for inftance, is introduced into
the city, and perfuades the Trojans to give
up Helen: Priam begs the body of Hector;
and no interpreters are mentioned, tho' Homer
is efteemed critically and hiftorically exact;
and, in each inftance, eloquence to which an
interpreter could not do juftice, was principally trufted. This is the opinion of Mr.
Wood, which, though often controverted,
has never been difproved. The fuggeftion of
a poet, however, on a poetical compofition,
deferves particular attention. Since the firft

G 4   reading

reading of this essay, one of our colleagues, whose hints I have often availed myself of with advantage, observes, that " poetry does not admit of the introduction of an intrepreter. The Christians and the Saracens, in Tasso, hold conferences *poetically*, without difficulty. Ulysses, in his travels, does the same with all he meets." In the present case, however, we want not this poetic licence, for the rival armies had one common origin ; and a passage in the Agamemnon of Æschylus, tho' it may seem to suggest some doubts, contributes to support the opinion that the languages were the same. When Cassandra is brought to Clytemnastra, she endeavours to persuade her to speak, adding, " if she has not the language of a Barbarian, resembling rather the twittering of a swallow, than articulate sounds, I will prevail on her by my arguments."* The persuasion, however, does not avail, and she is requested to make signs. The prophetic fit at last comes on ; her contorsions are violent, ὡς ніαίρετε, as of a beast newly caught in the toils, and she pours forth her vaticinations. The chorus express their surprize, not at her speaking their language,

* V. 1058.

though

though they at firſt ſuppoſed, that ſhe made ſigns for an interpreter, but that ſhe ſhould be ſo well acquainted with the different events, ſince ſhe came from a city beyond the ſea, (αλλοθεων) ſpeaking a different language. In this inſtance, Æſchylus expreſsly alludes to the language, and what might have otherwiſe paſſed without obſervation, now demands particular attention. The Cretan colony was placed among the Phrygians, a race, whom the Grecians ſtyled Barbarians. It was known from whence Caſſandra came, but it was not known that ſhe was the deſcendant of a Grecian family. From her country then aroſe the doubt of her language ; but, well knowing the prevalence of the Grecian tongue on the ſhores of Aſia, they are not ſurprized to find her acquainted with it. That ſhe was acquainted with the events, as ſhe came beyond the ſea, was ſingular. The word αλλοθεων has therefore no meaning, ſince ſhe confeſſedly ſpoke Greek, and the correction of the Scholiaſt, who ſubſtitues the word αλλοθεν, is ſupported by the whole tenor of the paſſage. Though this reaſoning appears to me concluſive, yet, as the Pelaſgic was the early language of Greece, as it was of eaſtern origin, and not materially
changed

changed by Cadmus, the fimilarity of it will be more readily believed. Thefe pofitions muft be at prefent admitted gratuitoufly : it will afterwards appear that they are not arbitrarily affumed, nor deftitute of proof.

The earlieft language of Greece is fuppofed by fome authors to have been the Pelafgic, brought from Afia by tribes which fixed their refidence in different parts of Greece, and at firft inhabited the whole diftrict from Thrace to Peloponefus. Pelafgus, the fuppofed founder, was ftyled the fon of Pofeidon, which, in the Grecian mythology, conftantly fignifies that the tribe came from a diftant coaft. The people afterwards called Pelafgi, moft probably received their name, as has been already hinted, not from a fuppofed founder or chief, according to the ufual fiction of Grecian genealogies, but from their early habitation. In the early hiftories of Greece, they are often called Ionians, which included, for many centuries, the Athenians ; fo that, as we fhall afterwards find, the Pelafgic letters refembled the Ionian, and the Athenian letters were fynonimous with both. It was the opinion of Cumberland, who had collected materials for a very extenfive enquiry on the origin of nations, rions, that the Pelafgi never attained that name in Afia, but were called Ionians, Javans, &c. the varied form of expreffing the defcendants of Juvan,* the fon of Japhet. When, therefore, we find the Afiatics very generally calling the Greeks Ionians ; when, from the inveftigations of Bochart, it appears, that the appellation, Ionians, was for ages the exclufive name of the inhabitants of the country from Thrace to Peloponefus,† we cannot doubt of their origin. The term Pelafgi was moft probably adventitious, from their wandering life, or from their fituation. The latter feems to me moft probable, for thefe Ionians who paffed the Ifthmus, though ftyled Pelafgi, had the additional title Ægialæi. After fome ages, when the Pelafgi had attained a firm eftablifhment, when the Pelafgi and Iones were become fynonimous, the former term was held to be equivalent to the latter and we hear of Πιλασγοι, on the coaft of Afia, diftinguifhed by the epithet διοι, becaufe, fays Euftathius, they alone are faid to have preferved the ufe of letters from the time of the deluge.—Euftath. in Iliad 2, v. 841.

* De Origine Gent. 379.   † Phaleg. l. 3. c. 3.

The

The oracle of Dodona was of Pelafgic origin, and it deferves particular attention, as the only remains of the eaftern mode of worfhip in Greece. In the following lines of Homer, this is particularly pointed out, and they are more fingular, as they confound the Cretan Jupiter with the eaftern Zuth, one of the appellations of Ofiris, who is undoubtedly the deity intended.

Ζιυ ανα Δωδωναιι Πελασγικι, τηλοθι ναιων,
Δωδωνης μεδεων δυσκειμερου.*

The leader of the Pelafgic race probably brought with his colony, its language, but of the early Pelafgic language, we know little. It is faid to have been the dialect of Linus, who was fuppofed to have fallen a victim to the jealoufy of Cadmus, becaufe he oppofed the reception of his new letters. But the hiftory of Linus and his fcholars Hercules, Thamyris, and Orpheus, has been generally confidered as, at leaft in part, fabulous. Paufanias has fhown, that his poetical account of the exploits of Bacchus, mentioned by Diodorus, refts on a doubtful foundation: that he left fome verfes on the origin of the

* Il. II. 433.

world

world, and the motion of the fun and moon,
according to another author, is generally dif-
credited. Homer is indeed fuppofed to mention Linus in his defcription of Achilles'
fhield, ' λινος δ'υπο καλον αειδε,'* which Pope, on
the authority of Paufanius, tranflates " the
fate of Linus fings." The prepofition υπο
however oppofes this interpretation, and Dr.
Clarke has come, probably, nearer the meaning, by tranflating " *chordaque* eleganter fucci-
nebat," adding, with his ufual concifenefs in
the note, " quomodo, in fcuto depigni potuit,
quem caneret Citharifta ?" †

Another early poet, unknown to antiquity,
is raifed to fame by Dr. Gillies, in his Hiftory of Greece, evidently from a miftake.
One of the defcendants of Melampus is called
Μαντις, a foothfayer: on this foundation he
makes Melampus a poet, and accufes Herodotus of knowing little of the antient bards,
when he afferted, that there were no poets
remaining of an æra antecedent to Homer.
Surely the hiftorian of *Greece* could not have
been mifled by finding, in the *Latin* tranflation, the correfponding term, " Vates."

* Il. E. V. 570.   † Vol. 2d. P. 178.

The

The origin of letters in Greece is very obfcure. Herodotus and Diodorus Siculus differ on this fubject ; and the little information
that can be obtained ; the little light to direct
us in this dark path, is from a few fparks fcattered in other authors. The Pelafgi, Herodotus informs us, were Barbarians, and he
profefles himfelf unacquainted with their language. Diodorus exprefsly obferves, that the
Pelafgic were employed previous to the introduction of the prefent Grecian letters, or
their prototypes, by Cadmus. It is generally
agreed, that thefe elements of words are of
eaftern, probably of Affyrian origin, and that
thefe of the Samaritan alphabet come neareft,
in their form, to the earlieft alphabets of Europe. They differ in one effential refpect,
that the eaftern writing is from the right to
the left.

Every thing that Herodotus relates of letters and antient infcriptions, is referable to
thofe of Cadmus only. They were brought,
he obferves, from Phœnicia, but adds, that
the Greeks changed the φωνη and the ρυθμος.
The former word probably means the found,
and the latter may allude to the order of the
letters, the direction of the writing, or the
modulation :

modulation: Ρυθμος is a word of very uncertain meaning, even in the later authors, and is evidently diftinct from accent, from quantity, and from emphafis : the only general idea, which it conveys, is the effect of a fucceffion of founds; and this may have been derived from order and arrangement in general. I am rather led to this explanation, from finding the Greek alphabet different, in its order, from the Samaritan, the Celtic, and the Etrufcan.

The language of Diodorus, Dionyfius, and Paufanius, is very different. The firft fays pofitively, that letters were known in Greece prior to the fuppofed Cadmus,* and in each there are fuch frequent allufions to *old* letters, fuch a diffimilarity ftudioufly pointed out between the old and the modern Greek letters, as to render the exiftence of an older alphabet different in power and in form from the prefent, highly probable. The author of this former alphabet has been called Pelafgus. Paufanius informs us, that he was the firft king of Arcadia, and has been faid to be an Argive; but, from whatever fource he may

* Bib. Hift. Lib. III. p. 296, Ed. Weffeling.

have

have fprung, he is defcribed as the general benefactor of the Arcadians, and fpoken of in the fame terms of glowing gratitude, which have graced the leaders of the more enlightened colonies in every part of Greece and Italy. In reality, this Pelafgus, like Medus, Ægyphus, Hellas, and the whole race of founders, introduced, feemingly, to account for an appellation, is an imaginary being. The Pelafgi were firft eftablifhed in Thrace, and the general advantages admitted to have been derived from the arrival of thefe ftrangers, fhow that they came from a more civilized, a more enlightened country.

Like all the Scythian colonifts from Afia, the Pelafgi taught thofe whofe territories they feized, the ufeful arts, particularly agriculture, and letters. Thefe were modified or fuperfeded by future, probably more enlightened, colonifts, feveral of whom have, in different regions, obtained the name of Cadmus. The whole Grecian hiftory of the moft celebrated Cadmus is, however, fabulous, founded on mifconftruction. The name Cadmonin fignifies an eaftern race, and what has been ignorantly tranflated ferpents' teeth, Bochart has fhown really to mean brazen fpears.

spears. Calamine, the ore of brass, is at this
time called cadmia, from an eastern radix;
and Bochart has shown, that a sentence, which
might be translated, ' he formed an army of
five men, armed, from the teeth of serpents,'
would, with more propriety, be interpreted,
' he raised a hasty army of men, armed with
(brazen) spears.' The great difficulty consists,
however, in ascertaining the existence and the
progressive changes of the early letters attributed to the Pelasgi. For this purpose, it is
necessary to examine how far history, or even
the mystic truths, that may be found under
the guise of fable, will assist the enquiry. It
seems to be an established fact, that the Pelasgi
were settled in Arcadia, but they were not
confined to Peloponnesus. They were established, we have seen, in Thrace and in Attica, (Herod. lib. viii. cap. 44;) and it is
worthy of notice, that the father of history
mentions their language, (lib. i. cap. 57,) to
have been that of the Athenians. This is
confirmed by Pausanias, in the Corinthiaca,
where he remarks, that, before the arrival of
the Heraclidæ, the language of the Athenians
and the Argives was the same. Again: whether we suppose Cadmus an allegorical per-

H   sonage,

fonage, whatever be admitted of the fable of
Linus, the writings of the fuppofed Orpheus,
&c. they all feem to meet in one point, that
a prior language really exifted. Paufanias,
probably, had feen fome traces of it, or at
leaft he has copied authors, who had preferved them. He mentions an interpretation
on the tomb of Chorœbus, in Attica, which was
read from the right to the left, and exprefsly
fpeaks of the old letters, which he calls Pelafgic, in oppofition to thofe of Cadmus. The
Athenians, alfo, who boafted of the invention
of letters, confidered theirs as diftinct from
the alphabet introduced by Cadmus, and the
Αττικά γραμματα are often mentioned, as equivalent to the Pelafgic.

It is obvious, however, that the Pelafgic
was loft in Greece as a language, even in the
time of Herodotus, and if any traces are found,
it muft be * in monuments and relics acci-

---

* A very fingular infcription was found by Tournefort,
(vol. i. p. 232) in the ifland of Delos, in the Ionic character,
differing very little from the Tufcan, and perhaps from the
Pelafgic. It feems fingular, that it is read from the left ;
but, if examined, it will appear to have been continued,
from a former line, and, and to have been originally written
in the alternate direction, called by the Greeks βυςροφηδον ;
for the four firft letters are unintelligible, and probably the
final letters of a word in the preceding line. This mode was
undoubtedly of early antiquity, and perhaps the intermediate
ftep to the change adopted in the direction of European writing.

dentally

dentally preferved, or in diftant regions, where it was carried, and efcaped the change which influenced literature after the arrival of the Cadonim. We are not without fome clue to affift this enquiry. Whether the colony of the Pelafgi, in Arcadia, preceded the other colonies in Greece, as Paufanias has exprefsly mentioned (Arcadica, p. 603) is uncertain; but Ænotrius, confeffedly the firft colonift in Italy from Greece, went from Arcadia. After fome viciffitudes, together with Pucetius and Japix fuppofed to be defcendants at no great diftance from the firft Pelafgus, he is faid to have fettled in Etruria, a country extending much farther than at a later æra, as it comprehended all the Campania : if then the Pelafgic letters exift, they may probably be difcover:d in the old Etrufcan monuments.

If the teftimony of the antients be examined, they will tend to confirm the fuppofitio., that the old Etrufcan language was the Pelafgic, and the fame w.th the earlier language of Athens. Tacitus, the moft inquifitive and philofophic of the antient hiftorians, obferves, that the Latins received their letters from the Arcadian Evander, adding, " et formæ literis

latinis

latinis quæ veterrimis græcorum."[*] Pliny obferves, that the Pelafgi brought letters to La-
tium, (lib. viii. cap. 56) and confirms the opinion, that the OLD Greek letters were nearly
the fame with the modern Latin, from the
teftimony of the infcription on the Delphic
table, (lib. vii. cap. 58.) . The treaty alfo between Servius Tullus and the Latins, exifted in
the time of Dionyfius, who obferves that the
characters were Greek, fuch as were FORMERLY
ufed in Greece.

If the forms of the letters, which are ufually
arbitrary, be the fame, it may be eafily fuppofed that the language did not vary greatly.
But there are arguments more conclufive than
thefe probable prefumptions ; and, in reality,
we find many words preferved in the Latin,
which we know were once Greek, though fuperfeded in the claffical authors by others. In
thefe refpects, no difference can be made between the Pelafgic and Cadmian languages,
nor is there any foundation from hiftory, to
fuppofe that there was any confiderable variation, except in the forms of a few letters, and
the addition, probably, of fome new founds.

[*] Annal. lib. xi. cap. 56.

The

The lines recorded by Tzetzes of an æra prior
to Cadmus, are evidently fictitious, and of a
later period. But, in a subsequent æra, the
Greek words resemble strongly the Latin.——
Thus, πορκος was antiently the Greek word for
hog ; and λανος or λαπος the old word, like the
Latin lana, for wool. Dr. Prideaux has observed also, in his differtation on the Arun-
delian marble, that the antient name of the
Greek nation, though loft in their language
even in the days of Homer, was preferved
in the Latin ; they were ftyled γραικοι or γραιοι,
long before the æra of the fuppofed fon of
Deucalion. Another argument of fome curiofity is the frequent termination of Latin
words in r, which, in claffical, or what may
be comparatively termed modern Greek, terminate in s ; though *they* alfo ufually terminated in r, before this euphonic refinement. If the decree of the Spartan fenate,
preferved by Severinus Boetius, be genuine,
it will afford numerous examples of this early
mode of writing. Timotheus the mufician,
to whom it relates, and who had attracted
cenfure for making fome alterations, probably fome improvements, in their lyre, is called
Τιμοθιορ. Μιλισιορ is ufed inftead of Μιλησιος, and

ταρ

ταρ ακοαρ inſtead of τας ακοας. Aϛιν, αϛιις αϛιιτ
are the old words for I have, thou hadſt, he
had. Aνιμος, a word almoſt in every ſenſe
equivalent to animus, is inflected alſo in the
ſame way: the old dative was ανιμοι, contracted
into ανιμυ, and again dilated into ανιμαιο, by the
Ionics; though originally very near to ανιμι.
The principal inflections of the Latin lego, and
the Greek λιγω, are the ſame, if the dipthong
ιι be changed into i.

The ſimilarity between the old Greek and
the Latin, would be more conſpicuous, if the
different changes of the conſonants were conſidered. Before the orthography of the words,
in either language, was ſettled by writing, the
changes were numerous; and, from theſe,
much of the apparent diſcordance can be
traced. At the end of this long eſſay, a few
examples muſt ſuffice. B and M often change
places: thus Μυρμηξ is βυρμηξ; the Latins as
frequently ſubſtituting the F for B, ſoon
formed the word for ant, formica. The Æo-
lians frequently change the β to r, and read,
for inſtance, inſtead of βαλανος, γαλανος from
which the Latins had their glans. The B and
π often change their places: the old way of
writing and pronouncing πυρρος was βυρρον, from
whence

whence came Byrrhum; of πυξον, βυξον, from whence the Latins had buxum. Πιεγος and *Turris* have been fuppofed by a fimilar con-verfion to have been the fame words, and they probably are fo from the Celtic tor. The old Latin word for wood, cala, from whence came caliga and calones, is the Greek Καλον from the Celtic, cail and coil. We have their de-rivatives in this country in *Kel*hydon (Clay-hidon) *Koly*dhon (Colyton), and in the old name of Scotland *Cale*donia.

The Hetrurians, we have feen, employed the Pelafgic letters, and probably ufed the characters brought from Arcadia. The Ta-bulæ Eugubinæ, a fingular Etrufcan monu-ment of great antiquity, publifhed by John Baptift Pafferius, affords many proofs of this kind, if compared with the earlieft Latin ; and authors, who have copied from others, when they remark that the antient Etrufcan language is the old Greek, are not aware that it in many refpects differs from what the prefent Greek ever was. The letters greatly refemble thofe of the Latins in the earlieft periods, of which records have been preferved ; the words are read from the right to the left, and their meaning is not to be elucidated by the lan-

H 4

guage

guage of Homer or Hefiod. Yet it muft not
be concealed, that the whole of our knowledge of the Etrufcan monuments is trifling
and obfcure. Gorius, in the Prolegomena of
the firft volume of the Etrufcan mufeum, (p.
48,) and afterwards, in a feparate differtation, entitled ' Diffefa dell' Alphabeti degli
antichi Toxani,' publifhed 1742, endeavours
to fhow, that it confifts only of 16 letters :
other authors, particularly Bourgonet, enlarge
the Tufcan alphabet to 25; and the Benedic-
tine monks of St. Maur, have added the c,
befides confidering the o as long and fhort, in
their Diplomatic treatife. In fuch uncertainty
it is needlefs to purfue the fubject. It is
enough to have fhown, that the language of
Etruria was probably the Pelafgic brought
from Arcadia, and primarily from the eaft,
that it is in its principal diftinctions eaftern,
and fo near the moft antient fpecimens of the
Latin language, as to leave little doubt of its
being the fource of that tongue which we have
fo long admired and affiduoufly cultivated.
We have too few remains to judge of the fimilarity in words or conftruction. From the
numerous inftances in which the Latin refembles the Greek, it is probable that the Cadomim

mim made no effential alteration in the fubftance of the language : the words that the
Arcadians carried to Italy were preferved in
Arcadia and Attica under the dominion of the
eaftern reformer. If Cadmus deftroyed Linus,
he could not annihilate the literary foundation he had eftablifhed : if he changed the
forms, the fubftance continued very nearly the
fame. If, as fome authors, particularly Cumberland and Squire, contend, Inachus and
his followers were of Afiatic rather than
Ægyptian origin, and expelled from Ægypt,
where, as colonifts, they had been fome time
eftablifhed ; if Cadmus or the Cadomim were
alfo Phœnicians, it will be ftill more probable that the literary innovations were not confiderable ; and that the languages of Greece
and Italy, as well as the inhabitants, were
truly Afiatic.

A. L.

On

On some of the more remarkable

BRITISH MONUMENTS

IN DEVON.

" Ad quæ nofcenda iter ingredi, tranfmittere Mare folemus. Ea fub
" oculis pofita negligimus feu quia ita natura comparatum ut prox-
" imorum incuriofi, longinqua fectemur : feu quod omnium rerum
" cupido languefcit, quum facilis occafio eft : feu quod differimus,
" tanquam fæpe vifuri quod datur videre, quoties velis cernere."

Plinii Epiftol. Lib. 8. *E.* 20.

NOTHING can more tend to the amufement, if not to the enlargement of the human
mind, than a retrofpective view of the earlier
ages of the world. From the contemplation
of the manners of mankind in a ruder and
more uncivilized period, a fund of curious and
rational entertainment may be drawn ; and,
perhaps, if we were to form a juft comparifon between the darknefs which then brooded

over

over the intellectual world, and the luminous
rays that now encircle it, the result may not
be lefs productive of inftruction.

The farther we go back into hiftory, and
the more minutely and impartially we enquire
into the condition of mankind, we fhall have
the more to wonder, at the flow progrefs
which the human mind made in the attainment of that knowledge, which (whether it
be confidered in the form of fcience or religion,) was ftored with a profufion of bleffings.
It might have been fuppofed that the genius
of human nature, fo intuitive and comprehenfive as we now find it, would at once
have grafped at a vaft number of advantages, which were fparingly difcovered by
mere accident, or by the moft gradual advances. Yet thofe who evolve the pages of
antiquity, will, with aftonifhment, perceive
what clouds of ignorance obfcured the intellect! what mifts of error! what wretched-
nefs! what barbarity! The antient Briton,
as the favage which then prowled among the
forefts, rufhed from his cave, or wicker habitation, in the purfuit of a fimilar prey, and
when acquired, fed on it in the fame voraci-
ous manner; while the Druid, the Prieft and
Tyrant

Tyrant of this wild race, shackled it with the chain of superstition, and terrified it with the perpetration of " deeds unutterable."

In a review of so dark a period, we shall with difficulty be induced to believe, that man was the same being we now find him. The posterity, however, of the savage who was rough as his native wilds, have been those who have chiefly contributed to the refinement of human nature; who have thrown a polish on human society; have adorned the globe which they inhabit; and have placed, within the attainment of every individual, the means of being as happy as elegance, science, humanity, and true religion will admit of in this present state of existence. Though the sketch I have taken of the first and rudest period of the natives of Britain, shows them to have been highly barbarous and uncivilized; yet an enquiry into their manners will not be unattended with amusement and advantage. The search also after any of those relics that may elucidate their history, will be deemed, by many, an undertaking of the most pleasing and instructive kind. I shall therefore, however I may fail in the latter, attempt the former, in laying before you a cursory
dissertation

dissertation on the monuments now subsisting
in this county, which we have reason to ascribe to the Britons, or to some of those ma-
rauding nations of the north, so repeatedly
making their incursions into this island; who,
whether of Gothic or Celtic origin, yet evidently adopted similar rites in their superstition, and have, in their respective countries,
left monuments of the same kind behind them
for posterity to contemplate.

Those remains of the British æra, which
we can with probability ascribe to it, are but
few; and are, in general, to be met with
in those wild and unfrequented parts, where
the hand of agriculture could have but little
prospects of reaping a produce that might
compensate its labors. The interest of the
husbandman seems to be inimical to the pre-
servation of such objects of the antiquarian's
veneration: in his language, they cumber the
ground, and the materials may be converted
to serviceable uses. 'Tis to this circumstance,
doubtless, that such rude monuments are so
rarely to be found in the more cultivated parts
of the kingdom, and that we hear of them
only on barren rocks or plains, in those spots
where

where ftrata of the fame ftone abound, and which appear to be

" Non raftris hominum, non ulli obnoxia curæ."

In the mountainous parts of Wales and Scotland, on the plains of Sarum, in the waftes of Derbyfhire and Cornwall, thefe huge monuments of the firft natives of this ifland are frequently difcovered. In our county they are rare ; the defcriptions of thefe to which I fhall now confine myfelf, were taken on the feveral fpots.

The CROMLECH is the moft confiderable monument of any that now remain. The only one in the county is fituate on a farm called Shel-ftone, in the parifh of Drewfteignton (fo named, I fhould conceive, not from the Norman Drogo, as Rifdon hath afferted,) but from this and other relics therein remaining, appropriated to the Druids, fimply deriving its appellation from the refidence of the Druids on the river Teign. The Cromlech here, is perhaps the moft perfect in the kingdom. The covering ftone or quoit hath three fupporters ; it refts on the pointed tops of the fouthern and weftern ones, but that on the north fide upholds it on its inner inclining

furface

A Cromleh at Drewsteington

surface somewhat below the top, its exterior sides rising several inches higher than the part on which the super-incumbent stone is laid. This latter supporter is seven feet high—indeed they are all of such an altitude, that I had not the least difficulty in passing under the impost erect, and with my hat on ; the height, therefore, of the inclosed area, is at least six feet. Of the quoit I made a measurement, and found the dimensions to be, from the north to the southern edge, 14 feet and half; and from the east and west it was of similar length. These edges or angles seeming to present themselves (as far as I could make an observation from the sun,) exactly to the cardinal points. The width across was ten feet. The form of this stone was oblate, not gibbous, but rounding from the under face, rising from the north about 13 inches higher than in the other parts ; yet so plane on its superficies, that I could stand on it, or traverse it without apprehension of danger. That the Cromlech was a monument of the Britons, there can be no doubt ; but that it was a Druidical altar, and of old, applied to sacrificial uses, cannot now be ascertained. Borlace and others who have treated

- this

this fubject, judge the fpecies of monument
to have been fepulchral; and there is reafon
for the fuppofition, fince they are often found
erected on barrows, which are avowedly fepulchral. Indeed, in Ireland, the matter hath
been fufficiently elucidated; for bones have
been abfolutely found in thé area which fome
of them inclofed. Though Borlafe, therefore,
failed in Cornwall, it refts on more than probability, that, to whatever other purpofes it
might have been applied the ufe and intent of
the Cromlech, that is, the crooked (or as fome
interpret the word, confecrated ftone,) was
primarily to diftinguifh and do honor to the
dead; and at the fame time to inclofe the ve-
nerated reliquiæ, by placing the fupporters
and covering ftone in fuch a manner as to be
a fecurity to them on every fide.

This opinion receives additional weight,
and is corroborated by the ufage of the northern nations; for though they were chiefly
Gothic, yet fome of their ritual obfervances
and religious cuftoms were analogous to thofe
of Celtic origin; indeed we may well fuppofe,
that in thofe early and barbarous ages, the
habits and cuftoms of men were nearly the
fame in every part of the globe; " for the
more

more mankind are confidered in a ftate of wild and uncivilized life, the greater refemblance they will be feen to poffefs in their manners, becaufe favage nature, reduced almoft to mere brutal inftinct, is fimple and uniform; whereas art and refinement are infinitely various."— Olaus Wormius 'authenticates the exiftence of monuments of this nature among the northern tribes, and the ufes to which they had been applied.' "Sed neque veteribus Gothis, aliifque Gentibus in Septentione, defuit *memoria majorum*, quin et eis exhiberent (quos humi recondere placuit) honorabiles ftatuas lapidum excelforum, prout hodie cernuntur mirâ compagine immenfa Saxa, in modum altiffimæ latiffimæque Januæ furfum tranfverfumque viribus Gigantum erecta." The ignorance of fucceeding ages not being able to comprehend how fuch ftupenduous edifices could be conftructed by the common race of mortals, have attributed them to giants and dæmons; but although we derive from the mechanical powers a variety of fuccours in the tranfporting and raifing large and ponderous bodies, of which we well know the founders of thefe monuments could not have the affiftance, yet it hath been well obferved, that

I   great

great things might be accomplifhed by men of
fuch mighty force, as we are certain many of
thefe antient tribes poffeffed in ftrength and
remarkable ftature, co-operating together.
The lances, helmets, fwords, and other arms,
which have been preferved in the mufeums of
the curious; the accoutrements of the heroes
of other times, are a full conviction of their
vaft fize, and are objects of curiofity and aftonifhment to thofe whofe anceftors are reputed
to have wielded them. This circumftance,
however, is not folely applicable to Europe,
for by our later difcoveries we learn, that the
Americans (particularly thofe of Peru,) un-
aided by the engines we apply to thefe purpofes, have raifed up fuch vaft ftones in building their temples and fortreffes, as the archi-
tect of the prefent times would perhaps not
hazard the attempt to remove. One may,
however, conceive, that perfeverance, united
with ftrength, might be enabled to convey
fuch immenfe ftones from one place to another, by means of the lever and artificial
banks. Down the flopes of thefe they might
caufe them to flide, and afterwards fet them
upright by letting them down into perpendicular pits; having, by the fame means, placed
                                          their

A Logan stone on a rock in the River Teing.

their tranfoms on them, they might clear away the mound which they had raifed. I fhall quit the difcuffion of the Cromlech with the conclufion, that moft probably they were ‘ tumuli honorabiliores’—that they were the appropriated monuments of chief Druids or of princes ; and this is confirmed by the appellation of the famous Cromlech in Kent, known by the name of ‘ Ket’s Coity-houfe,’ being the fepulchral monument, or quoit, over the body of Catigeon, a Britifh prince, who was flain in a battle, fought with the Saxons near Aylesford, in the year 455.

LOGAN-STONE.—In the fame parifh of Drewfteignton is a Rocking or Logan-ftone : its Britifh name I found to be yet retained by the country people, who call it a Logging-ftone, a ftupendous block of granite, detached and refting at its bafe on a rifing narrow point of another mafs, deep-grounded in the channel of the river Teign. An equipoife was thus formed, and though by accounts given in the neighbourhood, the motion had ceafed to be fo fenfible, as in former times, it was yet to be produced by preffing againft the ftone with fome force. It is doubtful whether this Logan-ftone was ever applied to religious ufes by the

I 2   Druidical

Druidical fuperftition; though we are certain that it cannot be artificial: that fuch, however, were conftructed where there were none naturally fo circumftanced, is extremely probable, for as they were employed in deceiving the common people, we may reafonably conclude, that fome methods would be ufed to fupply fuch a deficiency. The power of producing any furprifing effect from a natural caufe, difcovered, perhaps, by accident, and kept fecret from the people, was fufficient, with the addition of a few myfterious words or ceremonies, to pafs for preter-natural endowments. Thus Toland, in his hiftory of the Druids, is of opinion, that thefe holy Juglers made the multitude to whom monuments of this kind were facred, believe that they only could move them. The effect was fuppofed to be miraculous, and by it they condemned or acquitted the accufed, and often brought criminals to confefs what could in no other way be extorted from them. The dimenfions of this ftone are enormous; at the weft end it is ten feet high, and from the weft to the eaftern point, the length may be about eighteen feet. The local circumftances of it are almoft as extraordinary as the ftone itfelf.

The

The river Teign rolls its waters around, and it is feated among thofe wild romantic hills, whofe fhaggy fides are overfpread with fragments feparated from the craggs above—on the bold tufted creft of the oppofite eminence, in Widdon park, groups of deer are feen, during the mid day heats of fummer, inhaling the breezes of the hills, and filence would have kept a repofe uninterrupted, had it not been broken by the crafh of the fhattered rocks or the fhrill cry of the mountain kite.

   " Along this narrow valley you might fee
   " The wild deer fporting on the upland ground ;
   " And here and there uprife a ftunted tree
   " Or moffy ftone, or rock with ivy crowned :
   " Oft did the cliffs reverberate the found
   " Of parted fragments tumbling from on high ;
   " And from the fummit of a craggy mound,
   " The perching falcon oft was heard to cry,
   " Or on refounding wings to fhoot athwart the fky."

BEATTIE.

I know of but one other Logan-ftone in the county now extant, and that is found among

I 3

a

a carnedd of moorstone rocks on the downs in the neighbourhood of Ashburton; which, though the tender balance is now in a great degree destroyed, was so equipoised a few years since, as to have been an amusing instrument for cracking nuts. It now retains, and is known by no other name than that of the Nutcracker. The equilibrium of this also seems to have been affected by accident, by the operation of winds or rains, or by the decomposition of the smaller stones around, and in magnitude it is much inferior to that before noticed.

ROCK-BASON.——On a common in the vicinity of Dartmoor, among a number of carns, or series of granate rocks, heaped naturally on one another, there is one of an oblate form, serving as a cap to others, which is of a singular and curious appearance: its surface is rather gibbous, swelling into little inequalities, and is in four different places scooped out into cells of various forms; these are all indisputably the effect of art, and seem to have been intended for reservoirs to retain a liquid, that, falling on the superficies of the stone, was to be conducted to them by means of grooves or channels, which appear to be cut in it, in an
undulating

A Rock Bason

on a Karn called Mill-tor in the parish of Widdecombe.

J. Smale delin.   J. Allen fecit.

			Feet	Inches
Dimensions	of the Quoit	from West to South	12	0
		South to North	8	0
	of the Basons	Nº 1	2	9
		2	1	9
		3	1	3
		4	1	0

undulating direction. The sides of them all are rounded, and, diverging from the margin, are well adapted to the more ready reception of whatever shall be poured on the stone.— The lips seem to have been intended for letting out the liquid at will, for cleaning the basons, or for other purposes, and were probably stopped up when that liquid was to be retained. To what uses these caverned stones may have been applied, we have nothing left us but conjecture—no legend or tradition appears to throw any light of importance on the subject; and though as these monuments have been generally found among others, which are expressly dedicated to religious purposes, we may well suppose that they also had their appropriate uses : yet, whether they were altars for the immolating human victims, or (as Dr. Borlase supposes,) for the ritual of water libations, is a matter of uncertainty. That the antient nations, with but few exceptions, sacrificed men to their gods, is a point too well confirmed to be at all doubted. " Phœnices in bello et pestilentia amicissimos homines immolabant Saturno." And according to Lactantius, " Carthaginenses (who were a colony of Phœnicians) ab Agathocle victi, quum
iratum

iratum fibi Saturnum crederent, ducentos ei
nobiliffimos juvenes immolabant." Galli
Efum et Teutatem humano cruore placabant.
I have produced thefe feveral inftances with a
view of fhewing from what fources the Britons
probably derived their knowledge and obfer-
vance of this horrid right. Uncivilized nations have been marked for their fuperftition
and barbarity; living in a ftate of warfare with
all nature, among wild forefts and gloomy
woods, they are befet continually with terrors,
and keep themfelves armed with ferocity and
diftruft. Hence that thirft of revenge and
deftruction which favage tribes cannot dif-
poffefs themfelves of; hence that impious
prejudice which makes them imagine the
gods to be as fanguinary as themfelves.—
Thus, among the more humanized Greeks,
the deity, or the manes to thofe to whom the
facrifice was offered, were invoked to quaff
the blood of the immolated victim, of which
we have an inftance in the Hecuba of Euripides.

" Δεξαι χοας μυ τας δε κηλητηριυς
" Νεκρων αγωγυς ελθε δε ως πιης μελαν
" Κορης ακραιφνες αιγ' ο σο δωρυμεθα."

In

In Friezland, (fays an ingenious French author), and in feveral places of Germany, altars
are to be met with compofed of fuch immenfe
ftones, that they could neither be deftroyed by
the ravages of time, nor by the zeal of the firft
converts to Chriftianity. Thefe altars, according to the tradition of the inhabitants,
have ferved for thofe unnatural facrifices. In
Iceland alfo, an hiftorian of that country records an altar plated with iron, which was
feemingly confecrated for the like purpofe;
and what feems not inapplicable to the prefent enquiry, upon it was placed a vafe of
brafs, in which was received the blood of
the victims; befide it ftood a brufh, which
was made ufe of to fprinkle the blood upon
the bye-ftanders.

This was in an age when temples had been
erected, when the arts had introduced a variety of conveniences; when altars, plated
with iron, and brazen vafes had been fubftituted inftead of the rude mafs of ftone, and
excavated bafon. Thus then we collect that
human victims were facrificed, that their
blood flowed into fome fort of receptacle, and
that with it the people were fprinkled. In
the earlier ages all this might have been done,
and

and exhibited on such a stone as that above described.

The only argument Borlafe brings of any weight to invalidate this idea, is the difficulty of getting the victim on the rock, which in fome few inftances hath been found to be 20 feet high. It would indeed, I allow, be a laborious tafk to raife an ox or a heifer thither; but furely not fo in regard to a human victim. If the Druid could climb there for the purpofe of luftration, the perfon who was to be facrificed might either voluntarily, or by compulfion, be able to do the fame. The prieft alfo, from fo elevated a fpot, might more confpicuoufly difplay the horrid rite to the furrounding populace, and have it in his power more eafily to fprinkle them with the confecrated blood.

Tho' Dr. Borlafe, by his learning and ingenuity, hath made it appear that the rite of luftration among the Druids is not without fome traces in hiftory, and that it was very agreeable to the general tenor and caft of their fuperftition; yet, having fome pretext at leaft for a different conjecture, and fome ground to reft on, I fhall hope to derive a plea for having thus long trefpaffed on your patience, and

An Urn found inverted in a Barrow on Hald.

and shall quit the discussion with a reference to the plate for the figure, and dimensions of the stone and the several basons.

The BARROW on Haldown, and the URN found in it.——The barrow on Haldown known to the country around, by the appellation of the great stone-heap, which though originally of a conical form, as are all the tumuli in these parts, being now intersected by an opening made in the year 1780, affords a singular and conspicuous object to the subjacent country. The form of this barrow was nearly circular, being rather more than 200 feet in circumference, and in height about 15. By the aid of 14 men a passage into it was effected almost due east, about 8 feet wide ; at nearly the same space from the margin was discovered a dry wall about 2 feet high, which was separated from without by very large stones in the forms of piers or buttresses : on arriving near the centre were seen a great many huge stones (all of them flint) placed over one another in a convex manner ; and in the middle a larger stone nearly globular, 2 feet in diameter, covering a cell on the ground 2 feet square, formed by 4 stones of considerable size, which were placed upright on their edges.

edges. In this cave, or, as it is termed, Kiſt-vaen, the urn was found ; and what was rather a remarkable circumſtance, inverted, containing the aſhes and the burnt bones of a youth, as was probable from their being ſmall, and with little muſcular impreſſion. When the urn was removed, theſe appeared as white as ſnow, though, ſoon after they had been ex-poſed to the air, they loſt that whiteneſs. From the ſize of the tumulus and this circumſtance, there ſeems to be grounds for the conjecture, that the aſhes and bones here encarned, were the remains of a perſon of dignity, whoſe ſur-viving friends, in honor to his memory, had . taken care to have them *well burnt* and blanched by the intenſeneſs of the fire λευκα οςεα. Thus, among the Greeks, Homer, de-ſcribing the magnificent funeral of Patroclus, adds,

" Next the *white bones* his ſad companions place,
" With tears collected, in a golden vaſe."

For it was conſidered as the higheſt diſgrace which could be offered to the dead body, that it ſhould remain but *half burnt* ; and this in-dignity we find was put upon the corpſe of
Tiberius,

Tiberius, which Suetonius fays, was carried
" in amphitheatro femi uftulandum." This
urn is 13 inches high, 10 in diameter at the
mouth, and 5 at the bottom, near half an inch
thick, and holds about 10 quarts; it is made of
unbaked clay, fmoked, and difcolored by its
expofure to the fire, and confequently without
infcription or embellifhment.

One of the moft antient modes of fepulture
was covering the bodies of the dead with high
mounds of earth, or a collected mafs of ftones,
in later times called barrows, (or more properly burrows, a term derived from the Saxon
birighe, to hide or bury,) in the compofition
of which (whatever fanciful conjectures may
have been ftarted) there can be no doubt but
that the tumulus was formed of earth, or
ftones, or of an intermixture of each, as the
ftrata of the fpot around could furnifh. Thus,
in Wiltfhire, they are univerfally compofed of
earth and chalk, whilft, in this county, they
as invariably confift of ftones collected as convenience led from the grounds adjacent.——
That this cuftom prevailed not only among
the antient inhabitants of Europe, but in almoft every part of the world, appears from
old writers on the fubject, and from the difcoveries

coveries of modern travellers. Ifidore fpeaks
of it as a general ufage, " apud majores, Po-
tentes aut fub montibus, aut in montibus fe-
peliuntur." Bell, in his travels thro' China,
notices thefe fepulchral hills : and in Captain
Cooke's account of le Fooga, (one of the
Friendly Ifles,) he gives a defcription of one
of very large fize. All the old hiftorians of the
north are diffufe on the point; and tho' our an-
tiquarians in defcanting on thofe which remain
in this kingdom, are for referring every veftige
of this fort to the Druids ; yet, as this kind of
monument is fo fimple and obvious ; and as,
without doubt, it muft have prevailed among
many nations of very different origin, fo it cannot eafily be afcertained whether the barrows
on Haldown ought to be afcribed to our Gothic anceftors the Saxons and Danes, or to the
more antient inhabitants of Celtic race, the
Britons. From local circumftances, and from
the contents of the tumulus, a gleam of light
is not unfrequently thrown on thefe matters :
with refpect to thofe on Haldown, we might
be induced to afcribe them to the Danes, and
that perhaps without much temerity, when
we confider the numerous encampments in
the vicinity, which are generally imputed to
that

that nation. Battles may have been here
fought, and here may the chieftains flain,
have been intumulated; the fpot felected, always indeed an object of confequence, was
highly confpicuous; and this, the largeft burrow on the down, fhould feem to have been
raifed in honor of fome chief or perfon of eminence, for the tumulus was large, in proportion to the quality of the deceafed, and to
the affection, power, or opportunity of his
furviving friends: where, however, thefe local
references may be wanting, the contents, fuch
as urns, arms, utenfils may give a defignation
of the people.

The Romans, all the northern nations,
the Gauls, the Britons, (whatever might be
their general ufage,) certainly at times, and
on particular occafions, *burnt* their dead, and
collected the afhes and bones into *urns.* " Cineres et offa, cado five urna colligebantur;"
and then placed them in the centre of the
burrows. Thefe urns were of various forms,
elegance, and materials, and from hence,
conjectures are deduced, frequently decifive.
The Roman urns were generally of the moft
exquifite workmanfhip, and formed of precious metals, porphyry, and glafs. Virgil
notices

notices the bones of a perſon which were collected in a brazen urn :

" Oſſaque lecta cado texit Chorinæus aheno."

Among nations, however, leſs civilized,
the arts were in their infancy, and their productions were rude. Thus the urns found in
the burrows in theſe parts, are compoſed of
coarſe pottery, rather ſmoked than burnt, (as
in the preſent inſtance,) and often of clay unbaked. We may therefore refer them either
to the Britons or Danes, who continued Pa-
gans longer than the Saxons in this country.
The latter becoming Chriſtians ſoon after their
arrival in the iſland, left off the heatheniſh
uſage of burning bodies, though they ſtill retained the burrows.

From the cuſtom of burning with the dead,
or laying in the ſame grave the arms, ſpoils,
or implements of the deceaſed, the nation may
be alſo ſometimes traced; this likewiſe the
Romans practiſed, as noticed by Virgil.

" Hinc alii ſpolia occiſis direpta Latinis

" Conjiciunt igni, galeas, enſeſque decoros

" Frænaque, ferventeſque rotas—pars munera nota

" Ipſorum clypeos, et non felicia tela."

Tacitus

Tacitus relates the fame of the Germans, and we find the Scandinavians excited to it by their fuperftition; for Odin had affured them, that whatever was buried or confumed with the dead, would accompany them to his palace.

From the line in which thefe burrows (of which there are many,) on Haldown are ranged, it would feem that fome road had paft that way ; and indeed they have a direct tendency to the ftation now vifible, in the park of Lord Clifford at Ugbrook. The Roman fepulchres were often raifed near the common roads, and the reafon of it is affigned by Varro, who fays, " fecundum viam funt, quo prætereuntes admoneant et fe fuiffe, et illos effe, mortales."

Reflecting on the remote age in which thefe tumuli were formed, during which lapfe of time almoft all other monuments have had one common fate, we fhall not be furprifed that thefe are even now in being. Their fize, peculiar compofition, and the religious veneration in which they were held, exempted them from the ravages of time, or the more baleful depredations of avarice and facrilege. " Majores noftri ftatuas multis decreverunt, fepul-

K   -   chra

chra paucis, fed ftatuæ intereunt tempeftate, vi, vetuftate : fepulchrorum autem fanctitas in ipfo folo eft, quod nullâ vi moveri, neque deleri poteft." The profpect from this burrow, to which I now return merely to bid farewell, for its beauty and extent will not often, perhaps, be found rivalled—Mamhead's pine-clad hill, the caftellated grandeur of Powderham, the more immediate rural and picturefque fcenes of Bickham, Trehill and Oxton, the expanfe of ocean ftretching to the eaft, the cathedral towers of Exeter rifing on the north, between which (through a fertile wooded valley, decorated with towns and villas of every defcription,) are feen, flowing on, the widening waters of the river Exe ; thefe form the outlines of a fine picture, the variety and fplendor of which can never fail of exciting uncommon admiration.

N. E.

Hiftorical

Hiſtorical Outlines of Falconry.

AMONG the various proofs of the origin of a nation, their cuſtoms or uſages may ſometimes be admitted as no unſatisfactory evidence. On examining this evidence, we frequently find a nation in poſſeſſion of a cuſtom, that, from its ſingularity, excites attention; and, ſtruck by its appearance, we naturally look for ſome veſtiges of it in the neighbouring countries. But if, not finding it there, we diſcover the object of inveſtigation in a country remote, and at preſent unconnected with that in which it firſt appeared, our curioſity kindles in the proceſs; and we are gratified by enquiring how two people placed at ſo great a diſtance, and cut off, at preſent, from all communication, ſhould aſſimilate in a uſage, in itſelf uncommon; whilſt intervening nations, the neighbours of

K 2

both

both, are utterly unacquainted with it? This
enquiry muſt neceſſarily ſuggeſt the idea of an
affinity or connexion between theſe two countries at ſome early period, and may carry us
back, perhaps, to the very origin of the one
people as derived from the other; eſpecially
if, in this purſuit, we meet with additional
reſemblances.

Theſe obſervations were occaſioned by an
accidental notice of Hawking, or Falconry,
as a diverſion of the ancient Britons. This
curious and ſurpriſing art, whilſt familiar to the
earlieſt inhabitants of the iſland, was unknown
to the nations of Europe, for the Gauls were
ſtrangers to Falconry: the Germans, at the
ſame period, had never heard of its exiſtence,
nor had the Romans or the Greeks any accurate conception of it. On this quarter of the
globe it was almoſt excluſively poſſeſt by the
Britons. But the Aſiatics had been Falconers
before the date of hiſtory, and they ſtill preſerve the ſport. We ſhould purſue Falconry,
then, to the plains of Aſia; and in marking
its emigration to Britain from ſome country
of the eaſt, we can almoſt ſuppoſe ourſelves
following the progreſs of the Orientals themſelves, together with their art. To ſuppreſs
the

the idea is almost impossible; whilst viewing
Falconry in this country, we observe, at the
same instant, its independence on Europe,
and its close connexion with Asia. Whether,
however, the theory of such an eastern colonization be admissible or not, it is surely an
extraordinary circumstance, that Falconry was
thus confined to the British islanders and the
Oriental nations.

The survey of Falconry indeed, as existing
in this and other countries, without any view
to the origin of the Britons, might be sufficiently interesting—not that I shall industri-
ously avoid a conclusion to which my subject
has an obvious tendency.

In the examination of Falconry, I propose
to trace it, particularly in this island, from
modern times to the earlier ages; when, having advanced far into antiquity, we shall see
it, at every step, diminishing in Europe; till,
at length, it seems ready to disappear, ex-
cepting in this island. Here we shall perceive it eagerly pursued; and, arrived at this
point, we must extend our views beyond the
limits of Europe, if we would discover the
country whence it came.

K 3 The

The notion of Falconry, perhaps, was firft
fuggefted by fuch birds as flew particularly
high, and thus eluded the efficacy of miffive
engines. Certain it is, that birds of this defcription have always afforded the moft delightful fport to the falconer.* In tracing up
the art of Falconry from the prefent times to
thofe of our forefathers, we naturally turn our
eyes to thofe fpots on the ifland where it may
ftill exift, or has lately exifted. Thefe are few.
It is ftill practifed in the highlands of Scotland.† In Dorfet, a few years fince, it was
purfued by Mr. Sturt ; and in Norfolk by the
late Lord Orford. Their hawks, however,
were fupplied by Colonel Thornton ; and his
feat in Yorkfhire is at prefent, I believe, the
only fpot where Falconry can boaft a confiderable portion of its original magnificence. Under the aufpices likewife of this gentleman,
cormorants have been taught to fly at fifh,
and bring them to the lure.‡ After all, we

* See Buffon. Hift. Nat. tom. xvi. p. 239.
† See Birt's Letters on the Highlanders, vol. ii. p. 199,
and Pennants's Tour, p. 127.
‡ I have heard likewife of hawks being trained at Bridport.
A hawk made its efcape thence, not long ago, and was found
by the poffeffor of Grange, on his own grounds. He kept it
for fome time ; but one day, pouncing at a pigeon, the hawk
miffed its aim ; when it inftantly flew up to a vaft height, and
difappeared. Nor was it ever recovered—the bird being too
much afhamed of its failure, to offer its fervices again.

muft

muſt content ourſelves with viewing, in
the ſolitary inſtance adduced, a faint ſha-
dow of its ancient pomp, whilſt the Duke of
Ancaſter is ſtill hereditary falconer to the king
of England ; and whilſt one of the claims at
the coronation, ſtill kept up, is to preſent
him, while at dinner inWeſtminſter Hall, with
a pair of falcons.*

That Falconry was a favourite amuſement
of a Prince of Wales, but a ſhort time ſince,
may be collected from a letter of Shenſtone to
his friend Mr. Graves, relating to Somerville,
the author of the Chace. " Mr. Somerville's
poem upon Hawking, (ſays Shenſtone,) called
Field-ſports, I ſuppoſe is out by this time.

* The late Lord Orford (we are told) once looſed a heron,
and ſet his hawks after it. The conteſt between the heron
and the hawks was long and full of ſport ; when, at length,
the hawks were victorious, and brought the heron to the
ground. The heron, however, was not hurt. And in gratitude for the diverſion which this bird had afforded his Lordſhip, he ordered a gold ring to be made, with *E. Orford* and
the date of the year engraven upon it, and put it about the
heron's leg, and gave him his liberty. About ten years after,
Lord Orford received a letter, incloſing the above ring, from
the Imperial ambaſſador, who informed his Lordſhip, that
the Emperor had taken the encloſed ring from the leg of a
heron which his hawks had killed ; and ſeeing *E. Orford* upon
the ring, and obſerving the date, had ſent it to the Earl by
his ambaſſador, as a great curioſity. The ring was much
bruiſed and diſcoloured, but the inſcription perfect. This
incident hath a romantic air ; and, for a moment, we can
ſcarcely regard the event as fortuitous.

K 4   It

It was fent to Mr. Lyttleton to read to the prince, to whom it was infcribed. It feems the prince is fond of hawking." His royal highnefs is thus addreft at the opening of " the Chace :"

—————— O thou great Prince,
Whom Cambria's towering hills proclaim their Lord,
Deign then to hear my bold inftructive fong.
While grateful citizens, with pompous fhow,
Rear the triumphal arch, rich with the exploits
Of thy illuftrious houfe ; while virgins pave
The way with flowers, and, as the royal youth
Paffing they view, admire and figh in vain ;
While crowded theatres, too fondly proud
Of their exotic minftrels and fhrill pipes,
The price of manhood, hail thee with a fong,
And airs foft warbling ; my hoarfe-founding horn
Invites thee to the chace—the fport of kings,
Image of war, without its guilt. The mufe
Aloft on wing fhall foar, conduct with care
Thy foaming courfer o'er the fteepy rock,
And on the river-bank receive thee fafe ;
Light-bounding o'er the wave, from fhore to fhore.

No

No poem, under the title of " Field-Sports,"
appears to have been publifhed. It is probable, therefore, that Somerville, perceiving his
firft defign to be too extenfive, was afterwards
obliged to contract his views: and the Chace,
difencumbered from other field-fports, was
ftill dedicated to the Prince of Wales.* Notwithftanding thefe high honours, Falconry
has gradually declined in England. Not a
trace of it was to be found by Borlafe at the
weftern extremity of the ifland; though from
an incident which he has preferved, it feems
not to have been forgotten in Ireland in the
year 1738.† The farther we look into other
days, the more extenfive fhall we find this
diverfion in England. Familiar allufions to
any art or cuftom in the poetry of the times,
afford a ftrong proof of its general prevalence.
In " Holland's Leaguer," a comedy by Sha-
kerly Marmyn, 1633, is the following paffage:

> Before thefe courtiers lick their lips at her,
>
> I'll truft a wanton *haggard* in the wind.

From a paffage in *Vittona Corombona*, it appears, that haggard was a term of reproach,

* See Dodfley's Shenftone, vol. 3, p. 56.
† See Borlafe's Nat. Hift. p. 242, 243.

fome-sometimes applied to a *Wanton:* " Is this your perch, you haggards? fly to the stews!"—In Decker's " *Match me in London,*" 1631, we have—" your *Tassel-gentle,* she's lur'd off and gone." It appears from old books on this subject, that certain hawks were considered as appropriated to certain ranks. The *Tiercel-gentle* was appropriated to the prince. In Sir W. D'Avenant's " *Just Italian,*" 1630, this passage occurs ;

" They've *watch'd* my hardy violence so *tame.*"—

where the poet seems to allude to the management of hawks, which are tamed by keeping them from sleep. In Heywood's comedy, called " a Woman killed with Kindness," 1617, a humber of these terms relative to hawking, occur together :

Now she hath seiz'd the fowl, and 'gins to plume her,

Rebeck her not; rather stand still and check her.

So : seize her *gets,* her *jesses,* and her *bells.*

All these terms were, doubtless, familiar even to the London citizens ; otherwise they would never have found a place in popular comedy. In the reign of James the 1st, hawking was

pursued

purfued to fuch extravagance, that the famous falconer, Sir Thomas Monfon, (as we are informed in Weldon's character and court of K. James,) was at the charge of a thoufand pounds in Gofhawks, only for a fingle flight.*

The predeceffor of James, Queen Elizabeth, and all her court, feem to have regarded hawking with veneration. Yet the queen was difpofed to relax the feverity of thofe laws, which related to Falconry. Amidft all her defpotifm, fhe was not infenfible to the tyranny of the game laws. The heinous crime of ftealing the eggs of the falcon, fubjected the perpetrator to imprifonment for a year and a day. The term of a year and a day, however, was reduced in her reign to three months—but " the offender was to lie in prifon till he got fecurity for his good behaviour for feven years further."

In the time of Elizabeth the fport of hawking was ardently purfued thoughout the Britifh iflands ; and it appears from Carew, that the Devonfhire and Cornifh gentlemen in particular, " were greatly occupied at this time, in hatching, nurturing, and inftructing their

---

* See Weldon's Character and Court of King James, 1650, 12mo. p. 105.

hawks

hawks to fly at the partridge." They were likewife, as it feems from his relation, in the habit of ftealing hawks eggs.* Shakfpeare was obliged to hawking for a great number of metaphorical expreffions.† In the third part of King Henry the fixth, we have a noble allufion to Falconry; where Warwick exclaims,

" Neither the king, nor he that loves him beft,

" The proudeft he that holds up Lancafter,

" Dares ftir a wing, if *Warwick fhake his bells.*"

To underftand, therefore, the firft of our Engglifh claffics, it was neceffary to be acquainted with their terms of this art. Thus confidered, hawking rifes in importance, and merits attention as an object of literature. We meet with an allufion in Beaumont and Fletcher's Bonduca, fimilar to one in Othello. He that bafely

" *Whiftled his honour off to the wind.*"

That Spenfer was not ignorant of this diverfion, is proved by a great number of compa-

* Carew's Survey, p. 25.
† See Romeo and Juliet, Othello, &c. &c.

rifons.

rifons drawn from Falconry. In the firft book
of his Faerie Queen, we read,

" Long he them bore above the fubject plaine,

" So farre as Ewghen bowe a fhaft may fend,

" Till ftrugling ftrong did him at laft conftraine

" To let them downe before his flightes end.

" As *hazard hawke*, prefuming to contend

" With hardie fowle, above his able might,

" His weary pounces all in vaine doth fpend,

" To truffe the prey too heavie for his flight,

" Which, comming downe to ground, does free itfelfe
   by flight."*

A great number of didactic treatifes on
Falconry were written about this period;
among which was, " the Booke of Falconrye,
by George Fueberville, gent." printed in 1575.
The hiftorians of Henry the 8th have not
forgotten this favourite recreation of the Englifh, Scotch, and Irifh. Stowe tells us, " in
hunting and hawking many grave citizens (of
London) have, at this prefent, great delight,
and do rather want leifure than good will to

---

* See likewife book 2, B. 3. B. 6.

follow it."* With refpeﾐ to the hawks of
Ireland, Camden fays " they are not without
their praife : but thefe, as all other animals,
befides men and greyhounds, are of a lefs fize
here, than in England."† That hawking,
indeed, fhould have been greatly efteemed at
this junﾐure, is not to be wondered ; fince
Henry the 8th had conceived a " vaﬆ love for
the fport." And this paﬄion for hawking (as
Hall informs us) had nearly proved fatal to
him ; for, " on a time, as the kynge followed
his hawke (on foot) he attempted to leape over
a ditche, befide Hychyn, with a pole, and the
pole broke ; fo that if one Edmond Mody, a
footman, had not lept into the water, and lift
up his hede, which was faﬆ in the clay, he
had beene drow'ned ; but god of his goodnefs
preferved him."‡ It appears in Julian
Barnes's§ *Booke of Haukyng*, that in the reign
of Henry the 7th, there were hawks appropriated to all degrees of people, from an emperor down to the holy-water clerk. It was
the parliament of Henry the 7th, indeed, that
more peculiarly intereﬆed themfelves in the

* Survey of London, 1616. p. 147.
† Gibfon's Camden, p. 965.
‡ Union. an. 16. H. 8. fol. 139. B.
§ Printed by Caxton, 1486. cap. ult.

preſervation

prefervation of the falcon. Determined to give folemnity to the fport, they conferred a new dignity on the birds of rapine, by rendering them the objects of their guardian care. It was this parliament which ordained, " that no maner of perfon, of what condytion or degre he be, take or caufe to be taken, be it upon his owne grounde, or any other mannes, the egges of any fawcon, out of the neft, upon peyne of impryfonment of a yere and a daye, and fine at the kynges wylle."

We have feen that hawks of Ireland were " not without their praife :" but thofe of the Ifle of Mann were in ftill higher repute. It was for this reafon that King Henry the fourth, in his letters patent of the grant of this ifland to Sir John Stanley, (the firft King of Mann, of that name and race) obliged him, in lieu of all other fervices, upon the day of his and his fucceffors' coronation, to prefent him with a caft of hawks.*

In the reign of Edward the 3d, it was made felony to fteal a hawk. And here we have again an opportunity of illuftrating this art by the aid of poetry ; whilft we refer to Chaucer,

* Gibfon's Camden, p. 1061.

who

who had the honour of being appointed to feveral offices under government, by the third
Edward. Chaucer fpeaks of hawks, indeed,
in the language of a fportfman, calling them
by their different names of *Merlin* or *Marlin*,
Tercelet, *Sparhawk*, &c. In the " Nounes
Preefte's Tale" it is faid :

" He loketh like a Sparhauk, with his eyen."

In the " Squiere's Tale," where are many lines
relating to the falcon, is a curious defcription
of his mew. In the following lines from an
old ballad, Falconry is noticed as the royal
fport of thofe days :

" In fummer time, when leaves grow greene,
     " And bloffoms bedeck the tree,
 " King Edward would a huntyng ryde,
     " Some paftime for to fee.
 " With *hawkes* and hounde, he made him bowne,
     " With horne and eke with bowe ;
 " To Drayton-Baffet he tooke his waye,
     " With all his lordes arowe." •

• Reliques of Ancient Poetry, vol. 2. p. 76.

In

In the foreſt charter of Henry the third, the
privilege was granted, that " every freeman
might have in his own woods, aviaries of
hawks, ſparrow-hawks, falcons, eagles, and
herons."*

That Henry the ſecond was alſo attached
to Falconry, we learn from the report of Gi-
raldus. This hiſtorian informs us, that Henry
preferred the falcons of St. David's land, in
Pembrokeſhire, to all others.

By all the Norman princes, indeed, this
diverſion was purſued with a degree of enthuſiaſm ſcarcely credible. " In our times (ſays
John of Saliſbury)† hunting and hawking are
eſteemed the moſt honourable employments,
and moſt excellent virtues of our nobility.
But, by their conſtant purſuit of this way of
life, they became almoſt as great monſters and
ſavages as the animals which they hunt. Huſ-
bandmen, with their harmleſs herds and
flocks, are driven from their well-cultivated
fields, their meadows and their paſtures, that
wild beaſts may range in them at large. If
one of theſe great and mercileſs hunters paſs
by your habitation, bring out quickly all the

* Carta de Foreſta, cap. xi.
† J. Sariſburiens de nugis Curialium, l. i, c. 4.

L   refreſhment

refreshment you have in your house, or you can buy or borrow from your neighbours, that you may not be involved in ruin, or even accused of treason." This ardor of hunting and hawking was stronger than the consideration of religion, even in a superstitious age. Not only hamlets and villages were destroyed, but even the most sacred edifices thrown down, and all turned into one wide waste, to make room for animals, the objects of a tyrant's pleasure. Sanguinary laws were enacted to preserve the game: and in the reigns of Henry 1ft and William Rufus, it was less criminal to destroy one of the human species than a bird of prey, or a beast of chace. At this time the English ladies are said to have excelled the gentlemen in the art of hawking, which John of Salisbury, rather unpolitely, produces as a proof, that hawking was a frivolous amusement. Hawking appears to have been a favourite sport among the Britons of Wales in the tenth century. And, in the establishment of the British court, the head of the falconers was ranked among the great officers of state.* But, notwithstanding all his

* Howel Dha. l. 1, c. 1, and Florence of Worcester, p. 623. Frankfort edit.

honours,

honours, he was forbidden to take more than
three draughts of beer from his horn, left he
fhould get drunk and neglect his duty. It
feems that, in thofe days, a perfon of rank
fcarcely ftirred out without a hawk on his
hand—which, in old paintings, is the crite-
rion of nobility. Harold, afterwards King of
England, when he went on a moft important
embaffy into Normandy, is reprefented in an
old bafs-relief, as embarking with a bird on
his fift, and a dog under his arm. To " carry
his hawk fair," indeed, was thought a fufficient attainment for a nobleman's fon : this
was the fcience on which he plumed himfelf,
leaving literature to perfons of inferior degree.

The fondnefs of Edward the Confeffor for
hunting and hawking, is thus defcribed by
his hiftorian, William of Malmfbury. " It
was his higheft delight to follow a pack of
fwift hounds in purfuit of their game, and to
cheer them with his voice, or to attend the
flights of hawks taught to purfue and catch
their kindred birds. Every day, after divine
fervice, he took the field, and fpent his time
in thefe beloved fports."* In the fame hif-

* W. Malmf. l. 2. c. 13.

tory

tory we fee Atheftan requiring of the Welch
—" Volucres, quæ aliarum avium prædam
per inane venari nofcerent."

Alfred the Great, though he hath gained
the credit of a wife ftatefman and a philofopher, feems to have placed his fupreme happinefs in hawking—if we may judge from the
language of Affer, the hiftorian and the friend
of the king. It is with rapture that Affer obferves: " His felicity in hunting and hawking, as well as in all the other gifts of God,
was really incomparable, as I myfelf have
often feen."*

In the times of Ethelbald, fo deeply were
the princes and nobility of Europe enamoured
of Falconry, that they conftantly carried their
hawks with them in all their journies, and
fometimes into battle. Nor would they part
with their birds, even to procure their own
liberty, when taken prifoners. The nobleman, in fhort, who refigned his hawk, was
confidered as refigning his nobility.†

Hawking feems alfo to have generally obtained among the Roman Britons of the fixth

* Affer. vit. Æfredi, a Camd. edit. p. 5. Flor. Wig. in
ann. 871. p. 310. Spelman. Gloff. p. 6, 7.

† Memoirs des Infcript. t. 9, p. 542.

century.

century. Gildas, in a remarkable paſſage of his epiſtle, ſpeaks of Maglocunus, on his re-linquiſhing the ſphere of ambition, and taking refuge in a monaſtery, and poetically com-pares him to a dove, that haſtens away at the noiſy approach of the dogs, and with various turns and windings, takes her flight from the talons of the hawk.*

Thus univerſal was the love of Falconry among our progenitors.

The ſport was not purſued with much leſs enthuſiaſm on a great part of the continent of Europe, during the extenſive period through which I have paſſed. But here too large a field would open for the preſent eſſay. I ſhall content myſelf, therefore, with adverting to the anecdote of Lord Orford's heron, which brings proof that Falconry was, about twenty years ago, inveſted with no mean honours in Germany; and, from this juncture, up to the ſixth century, (the point to which I have juſt traced Falconry in Britain,) we might catch a glance of the aerial plunderer, where-ver we directed our views, whether to the Germans, the Gauls, the Italians, or to any

* Gildas—Gale—p. 20.

L 3

other

other of the European nations. It will foon
appear, indeed, contrary to the ideas of every
profeffed writer on the fubject, that Falconry
is to be traced, not only in this ifland, but in
other parts of Europe, far beyond the fixth
century.

The grand falconer of the French King is a
well-known office,* which hiftorians notice
about the year 1250: and at this crifis Falconry was firft invented, according to the
opinion of no fuperficial antiquaries. This,
however, is a moft extraordinary miftake,
that could only have originated in their want
of attention to the fubject. It is a miftake,
which Sir Henry Spelman very juftly expofes,
yet he hath fallen himfelf into an error, for
which it is ftill lefs eafy to account, after the

---

* The royal eftablifhment for hawking in France, was as
follows :—Four captains for as many feveral forts of game,
750 livres each. Four lieutenants, or affiftants to them,
300 livres each. Four mafter falconers, 300 livres each.
Thirteen riders, 250 livres each. Four keepers of the
hawks, 275 livres each. For keeping of forty birds, 4290
livres. For keeping of eighteen fpaniels, 1314 livres. A
keeper of the fpaniels, 275 livres. The captain general of
thefe falconers had alfo a penfion of 2000 livres, and 5000
more allowed him for the hawks which flew at hares, and
lodgings for fervants. There was befides, a captain general
of all the king's private falconries, diftinct from the great
falconry, all his allowances 23,861 livres.—Lewis the 14th
kept for his fports 3,000 dogs and 400 hawks.

Hift. and prefent State of France, vol. 1. *London,* 1717.

pains

pains he feems to have taken in the inveftigation of our art. His view of Falconry, indeed, is limited by the circle of his cuftomary
enquiries, as a legal antiquarian. Beyond this
circle he dares not venture. With refpect to
the opinion, that hawking fprung up in Europe about the year 1250, (or in 1246,) he
thus fpeaks : " Mihi locus peroportune jam
fe offert, ut de antiquitate nobilis illius artis
acceptoricæ, five aucupandi cum accipitre
quædam annotem ; id vel maxime faciendum
cenfeo, ut* Blondo refpondeam, ipforumque
opinioni, qui eam non inventam effe exifti-
mant, ante ætatem Frederici Barbaroffæ."
" Taceo Gaufredum, Ducem Britanniæ, iter
Romam carpentem, ideo à tumultuofâ mu-
liere, caput lapide percuffum, occifumque,
quod accipiter ejus, mulieris gallinam invafe-
rat, † an. dom. 1008." " Ex antiquis legibus manifefte conftat, non folum inventam
eam effe ante mille plus hinc annos, fed pro
more etiam noftris fæculi et difciplinæ, à
Gallis Germanifque illuftratam. Hodiernas
enim artis voces (quà latinè reddi poffunt)

* Decad. 2 lib. 7.—P. Jovius, alfo, in his Hiftory of
Mofcovy, affirms that hawking was altogether unknown to
the ancients
† Hift. de Bretaigne, l. 3, c. 21.

multæ

multæ deprehenduntur in illis legibus."
" Tantumque admirationis in hoc voluptatis
genere pofuere olim veteres illi, ut lege etiam
prohiberent, ne quis fpatham, vel accipitrem
fuum, in ipfam capitis redemptionem cœge-
retur dare : fcilicet cum hic non minus vitæ
effet folatium, quam illa libertatis vindex
atque præfidium. Quin et ipfos, qui vel
canem, vel accipitrem alterius furtim fubtra-
herent, omni ludibrio et dedecore fugillandos
decernerent."—" Majorem adhuc loqui vide-
tur, hujus artis antiquitatem, quòd in notitia
occidentalis imperii ordo militum qui fagit-
tarii venatores dicti funt, aufpicium nominis
fui, accipitrem gerunt in clypeo pro infigni."
There is no doubt but Falconry was practifed
in Gaul and Germany, as Spelman here reprefents it : and it is generally faid to have been
introduced into Italy by the Lombards in the
fixth century : it is mentioned about the time
of Alaric the Goth, by Julius Firmicus.* But

* The laws of Italy, efteemed the Sword and the Hawk
as of equal dignity and importance in the hands of a noble
Lombard. See Script. rerum Ital. tom. 1, part ii. p. 129.
This is the 16th law of the Emperor Lewis the Pious. Memoires fur l'ancienne Chevalerie par M. de St. Palaye, tom.
iii. p. 175.—In the laws of Rotharis, there is a more early
mention of the Art of Hawking, No. 322.—In Gaul, in the
5th century, it is celebrated by Sidonius Apollinaris among
the talents of Avitus, p. 202, 207.

hawking

hawking was known long before in Italy : it was known long before in many parts of Europe: it was known in this country, probably, before many parts of Europe were peopled. Yet, even Warton, the moft refined and enlightened of our antiquaries, was fatisfied with the vague and vulgar notion—obfcurely telling us, that "Falconry was imported into Europe from the Turks and other eaftern nations, where it became chiefly cultivated by the Englifh." I am firmly of opinion, indeed, that our art was actually imported into this ifland from the eaftern nations, but many ages before the exiftence of the Turkifh empire.

That the art of hawking was practifed among the Romans immediately after the days of Vefpafian, we have the moft unqueftionable proof.* Martial, in the 216th epigram of the fourteenth book, thus evidently points out this diverfion :

.Prædo fuit volucrum, famulus nunc aucupis, idem

    Decipit, et captas, non fibi, mæret aves.

* Mart. lib. xiv. E. 216. Opp. Cyneget. lib. 1.

                           But,

But, immediately before this, the Romans were ignorant of the fport. That they had never, before this crifis, adopted it as a diverfion, is proved by the filence of their authors, who profeffedly treat on the arts of hunting, and the hiftory of animals.

To whom, then, were the Romans indebted for their knowledge of Falconry, as Martial defcribes it? probably to the Britons. Martial was particularly attentive to the Britons. No fooner was the Bafcanda Britannica imported from this country into Italy, than Martial feized an occafion of celebrating its curious texture. In the fame manner, I am affured, on his firft obfervation of Falconry, he was pleafed with its novelty, and made it the fubject of an epigram.

It is a certain fact, that, in Britain, the Romans viewed the falconer with admiration, immediately imitated his art, purfued the diverfion with ardor, and greatly improved it by the introduction of fpaniels into the ifland.

Before the Romans thus imitated the Britifh fportfman, and communicated their recently-acquired knowledge to their countrymen at Rome, Falconry feems to have been monopolized by the Britifh iflands, (on this

quarter

quarter of the globe) if we except only a particular part of Thrace.

Of the Thracian falconers, Pliny's description is curious. It wants only clearnefs; and the obfcurity muft have originated in the darknefs of the writer's own ideas concerning the thing related. The following are the hiftorian's words: " In Thraciæ parte fuper amphipolim, homines atque accipitres focietate quadam aucupantur. Hi ex fylvis et harundinetis excitant aves : illi, fupervolentes, deprimunt. Rurfus, captas aves dividunt cum iis. Traditum eft, miffas in fublime fibi excipere eos : Et, cum tempus fit capturæ, clangore ac volatûs genere, invitare ad occafionem."*

The Thracians and Britons were then at this crifis, the only followers of the fport. And, among the former, it was purfued merely by a particular diftrict of the country. That Falconry was thus confined to Thrace and Britain, is further evident from the manner in which it is alfo defcribed by Ælian, and perhaps Homer. Ælian feems to mention, with aftonifhment, that tacit league and common chace between the hawks and the Thra-

* Lib. 10, c. 8.

cian

cian fowlers. " Ακυω δε οτι εν τη θρακη και ανθρωποις εισι συνθηροι εν ταις ελειαις αγραις. Και ο τροπος—οι μεν ανθρωποι, τα δικτυα απλωσαντες, ησυχαζυσιν. Οι δε ιερακες, υπερπετομενοι, και φοβυσι τυς ορνεις, και συνωθυσιν εις τας των δικτυων περιβολας. Των εν ηρημενων οι θρακες μερος αποκρινυσι και εκεινοις, και εχουσι αυτυς πιστυς, μη δρασανΙες δε τυΙο, εαυτυς των συμμαχων εΙερηνσαν." *.

The paffage in which Homer is fuppofed to allude to Falconry, occurs in the 22d book of the Odyffey :

Οἱ δ', ὡστ' αιγυπιοι γαμψωνυχες, αγκυλοχΙιλαι,
Ἐξ ὀρέων ἐλθοντες, ἐπ' ὀρνίθεσσι θορῶσι,
Ταὶ μέν τ'ἐν πεδίῳ νέφεα πλώσσυσαι ιενΙαι,
Οἱ δί τε τὰς ολέκεσιν ἐπάλμενοι ᾽υδέ τις ἀλκὴ
ΓίγεΙαι, υδέ φυγή χαίρυσι δὲ τ'ἀνέρες ἀγρη. †

Not half fo keen, fierce vultures of the chace,

Stoop from the mountains on the feather'd race.

When the wide field extended fnares befet,

With confcious dread they fhare the quivering net :

No help, no flight ; but, wounded every way,

Headlong they drop : the fowlers feize the prey.

* De Animal. lib. 2, c. 42.

† Lib. 22, verf. 320, &c. Xenophon, in his Cynegetics, would probably have noticed Falconry, had he been apprized of its exiftence.

Euftathius

Euftathius and Dacier are decidedly of opinion that thefe lines relate to Falconry.

Falconry, then, as an European fport, eemsf to have been almoft circumfcribed within the limits of Britain ; and it was univerfal among the Britifh chiefs. Every chieftan, among the ancient Britons, maintained a confiderable number of birds for the fport. This appears from a remarkable paffage in the poems of Offian ; in which a peace is endeavoured to be gained by the proffer of " a hundred ma-naged fteeds, a hundred foreign captives, and a hundred hawks, with fluttering wing, that fly acrofs the fky."* That one of the moft northerly chiefs, the private head of a clan, and an inhabitant of a country ill-adapted for the exercife, on account of its hills, fhould offer no lefs than a hundred hawks to the enemy, not only proves the pre-valence of this diverfion among the Britifh chiefs, but the uncommon fpirit with which it was purfued.

Here, then, we have gained our higheft point, where Falconry feems to exift in this ifland, unknown to the countries around ; or,

* See Offian, vol. i. p. 119.

if

if cafually obferved, marked only with aftonifhment.

A queftion, then, arifes—was Falconry invented (as Druidifm is idly reported to have
been) in Britain?—was it indigenous, fpringing up fpontaneoufly in Britifh foil?—Or,
was it an exotic, imported into this ifland,
from fome diftant country?

As we difcover it no where elfe in Europe,
at this period of high antiquity, (except a
ftraggling plant in the country above Amphi-
polis) let us ftretch our views to Afia. Here
we find it luxuriantly flourifhing. To the Indians, the Arabians, the Perfians, and all the
people of the eaft, Falconry feems to have
been familiar from the higheft antiquity. In
the Fables of Pilpay, (an Indian Bramin) and
other oriental writings, hawking is often defcribed. In the eaftern countries, fome of
the wilder quadrupeds, fuch as deer, and
gazelles or rock-goats, have been always the
chief objects of the falconer's purfuit. Arrian,
the Roman philofopher and hiftorian, who
wrote about 160 years after Chrift, feems to
have been well acquainted with the oriental
mode of hunting. This writer, fpeaking of
men, who, from a vain idea of infecurity, are
often

often hurried into actual danger by their fears, compares them to deer purfued by falcons, and flying into nets.* The hunting of wild animals with the falcon, is ftill practifed in the eaft; though not exactly in the manner that Arrian defcribes it. We do not find that nets are at all ufed in the fport. The fportfman trufts to his falcon alone: and the gazelle or rock-goat, it feems, hath fufficient reafon to fear the falcons of his enemy. In all countries, indeed, where the gazelles are found, they are purfued by falcons; and this admirable manner of hunting makes one of the principal amufements of the higher ranks of people, all over the eaft. The Arabians and Perfians, in particular, breed up, for this purpofe, that kind of hawk called the Falcon-gentle; with which, when properly trained, they go forth on horfeback among the forefts and the mountains; the falcon darts on his prey, and is taught to fix his talons in the neck and throat of the animal. Haffelquift, who made a voyage to the Levant, purpofely to trace out the natural hiftory of Paleftine, and of the neighbouring countries, informs us, that he

* Arrian, l. 2, c. 1.

had

had once an excellent opportunity of feeing this fport near Nazareth in Galilee.

The great attention of the Orientals to hawking, is evinced by the vaft number of falconers kept by their princes. Mahomet, when he made war in Caramania, is faid to have difcharged from his camp feven hundred of Amarath his father's falconers. Hence it appears, that in that æra, Falconry was very extenfively practifed. Nor is it, by any means, in a declining ftate at the prefent moment, if the Grand Seignieur (as we are informed) keep fix thoufand falconers in his fervice. But there are few eaftern ufages, that undergo the flighteft change: as they exifted at the remoteft periods, they generally remain to this day. I fhould not omit, that the Chinefe have been falconers from the moft ancient times. Hawks perched on the hands of fportfmen, and in various other fituations, are often reprefented in Chinefe paintings. Falconry then, of which the Europeans had, in general, no idea, in the days of the firft Britifh princes, was familiar to the Afiatics at the fame time that it was the favourite amufement of the Britons. That it was imported, therefore, from

from some part of the east into this country, is no improbable conclusion.

The Aborigines of Britain, according to the vulgar opinion, were a colony from Gaul. But they resembled the Gauls in few particulars. In their religion, their language, their usages, and their diversions, they were very unlike the Gauls, and indeed the European tribes in general. But I could prove, that, in all these points, they approached very nearly to the Asiatics. The British war-chariot had its prototype in the east. It was too incommodious a vehicle in an island, almost every where rising into hills or declining into vallies, to have been first invented in Britain. It was certainly imported into Britain by its primitive inhabitants ; and the perseverance of the Aborigines, in still using this chariot for the purposes of war, after they had colonized the island, notwithstanding the inconvenience of their new situation, seems, itself, to point out their origin. In the same manner, our love of Falconry, notwithstanding the inequalities of ground I have just remarked, so ill-suited to the sport, strongly speaks our descent from the eastern nations, whose fine champaign

M   countries

countries may be ranged by the falconer, without interruption, and with little danger.

From what part of Afia the Aborigines of Britain came, is a point which it fuits not my prefent purpofe to difcufs. Nor by what channel we received our firft colony, have I leifure to enquire. For ample information on this fubject, I would refer you to Mr. Pinkerton, Colonel Vallancey, and Sir W. Jones.

That this ifland was not originally colonized from Gaul, about 1000 years before Chrift, (which is the generally-received hypothefis) is evinced beyond all contradiction by the concurrent teftimonies of thefe eminent antiquaries. And, that it was peopled from the eaft, they feem to have as clearly proved. But, whether our firft colonies came hither immediately by fea, or progreffively advanced towards this ifland over the north of Europe, it may be difficult to determine. From our evident independence on the continent in various inftances, I fhould prefer the former opnion. The mercantile voyages of the Phenicians are well known; and a colonial voyage might have been as eafily performed as a mercantile one. According to Pinkerton, the Scythians, the Getæ and the Goths, were all one people; the

the firſt grand Scythian empire was in preſent Perſia, and the Scythians came from preſent Perſia into Europe by a north-weſt progreſs. Admitting this theory, we need not wonder that Falconry ſhould at one time appear only in Thrace and in Britain, ſince the Thracians were no other than Getæ or Scythians, and ſince the Aborigines of this country were Scythians alſo. Nor have we, in this caſe, any reaſon to be ſurpriſed at the Barbarians of the ſixth century exhibiting their ſkill in Falconry wherever they made their incurſions; ſince the Lombards and the Goths had no common origin. By ſuppoſing, however, this colonization of Britain, in conſequence of the north-weſt progreſs from Perſia, we muſt preſume that Falconry was practiſed at this early period, in the intermediate countries at leaſt between Thrace and Britain.

Such then is the ſlight hiſtorical outline of Falconry that I propoſed to draw; a diverſion which, though no longer purſued with enthuſiaſm in Europe, and almoſt abandoned in this iſland, is ſtill univerſally followed in thoſe countries of Aſia, where it originated; a diverſion which was followed in Britain from the earlieſt times, and which our continental

neighbours

neighbours to the fouth, when they firft faw
it, beheld with wonder! Nor is it difficult to
imagine, that the European nations fhould
gaze with eager curiofity on an art which
taught the birds of the air to acknowledge
the voice, and execute the commands of their
mafter: it was an act which bore a refemblance to the fpells of the Perfian enchanter;
and the magic which could charm the ftars
from their courfes, was fcarcely lefs aftonifhing than that power, which, acting on the
rapacity of the falcon, could urge it through
the fields of heaven, or fuddenly arreft it in
its flight—which could point its unerring
talons to its prey, yet bring to the earth the
bloodftained victor, laying its acquifitions at
the feet of man; and thus, in the very moment of its triumphs, convert its ferocity into
gentlenefs.

A CHRO-

A
CHRONOLOGICAL ESSAY

O N

PTOLEMY's MODE of COMPUTATION.

December 13th, 1792.

" Remque Ordine pando."

VIRGIL.

I PROPOSE, in the differtation now prefented to you, to difcufs, and if I can, afcertain
a truth upon which the neceffary precifion
and regularity of chronological information,
in a good meafure, depend. Should, indeed,
the object of this paper be attained by me,
the character of the moft ufeful and moft celebrated annalift of antiquity, I mean Ptolemy
of Alexandria, will be refcued from the mo-
mentous charge of error and difcordance in

M 3

his

his computations. As hiftory itfelf is * " nihil
aliud quam annalium confectio ;" and as
Bacon juftly obferves, that †" chronica nomine
et celebritate excellere videntur," this fociety
will, doubtlefs, approve a defign to remove
the caufes of perplexity from the canon, antient hiftory's moft exact regifter.

Moft writers imagine that the above author
invariably afcribes the year of a king's death
to him who began the year. From the greateft
part of chronologers, who are united in this
opinion, we may except Sir Ifaac Newton
alone. However, it is of fmall import who
are on one fide or the other. That thefe chronologers are totally erroneous, is a point to
be determined by *facts* and not *authorities* ;
and this is the point which I mean to prove.
Perhaps I fhall put beyond the reach of difpute this pofition, that Ptolemy always afcribes the year of a king's death to his fucceffor.

Mr. Dodwell, in his notes upon the " mi-
nores Geographi," has found fault with the
chronology of this canon in the Egyptian
kings ; in his appendix to the " Differtationes

* De Oratore.　　† Augmen. Scien. lib. 2d. c. 7th.

Cyprionicæ,"

Cyprianicæ," he has *defended* the same chronology. But I shall leave him to answer himself, and chuse rather to consider the last part of the canon relating to the Roman emperors, because we know exactly the days of inauguration and death of almost all. This will give us Ptolemy's rule to a certainty in that part of the canon; and none have doubted but that he follows one and the same rule throughout the whole. If indeed we had not this method of determining it, I should however be inclined to my own opinion for this general reason. It is confessed the whole civil year from Thoth to Thoth, is ascribed to *one* king, either the deceased or the successor, and is never divided between them, after the manner of the Romans of old, and of ourselves at present; but if so, then, certainly, it is much more probable that they complimented the living with it, than the dead. The year was indeed ascribed, as it ought to be, to the king who begun it, and continued so as long as he lived; but upon his death it was ascribed to his successor in the latter part of it, for the very same reason upon which the former part of it had been ascribed to the other; and since the whole year could

M 4

not

not be afcribed to both, the laft poffeffor had
a fort of right to retain it, and the deceafed
yielded up the year as well as the crown.——
This, I fay, is fo natural and reafonable to
believe, that it would weigh much with me,
without any other argument. We find this to
have been the cafe in fact, among the Jews.
Herod died about the *latter* end of the year,
Anno Ur. C. 750, in the 37th year of his
reign; and yet Archelaus was banifhed in the
10th year of his reign, before the autumn,
An. Ur. C. 759; that is, as Kepler long ago
obferved, and as the Talmudifts acknowledge,
Archelaus's reign was not reckoned from the
death of his father, but from the Nifan proceeding; nor was this the cafe only among
the Jews. The Eyptians (which is more to
our purpofe, as Ptolemy was an Alexandrian)
ufed the fame way of reckoning. The Dioclefian æra was Egyptian. Dioclefian was declared emperor September 17th, A. Chrifti,
284, but the years of Dioclefian were reckoned
from Auguft 29th, that is the Thoth preceding. In fhort, the fixed years of the Egyptians beginning with Auguft 29th, are called
by Cenforinus the Anni Auguftorum fecundum
Egyptios. But why were they fo named?
Not

Not from Auguftus Cæfar; for then they fhould have been named Anni Augufti, or a victoriâ Augufti; whereas, if I miftake not, " Auguftorum" implies, that thefe years in the Egyptian way of reckoning were wholly coincident with the years of the feveral Augufti or emperors, which was not true of the Roman years, that were always divided pro ratâ between the predeceffor and fucceffor. But to come to particulars in the canon itfelf:

According to Dion, Auguftus beat Antony at Actium, Sept. 2d, anno U. C. 723; about a year after he took Alexandria; but the day is not mentioned. Dion, however, tells us * that the Roman fenate decreed thereupon, among other honours, τηντε ημεραν 'εν η̃ 'Αλεξανδρίια 'εάλω αγαθηντε ειναι, και ιστα επειτα ετη αρχην της απαριθμησεως αυτων νομιζεσθαι. But who were to reckon from this day, and in this manner? not the Romans; they neither began their year nor the reign of Auguftus from that day; neither were they the Afiatics and Syrians: for all thefe falling under the power of Auguftus upon the defeat of Actium, reckoned his years from *that* victory, as appears by their coins. The decree, therefore, muft relate to the Alexan-

* Lib. 51. p. 457 Ed. Leunclavii 1606.

drians,

drians, and accordingly we find that Philo,
Clemens Alexandrinus, and, agreeably to Cenforinus, the Egyptians in general reckoned the
year of the Roman emperors from thence.
They had a fixed year too, from this time
forward (like the Julian year) which, doubtlefs, they would not have received but in obe-
dience to their new mafters and conquerors.
Geminus tells us, in his time, that it was a
point of their religion to keep the Thoth vague
and unfettled. We may fuppofe, therefore,
that the Thoth was fixed by virtue of this decree, and confequently that Auguft 29th was
the day on which the city was taken, anno U.
C. 724. Ptolemy, therefore, has juftly made
the reign of Auguftus to commence with the
year of Nabonaffar, 719, and of courfe concluded the reign of Cleopatra with the year
of Nabonaffar, 718, though fhe lived for fome
time after. Petavius, indeed, fuppofes that
fhe killed herfelf on that day ; but it is certain, from Dions' account, that fhe had an
interview with Auguftus after the city was
taken, tried all her wiles with him, and did
not deftroy herfelf till fhe defpaired of not
being perfonally led in triumph ; nor could
fhe even then execute her defign immediately,
                                    guarded

guarded and narrowly watched as fhe was by
Epaphroditus. She was forced to pretend a
readinefs and defire to go to Rome in order
to impofe upon him, and make him lefs
watchful of her ; fo that it is certain fhe lived
for fome time in the year of Nabonaffar, 719,
though Ptolemy concludes her reign with the
former. But I do not infift upon this inftance, becaufe Auguftus came in by conqueft
upon the firft day of the year, and put an end
to her reign, though not to her life.

Auguftus died Auguft 19th, An. U. C. 767,
and the next day, Auguft 20th, was the Thoth,
anno Nab. 762, and the firft day of the reign
of Tiberius ; Ptolemy, therefore, has properly ended the reign of Auguftus with anno
Nab. 761, and afcribed 762 to Tiberius ;
but this inftance proves nothing, becaufe Auguftus lived to fee the laft day of his laft year,
and Tiberius commenced his reign and the
new year together.

Anno U. C. 789, Auguft the 14th, was the
Thoth, anno Nabonaffar, 784, and Tiberius
died on the 16th March following. This is
fully to our purpofe, for Ptolemy ends the
reign of Tiberius with anno Nabonaffar, 783,
and afcribes the whole year, 784, of that æra

to

to Caius; that is, he anticipates his reign about seven months, beginning it with the Thoth preceding the death of Tiberius.

Anno U. C. 793, August 13, was the Thoth, anno Nab. 788. Caius was killed on January 24th following, and yet Ptolemy ends his reign with anno Nab. 787, and ascribes all the year, 788, to Claudius. This, therefore, is to the point likewise.

Anno U. 807, August 10th, was the Thoth anno Nab. 802. Claudius died the 13th of October following; but Ptolemy, as in the former instances, ascribes the year of Nab. 802, to Nero, and ends the reign of Claudius with the former year.

Anno U. C. 821, August 6th, was the Thoth anno Nab. 816. Nero killed himself on June 9th preceding, that is, anno Nab. 815. Vespasian, according to Tacitus, was declared emperor by Tiberius Alexander, prefect of Egypt on July 1st, the year after, or anno U. C. 822, which was still within the year of Nab. 816. Ptolemy, therefore, could not carry back the reign of Vespasian farther than the Thoth of that year 816. And yet this was near two months short of the death of Nero on June 9th, anno Nab. 815. In this
case

case therefore, Ptolemy gives Nero the whole
years in which he died, and reckons the reign
of Vespasian from the thoth following; nor is
this contrary to the reason of his former rule;
for where one emperor dies, and another succeeds in the *same* year, both of them have
some title to that year; which, since it cannot be ascribed to both, the living, that is, the
successor is to be preferred; but where the one
dies and the other succeeds in *different* years,
i. e. where a Thoth comes between, there each
of them may have his year, because their
claims interfere not with one another. And
since Vespasian's reign, by Ptolemy's rule
must be reckoned from Thoth anno Nab. 816,
and could not commence before; the year
815 was of necessity ascribed to Nero, because
from his death, June 9th, to the thoth following, viz. August 6th, there was not time
enough for an intermediate reign, nor for an
interregnum, as Ptolemy reckons nothing less
than one year. Eusebius and the Chronicon
Alexandrinum reckon the same way, and omit
Galba, Otho, and Vitellius.

A. U. 831, August the 4th, was the Thoth
anno Nab. 826. Vespasian died *June* 24th
following, and was immediately succeeded by
his

his fon, to whom Ptolemy therefore afcribes all that year 826, and fo begins his reign above ten months before the death of his father.

Anno A. U. 834, Aug. 3d, was the Thoth anno Nab. 829, in which year, Sept. 13th, Titus died, and Ptolemy afcribes the whole year to his fucceffor Domitian.

Anno U. C. 849, July 30th, was the Thoth of an. Nab. 844, and Domitian was killed about two months after, viz. Sept. 18th ; Ptolemy therefore concludes his reign with anno Nab. 843, and afcribes the next year wholly to Nerva.

Anno U. C. 850, July 30th, was the Thoth anno Nab. 845. On the calends of January following, Trajan was conful the fecond time with Nerva, and was at that time emperor ; for Pliny fays, * " fecundum confulatum imperator quidem *fub* imperatore tamen inivifti," but how long before this he was adopted and affociated in the empire, does not appear. January 27th, that year, Nerva died, and Trajan remained emperor alone. Ptolemy, therefore, according to his rule in the former cafes, has very rightly afcribed all that year

* Panygeric.

of

of Nab. 845, to Trajan, even though we
fhould reckon his reign only from the death of
Narva, and not from his adoption.   Accordingly he has recorded an obfervation made on
January 10th, this year, anno primo Trajani;
and Petavius * erroneoufly fuppofes this a difficulty, and then as erroneoufly folves it by
conjecturing, that Ptolemy had followed a
faulty catalogue of the Roman emperors.
Scaliger, to fave the credit, as he affuredly
thinks, of Ptolemy, cuts off one year from
Domitian, and Cardinal Norris, though he
objects both to Petavius and Scaliger, with
equal abfurdity offers no folution, which, as
we fee, was indeed unneceffary.

A. U. C. 870, July 25th, was the Thoth an.
Nab. 865, and Trajan is fuppofed to have died
on Aug. 10th following.   Ptolemy therefore
fhould have begun the reign of Adrian with
the year of Nab. 865, but inftead of fo doing,
he begins it with anno Nab. 864.   Here there
is a real difficulty, and feemingly an anticipa-
tion of one year, which Petavius and others
have obferved, but afcribed to a wrong caufe.
It can be no fault in the reading, nor yet a flip
of memory, becaufe he has no lefs than fix-

---

* Nat. Contemp. p. 2. lib. 4th. c. 6.

teen

teen obfervations made in different years of
Adrian's reign, and in all of them he com-
putes 864th year of Nabonaffar to be the firft.
Let us fee, then, when the death of Trajan
really happened. Spartian tells us of Adrian,
quinto iduum Augufti die legatus Syriæ literas
adoptionis accepit quando et natalem celebrari
juffit. Tertio Iduum quando et natalem Im-
peratoris inftituit celebrandum exceffus ei Trajani nuntiatus eft. He received the news therefore, of his adoption, Auguft 9th, and of the
death of Trajan Auguft 11th, anno U. 870.
Trajan, according to Eutropius and Xiphilin,
reigned 19 years, 6 months, and 15 days.
Reckon this time from the death of Nerva,
January 27th, inclufively, and it brings us to
Auguft 10th, where Petavius and others place
the death of Trajan. But this cannot be true,
for if Trajan died Auguft 10th, at Selinus in
Cilicia, Adrian could not receive the news of
it the next day at Antioch in Syria. Dion
fays, that his father Apronianus, who was at
that time governor of Cilicia, had often told
him that Trajan's death was concealed ημεραστιναι
by Plautilla and Attianus, who, in the mean
while, wrote letters in the emperor's name to
the fenate, and forged the inftruments of
Adrian's adoption. Trajan, therefore, muft
have

have been dead before Auguft, but how long before, Dion does not tell us. Let us reckon then his reign of 19 years, 6 months, and 15 days, from the time of his adoption and affociation into the empire with Nerva, and not from the death of Nerva. This time, as I before obferved, was before the calends of January, preceding the death of Nerva, and confequently the reign of Trajan, reckoned from thence, will end before the 25th of July, *i. e.* before the Thoth anno Nab. 865. Again, Eutropius tells us, that Trajan was 63 years, 9 months, and 5 days old when he died; but Pliny fays, that he was born on the fame day of the fame month on which Domitian was killed on, Sept. 18th. Reckon the odd months and days of his age from thence, and his death will fall on June 23d. Perhaps it will be thought too long a time for his death to have been concealed from June 23d till Auguft, and therefore I fhall leave the day of his death as a thing uncertain. Now if it happened after July 25th, *i. e.* after the Thoth anno Nab. 864, then Ptolemy fhould have begun the reign of Adrian with anno Nab. 865; but if the death of Trajan happened before July 25th, *i. e.* before the Thoth anno Nab. 865,

then

then Adrian fucceeding by virtue of the pretended adoption, really fucceeded in the year
Nab. 864, though he received not the news
of his fucceffion till Auguft following. In
this ftate of uncertainty about the death of
Trajan, it is more reafonable to fuppofe that
Ptolemy had fome certain account of it, which
we have loft, than to think that he could miftake the years of an emperor's reign in his *own*
times, and confequently we may fuppofe that
he has, according to his general rule, afcribed
the year 864 to Adrian, becaufe Trajan really
died in the latter end of the year. However,
I fufpect that the true reafon might be different, and Theon's continuation of Ptolemy's
canon helps us to determine this matter.
What I fufpect is this, Ptolemy made not the
Imperial years coincident with the civil years,
merely for the convenience of reckoning; but
likewife becaufe it was conformable to the cuftom of his countrymen the Alexandrians, for
whofe ufe principally he wrote. He has likewife made ufe of the vague form of year for
the fame reafon, becaufe this was in ufe
among them during the former times of the
canon. But from the time of Auguftus, the
Egyptian year was fixed, and confequently
in

in the popular way of reckoning the Anni Auguftorum or Imperial years, began with Auguft 29th, or the fixed thoth. Ptolemy,
however, keeps to the vague form of years in
his obfervations within the times of the latter
part of his canon, as well as within the former,
becaufe all his tables were calculated to that
form, and it was not worth the while to make
his tables anew for the fake of a few reigns.
Nor was the inconvenience of it any more
than what we have experienced in the different reckonings by the new and old ftile.
I fufpect then Ptolemy in reckoning the *years*
of the emperors from the time of Auguftus,
followed the fixed form of year, becaufe that
was conformable to the popular way of reckoning, and of courfe more intelligible; but
as to the day of the month he followed the
vague form in conformity to his own tables,
becaufe the day of the month might eafily be
reduced from one form of the year to the
other. To apply this to the reign of Adrian,
Spartian fays, that he ordered the 11th day
of Auguft to be kept as the day of his acceffion : this was anno Nab. 865, according to
the *vague* form of year beginning at that time
with July 25th, but in the *fixed* form of year,

beginning

beginning with Auguſt 29th, and in the popular way of reckoning it was anno Nab. 864. Ptolemy therefore calls 864 the 1ſt year of Adrian, agreeable to the common mode of reckoning among his countrymen, who, by theſe means, more readily underſtood him. For inſtance, he tells us, that in the 17th year of Adrian, anno Nab. 880, upon the 20th day of Payni there was an eclipſe ; they immediately underſtood the 17th of Adrian and anno Nab. 880, to be coincident according to the popular way of reckoning, and the fixed form, from whence they could eaſily reduce the day of the month by a certain rule, which Theon has given us in his commentaries upon this canon.* But if Ptolemy had called this year the 16th of Adrian, as he muſt have done in caſe he had begun his reign with anno Nab. 865, the reader would then have been led to think of the year 879, according to the vulgar computation, and would have had no way of correcting his miſtake but by recourſe to the day of Adrian's acceſſion ; which day, in all probability, was not much attended to by a nation who did not compute from that day,

* Vide Obſer. in Theonis Faſt. &c. p. 34, &c.

.· but

but from the Thoth of their own civil year. If this conjecture is right, then all the Imperial years in the canon from the reign of Cleopatra are to be computed from the *fixed* and not from the *vague* thoth ; but this can make no difference, unlefs when an emperor's acceffion to the crown falls *between* the *two* thoths, of which we have no inftance befides this of Adrian.

Antoninus is the laft emperor in this canon, and Ptolemy begins his reign with anno Nab. 885. Here again Petavius and others exclaim, that Ptolemy has anticipated this reign by one year. But how is this poffible ? Ptolemy has recorded many obfervations made by himfelf in the 17th, 18th, 19th, 20th, and 21ft years of Adrian, and in the 1ft, 2d, 3d, and 4th years of Antoninus. Now if we could fuppofe him guilty of an error in reckoning the year of Adrian, yet it is abfurd to think that he could continue that error into the next reign, and record his obfervations, as if made under Antoninus for a full year before he was acknowledged emperor. Ptolemy all along mentions the Nabonaffarean as well as the Imperial year, and therefore the latter year (viz. the Imperial) was only added for the better

afcertaining

afcertaining the time, and for preventing all
error and miftake; but it would be fo far from
anfwering this end, that on the contrary it
would occafion error and miftake if Ptolomy
defignedly anticipated thefe reigns and reckoned them differently from the common manner of his countrymen. Neither could fuch a
different way of reckoning be accidental, for
it is inconceivable, that he fhould defignedly
fet down thofe years, and yet take no care to
do it with accuracy, or that he fhould fall into
an error about the year of the reigning emperor, and continue in the error for fo many
years together, without perceiving it either
his own enquiries, or by converfation with
others. In fhort the miftake is not Ptolemy's,
but is a miftake of thofe who find fault with
him. Petavius himfelf places the death of
Adrian on July 10th, A. U. C. 891, i. e. anno
Nab. 885, for the 20th of July was the Thoth
of the Nab. year 886. Onuphrius, Goltzius,
and moft other writers, agree in this time of
Adrian's death, and Antoninus's fucceffion.
Since therefore it is confeffed, that Antoninus
began his reign in the latter end of the year
Nab. 885, it follows that the whole of the
year, according to the method of Ptolomy
and

and of the Egyptians, was to be afcribed to
him, and confequently the canon is right in fo
doing. I muft, however, obferve to you,
that Cardinal Norris, notwithftanding this general confent of authors about the time of
Adrian's death, has undeniably proved him
living A. U. C. 892, but then at the fame
time he proves that Adrian being old, in-
firm, and incapable of the bufinefs of the empire, Antoninus was acknowledged as emperor from July 10th, A. U. C. 891, that the
Roman writers dated his reign, and Antoninus
himfelf computed his decennalia from that
time,* fo that this does not affect Ptolemy.
For if Antoninus was acknowledged emperor
at Rome, and by the Latin writers, there can
be no doubt but that he was acknowledged
fuch in the provinces and at Alexandria; and
confequently if the year Nab. 885, was the
firft or the year of inauguration of Antoninus,
the former year muft of courfe, in the method
of the canon, be the laft of Adrian. This,
therefore, evidently fhews that the laft year of
any reign in the canon is fo far from being
the year of the *king's death*, that it does not

* Differ. de Vet. Decennal.

fo much as imply him to have died even in
year following. All that it ſhews is, that ſuch
a year was the laſt year ended or compleated
by that king; or rather that his ſucceſſor was
inaugurated or acknowledged in the year following; whether the death of the king happened in that *laſt year,* as in the caſe of Auguſtus and Nero, or in the year following, as
in the caſe of Tiberius, Caius, &c. or ſtill
later, as in this caſe of Adrian. In *all* theſe
caſes it is undeniably evident that the *next* year,
i. e. the *firſt* year of the ſucceſſor was always
the ſame with the year of his acceſſion or inauguration.

I have now, I truſt, ſufficiently proved my
point, upon which the uſe and credit of the
" Canon" reſt. If the rule laid down, had
been properly attended to, Ptolemy would not
have been charged with error by ſo many conſiderable writers. Every one who had any
ſkill in chronology has ſaid ſome ſtrong things
in praiſe of it. Calviſius, who firſt publiſhed
it from MSS. ſays it is "omni auro pretioſior."
Canon certiſſimus, ſays Dodwell. "The undoubted meaſure of time among all the aſtro-
nomers, both Jews and Gentiles," ſays Biſhop
Loyd; yet, if you ſuppoſe the year of any
king's

king's death to be afcribed to that king, as the laft year of his reign, this invaluable canon and infallible guide, " hic exactiffimus temporum character, fallere nefcius," as Bifhop Beveridge ftiles it, will be faulty and delufive in almoft every inftance.

I fhall conclude the effay with fome fhort and general remarks on this Canon, to facilitate the ufe and comprehenfion of it, and on the Nabonaffarean æra, which Ptolemy has adopted.

It has been a very prevailing opinion that this æra was ufed at Babylon from the time of Nabonaffar; and that Berofus was the author of this canon as far down as the time of Alexander.—I am of a quite contrary opinion. There is not one word mentioned of Nabonaffar or the æra Nabonaffar in any author now extant, before Ptolemy, *i. e.* about 140 years after Chrift. It appears too from Ptolemy himfelf, that all the Babylonifh obfervations were dated in fuch a year of the reign of fuch a king, juft as we now date contracts by the year of the king's reign; fo that this table was Ptolemy's own work. When an aftronomer has once

fettled

settled the annual, monthly, and diurnal motions of the planets, and formed them into
tables, 'tis also necessary that he should determine the places which the planets 'Επιχυσι in
the heavens at the very end or beginning of
some certain year, and this is called the 'Εποχὰ
from whence the motions of the planets, according to the time from that epocha, are to be
compleated. Thus the Christian astronomers
usually fix their epocha at the beginning of the
1 st year of Christ; the Jews, of the 1 st year of
the world. Now Ptolemy says, that he fixed
his in the beginning of Thoth, or the 1 st day of
the 1 st year of Nabonassar. 'αφ 'υ χρονυ, says
he, και πας παλαιας τηρησεις εχομεν 'ως 'επιπαν μεχρι τε
δευρο διασωζομενας. This is the only reason that
Ptolemy gives for placing his epocha there,
namely, that it would take in the antient observations; but as to Nabonassar's being Be-
lesis, or the founder of the Babylonish monar-
chy, or of a college of astronomers, or that this
æra was used by the astronomers at Babylon,
he does not say one word. And yet these
would have been proper reasons, if he had
known any thing of them, or had regarded
them. On the contrary, when he mentions a
Chaldee observation, he *first* sets it down as
made

made in fuch a year of fuch a king, but what was that to his purpofe? nothing at all, unlefs he found it fo recorded in the books of the Chaldeans, and intended to copy them exactly. When this was done, there was no ufe to to be made of it, till the diftance of the time from the epocha was determined; and there-fore after the year of the king, he adds of himfelf " which is fuch a year from Nabon-affar, and fometimes, which is fuch a year from *our* epocha, plainly intimating, that this æra was his own invention; and confequently that the canon was made by him for the more readily reducing the years of the kings to this æra, and thereby examining the obfervations of the Babylonians. However, though this was the work of Ptolemy, yet it is of much more authority than the chronology of Hero-dotus, Ctefias, or other authors. For (1ft) Ptolemy was obliged to take more care, and ufe the utmoft exactnefs in fettling and con-necting the years of his reigns; becaufe, if he had erred but one year in fettling the time of the obfervation, it would have been ufelefs, and could never have anfwered to his aftrono-mical tables. 2dly, Every aftronomical ob-fervation was a proof of the truth of the

canon;

canon; for if, by calculation, he found the motion of the planets to anfwer to the obfervation, this was a proof that he had fixed that year of the king's reign rightly; but if the obfervation did not agree with the calculation, this was a proof that there was fome error in fixing the time, provided that the obfervation might be depended on. 3dly. When this canon of the kings reigns was made, it could not eafily be corrupted like other books in tranfcribing, becaufe the double column of numbers, whereof one contained the whole reign of each king, and the other the aggregate or fum total of all the reigns from Nabonaffar, ferved to correct each other, and would at once difcover any error that might have crept into it. 4thly. The feveral obfervations preferved in his Μεγαλη συνταξις, or Almageft, with the year of the king, and year of Nabonaffar in which it was made, are ftill fo many fure proofs of the integrity of this canon.

So much for the author, antiquity, and credit of it. I fhall add a few rules to be obferved in it. 1ft. It was Ptolemy's defign only to fix the number of years of the beginning and end of each king's reign from his epocha, the Nabonaffarean; therefore, if any

king

king reigned lefs than one year, he did not infert him in this canon. Thus Laborofoarchod, who reigned nine months after Nerigliffar, is omitted; fo too Smardis, who reigned feven months after Cambyfes, is omitted. The Chinefe do the fame to this day. They omit fuch reigns in their fafti, though they mention them in their hiftories. 2dly. In whatever part of the year any prince fucceeded, Ptolemy reckons that whole year to his reign, beginning it from thoth, or the firft day of that year: this, I think, was the method of all the eaftern people. The Talmudifts fay it was the conftant method of the Jews, and it is demonftrable in the cafe of Herod and his three fons. Dr. Prideaux has erred moft egregioufly, when he tells us, this canon begins each reign from the thoth *following* inftead of the thoth *preceding*. 3dly. If a prince died in the middle of the year, and his fucceffor lived to begin the *next* year, but did not compleat twelve months, then this intermediate prince being omitted in the catalogue, his next fucceffor could begin his reign no higher than the thoth preceding, and therefore his predeceffor's reign muft be brought down beyond his death to the thoth following.

This

This I fhewed in the former part of this effay.
4thly. If there are two competitors for the
crown, or two princes reigning jointly at the
fame time, Ptolomy fets down, as I hinted
before, the conqueror, or the furvivor only,
becaufe the whole reign of the former was
included within that of the latter, and therefore it would have been of no ufe to his purpofe to have mentioned both of them.   This
is evident in feveral of the Egyptian and Perfian kings, and this, I think, is the reafon
too, why he did not fet down Darius the
Mede, or Aftyages, in this catalogue.   Ptolemy therefore appears to have concerned himfelf only about whole years.

The form of the year and the months are
undoubtedly Ægyptian.   That the Chaldeans
ufed the fame year and begun it with the fame
day as the Egyptians, may be probable, but
is not certain.   The year contained 365 days
only, and confequently four of them contained
one day lefs than four Julian years; fo that
365 multiplied by 4, or 1460 Julian years
contained 1461 Egyptian or Nabonaffarean
years.   Of thefe 1461 years one fingle year
began upon the intercalated day in the Julian
year between the 23d and 24th of February.
Of

Of the reſt every 4 began upon a new day in the
Julian year, going backwards. Thus the 11th
year of Nabonaſſar began upon the Biſſextilis
calendas martias anno periodi Julianæ 3977,
and ended upon the 22d of February. The
12th, 13th, 14th, and 15th began upon the
23d of February. The next 4 upon the 22d,
and ſo on in a retrograde order. Subtract 11
therefore from any given year of Nabonaſſar,
and divide the reſidue by 4, the quotient will
ſhew the number of days to be counted back,
incluſively, from the 23d of February; the
next day backwards is the beginning of the
year, and the remainder ſhews whether it is
the 1ſt, 2d, 3d, or 4th year beginning on that
day. The 1ſt year of Nebuchadnazzar is annus
Nabonaſſarius 144. Subtract 11, and divide
the reſidue 133 by 4, the quotient will be 33,
and the remainder 1. Count back 33 days,
beginning with February 23d, and the laſt
day will be January 22d; therefore this year
began January 21ſt, and was the firſt year of
the four beginning on that day. Again, from
anno Nabonaſſar 747, ſubtract 11, and divide
the reſidue 736 by 4. The quotient will be
184, and the remainder none, but the remainder ought to be ſomething; therefore in
this

this and like cafes make it 41, which makes the quotient 1 lefs, namely, 183. Count back 183 days, beginning with February 23d, and the laft day is Auguft 25th; therefore this year begun Auguft 24th, and the remainder fhews it to be the 4th or laft year beginning on that day. Upon the 1ft of January following begun the year before Chrift, and the 4713th year of the Julian period; confequently the firft year of Chrift begins in January, anno Nabonaffaris .748. This will be fufficient to fhew you how to find the beginning of thofe years of Nabonaffar, and to connect them with the years of the Julian period, or of the vulgar æra.

AN

AN

ESSAY ON THE IRIS,

Demonſtrative of the MOTIONS and EFFECTS of that
MEMBRANE on the PUPIL; with ſome OBSER-
VATIONS which lead to a new Theory of Muſcular
Motion.

THE Iris is that membrane of the eye,
which is ſeen through the tranſparent cornea,
and divides the ſpace between the cornea and
cryſtalline lens into two cavities of unequal
ſizes.

This membrane has an aperture nearly in
its centre, through which the rays of light paſs
to the retina, and the choroide coats, where
the images of external objects are formed.

This aperture is called the pupil.

The pupil is found to alter in its dimen-
ſions from different circumſtances; at preſent
I ſhall conſider it only as affected by the ad-
O   miſſion

miſſion of more or leſs light into the viſual
organ. It is remarked by all writers on this
ſubject, that when the eye is expoſed to a
ſtrong light, the pupil is diminiſhed ; and on
the contrary, if the light is weak, the pupil
is enlarged.

Theſe alterations are called by phyſiologiſts,
the contraction and dilatation of the pupil, and
depend upon a difference in the breadth of the
Iris, from ſome internal motions effected in
this membranous zone, by the ſtimulus of
light; for it is obvious to every obſerver, that
the Iris is narrower acroſs the ring in the dilated, than in the contracted ſtate of the pupil.

Before I proceed farther, it will be neceſſary to enter into a minute anatomical inveſtigation of the ſtructure of the Iris.

This membrane is not convex before and
concave behind, as deſcribed by moſt anatomiſts, but plain on both ſurfaces.

It is connected to the ligamentum ciliare
by its proper veſſels, and ſeems to conſiſt entirely of a vaſcular ſtructure and a delicate reticular ſubſtance.

To a common obſerver it certainly appears
convex on its anterior ſurface, when viewed
through the medium of the denſe and convex
cornea ;

cornea; but this deceptio vifus depends upon the convexity of the cornea and the different refractions and reflections of the rays of light that fall obliquely on the cornea, and is in a great meafure explained by the laws of optics.

As the cornea is convex on its outer fur_face, the obferver fuppofes the Iris to be con_vex likewife, for he fees it indiftinctly thro' the cornea, and thus it appears to moft ana_tomifts and furgeons.

Vifion is rendered indiftinct from the rays of light paffing from the rarer medium of air, to the denfer and convex cornea, the oblique rays being refracted in their paffage through the cornea; and another circumftance occurs in this inftance, that renders the vifion con_fufed, viz. the cornea acting in fome meafure as a convex mirror; yet to my eyes, who am acquainted with the true form of the Iris, it now appears plain, although, before I was fatisfied of the truth of this obfervation, it feemed convex anteriorly.

If any doubt fhould remain on this fubject, the famous experiment of Monf. Mery, and which was fo elegantly and lucidly explained

by

by Monf. de la Hire, will immediately confirm this affertion.

In the Memoires de L'Academie royale
des Sciences for the year 1704, p. 261, Monf.
Mery afferts that the Iris is plain, and mentions a curious experiment that he made,
which proves it, viz. by immerfing the head
of a living cat in water, and expofing the eyes
to the rays of the fun, when he obferved that
the pupils were dilated ; which muft have
ftruck him as a very extraordinary phænomenon, fince the pupil of the cat and other
animals would have become fmaller, if the
eyes had been expofed to the light of the fun
in air. This difference Monf. Mery accounts for, on the fuppofition of the circulation being impeded, owing to the refpiration
being ftopped by the immerfion of the animal ; but the alteration in the pupil is too
fudden to be accounted for from this circumftance: the pupil is dilated as foon as the
animal is immerfed ; and I hold with the explanation of Monf. de la Hire, that there is a
confiderable difference in the eye expofed to
the light in air, or water, viz. the eye in
water is to be confidered as a plain furface,
the convex cornea being now furrounded by
water,

water, and as the furface of the water is plain, and the denfities of the cornea and water being nearly equal, the Iris and parts at the bottom of the eye are as diftinctly feen of their true forms and colours, as if they were covered by water alone. His words are thefe, M. de L'Academie, 1712, p. 73. "La cornèe ètant à l'air fait l'office dún Miroir, parcequ'elle eft polie, & d'un Miroir convexe a caufe de fa figure. Elle a donc au de-là d'elle fon foyer, qui eft meme affez vif, & elle renvoye à celui qui la regarde fa propre image, qui par fa vivacitè l'empeche de vóir aucun autre objet au dè là de la cornèe. Mais quand cette même cornée eft dans L'Eau, le peu de différence qu'il y a entre fa denfite & celle de L'Eau fait, qu'elle eft phyfiquement homogène, elle n'eft donc plus un Miroir convexe, elle ne tient lieu que d'une furface d'eau qui feroit plane, & on voit au travers d'elle cè qu'on auroit vu au travers de L'Eau."

But Monf. de la Hire does not explain the dilatation of the pupil. I am of opinion that it may be accounted for from a very fimple principle, which feems to have efcaped both the fagacity of Monf. Mery and Monf. de la Hire.

O 3

It

It has already been obferved that the dilatation of the pupil is greater in the proportion
of the diminution of the light. I fhall now
prove that lefs light is admitted, when the
organ is in water than in air, and confequently the pupil is more dilated.

The cornea is to be confidered in this cafe,
(viz. in water) as forming an horizontal plane
by means of the circumambient water; of
courfe it follows that the difference in refpect
to the quantities of light paffing through the
pupil will be in the proportion of the difference of the extent of the convex cornea in
air, and in water, in which laft ftate it is to
be confidered only as a plain furface, of the
fame diameter as the cornea; the oblique rays
are now excluded, and the dilatation is accounted for from the fame principle as before
obferved, viz. from the admiffion of lefs
light.

Arteries, which arife from the external and
internal carotids, and are called optic and opthalmic, pafs to the Iris; thefe have been reprefented in figures by Ruyfch, by Haller,
and in a moft accurate and elegant manner by
Zinn.

Veins

Veins are likewife derived to this membrane. Figures of thefe may be feen in the
above-mentioned authors.

The nerves alfo, (notwithftanding their
minutenefs,) may be traced to and in the Iris;
thefe come principally from the third pair of
the head or motor oculi and opthalmic branch
of the fifth ; twigs from thefe form the len-
ticular ganglion from which the nerves pafs
on the outfide of the optic nerve, pierce the
tunica fclerotica, and run between it and the
external choroide coat to the Iris ; thefe are
moft beautifully and accurately depicted by
the lynx-eyed Zinn.

Anatomifts likewife fuppofe the exiftence of
abforbent veffels here ; and I have always confidered the Iris as a gland ex officio, fecreting
the aqueous humour, by and in which it is
fluctuated and expanded.

To an anatomift nothing can appear more
beautiful than the Iris. It is indeed the inner
curtain of the eye expanded in a clear and
colourlefs fluid which itfelf fecretes and is
acted upon, as I fhall prefently demonftrate
by that very light, which it is to admit or
exclude in different quantities, for the purpofe of accurate vifion.

It

It is remarkable that the light cannot act upon the Iris primarily, but in a secondary manner only; and that it does not contract by stimuli immediately applied to its surface, either in living animals or those recently dead, as other muscles do. This has been proved by the illustrious Haller, in his Opera Minora, by a great variety of experiments; and since that time by others, invented and executed by the ingenious Abbe Fontana. Light was thrown by him upon the anterior surface of the Iris, between two hollow black cones, in such a manner, as to produce a bright ring of sunlight on this membrane, in an animal placed in a dark chamber: the light was not permitted in this experiment to pass through the pupil, and no alteration took place in the Iris.

The same result was found when electric light was thrown in circles on the Iris in a similar manner.

If we examine an human Iris of a light blue colour with magnifying glasses, or view our own (if of the proper colour) in a deep concave metal speculum, to which a convex lens may be added and move a lighted candle nearer to or farther from the eye, the Iris is

put

put in motion and the pupil is increafed or diminifhed at pleafure.

This moving image of the Iris is one of the moft beautiful that can be imagined.

Fibres appear in the Iris in great numbers, and thefe feem to conftitute the whole of that membrane, are of a white colour, are placed in a radiated direction, and terminate in a beautiful circular fringe, which forms the boundary of the pupil.

Upon bringing the candle near the eye, we may obferve foon after the admiffion of the light, an alteration taking place in the Iris, and the pupil decreafes in proportion as the Iris increafes in breadth.

But if the light be removed to a greater diftance, the pupil foon increafes, owing to the diminution of the breadth of the Iris. Thefe motions of the Iris do not take place in the fame inftant that the light is admitted or excluded, for it takes fufficient time to mark the periods by a ftop watch. When the pupil is diminifhed the white fibres of the Iris, (which are blood veffels, for they become of a red colour in our fubtile injections of the Iris, which are coloured with vermilion,) are nearly rectilinear. On the contrary, when the pupil
is

is dilated the white fibres form ferpentine lines. Thefe facts being premifed, I fhall next endeavour to explain the manner in which these curious and important phænomena are effected.

I am of opinion that the blood veffels of the retina and choroide coats, the firft of which is tranfparent, are capable of being ftimulated by light; or in other words that the light caufes a greater derivation of blood to the fanguiferous fyftem of the parts, forming the internal camera of the eye; and as the blood veffels of the Iris and choroide coats arife from the fame trunks and anaftomofe freely together; it follows, that in proportion as more blood is derived to the retina and choroide coats; that the Iris will receive lefs blood during the time that the light paffes in great quantities through the pupil, and this will increafe the breadth of the Iris, by the blood veffels being abfolutely fhortened, but lengthened in the direction of right lines.

On the contrary, when there is lefs light, the Iris will receive a greater quantity of blood, and the veffels of this membrane will form ferpentine lines;* and although the

* It is a fact well known to practical anatomifts, that the blood veffels, efpecially the arteries, become tortuous in proportion to their turgefcency.

veffels

veffels are abfolutely lengthened, yet in the fame proportion as they are abfolutely length-ened, they are fhortened in right lines, the Iris is diminifhed in breadth, and the pupil confequently dilated.

THE

THE

Continuation of an ESSAY on the IRIS,

Demonſtrative of the Motions and Effects of that Membrane on the Pupil;

With OBSERVATIONS and EXPERIMENTS on

MUSCULAR MOTION.

IN the former part of this eſſay, I deſcribed the anatomical ſtructure of the Iris, and con‑ſidered minutely the alterations produced in the pupil, by the motions of this membrane, owing to the admiſſion and excluſion of light in the viſual organ. I have ſtill ſome farther obſervations to make on its phyſiology; and having concluded the hiſtory of the Iris, I ſhall next explain the manner in which the muſcular fibres of animals effect (what is com‑monly called) their Contraction or Vis Motrix. I ſhall next endeavour to deſcribe the true ſtruc‑ture of theſe fibres, and what takes place in the
muſcle

mufcle during its action; in other words, I shall lay before you a new theory of Mufcular Motion. This theory is a reafoning from experiments made on living and dead animals, and is the beft induction I have been able to make, from a long and almoft continual re-flection upon the facts. As the Iris, which is certainly a mufcle, produces its actions, in the way I have endeavoured to demonftrate in the firft part of this effay; it is therefore probable that all the other mufcles effect their motions in a fimilar manner; and I shall bring fome experiments to confirm this opinion. The manner in which phyfiologifts in general have explained the motions of the Iris is very different from that which I have endeavoured to illuftrate. It was impoffible for them not to have obferved the motions of the Iris in the human fubject and other animals, efpecially the cat, in which, as well as in many of the nocturnal kind, the motion, for obvious reafons, is very extenfive.

They fay this motion depends upon the ftimulus produced by light falling on the vifual organ, exciting mufcular action in the membrane Iris; and almoft all anatomifts have fuppofed, and fome have defcribed, circular

cular fibres like a fphincter mufcle in the Iris, furrounding the pupil. Upon the moft accurate examination of the Irides of all animals that I have diffected, and many that have been examined by others, no circular fibres have been difcovered. However, they have fuppofed the exiftence of fuch an orbicular mufcle, becaufe they have not been able to account for the diminution of the pupil without it. If the exiftence of this mufcle be allowed, it is ftill impoffible to explain the action or motion of the Iris in the dilated ftate of the pupil; for although it be granted that this fphincter can effect the contraction of the pupil, yet the privation of light would not produce its dilatation; the manner in which the dilatation is performed, is generally paffed over, and the phænomenon is remarked, without any attempt to account for the modus operandi.

In the dilated ftate of the pupil, the Iris has been confidered by all phyfiologifts in its paffive or relaxed ftate; when the pupil is diminifhed in fize or contracted, (as it is commonly called) they fuppofe the Iris to be in its active ftate. My ideas are exactly oppofite; I have proved that the Iris is in its active
tive

tive ſtate when the pupil is dilated, and in its
paſſive ſtate when the pupil is diminiſhed.
The veſſels of the Iris are diſtended, and contain more blood in the dilated, and are relaxed from containing leſs blood in the contrary ſtate of the pupil. Theſe changes in the
Iris and pupil, I have demonſtrated in a former
part of this eſſay, depend upon the blood being derived to the retina and choroide coats
in greater quantities, whilſt a ſtrong light is
in contact with them, and the reverſe when
the light is decreaſed.

I account for the pupil being dilated in
amauroſis or gutta ſerena from the retina being in a paralytic ſtate, and therefore the
parts within, before noticed, are incapable
of being ſtimulated by the light. As the
blood is not derived in greater quantities to
theſe coats, within the cavity of the globe,
owing to the paralyſis of the retina, the Iris
receives a greater proportion of blood, and
its veſſels are thrown into ſerpentine lines,
from their diſtention : they are conſequently
ſhortened in right lines proportionate to their
abſolute elongations ; the Iris is narrower in
breadth, and therefore the pupil is dilated.

The

The dilatation of the pupils is generally found to take place alfo in cataracts, in proportion to the degree of opacity in the cryftalline lenfes; for as lefs light will pafs in this cafe to the retina and choroide coats, from the ftimulus, viz. the light being diminifhed; the derivation of blood to the parts lining the cavity of the globe, will be leffened in the fame proportion. I fhall next apply this theory of the motions of the Iris to the explanation of mufcular motion.

On MUSCULAR MOTION.

On the Structure of Muscles.

THE inorganic bafis of all parts of animals, except, perhaps, the cuticle is the reticular fubftance.

The inorganic bafis of mufcles is formed by the fame fubftance.

The inorganic bafis of the nerves alfo appears to me to be formed of this fubftance,

including

including within it a particular kind of matter fimilar to the brain.

In the compofition of a mufcle we difcover
arteries, veins, abforbents, and nerves; the
three firft of thefe are made entirely by the
reticular fubftance. Nothing farther can be
difcovered entering into the compofition of
a mufcle.

The tendons fhould be confidered as inelaf-
tic cords, equally diftinct from the mufcles,
with the bones, and ferving to fix the mufcles
to the bones.

To prove that this idea is correct, it may
be obferved that the tendons of fome animals
are perfect bones, as in the lower extremities
of turkey-fowls, &c.

Anatomifts have fuppofed a kind of fubftance fui generis, entering into the compofition of the mufcular parts of animals, which
they have called mufcular fibres (fibræ mo-
trices.)

Some have imagined that thefe fibres confifted of veficles of different forms, and from
the infarction of thefe bladders they have conceived the mufcular contraction to be effected.
Some have confidered the fibres as hollow
cylinders, and capable of diftention in muf-

P   cular

cular action.* These opinions, founded on the
suppofition of veficles and hollow fibres diftinct from the blood veffels, are now fully
and juftly controverted by the modern anatomifts, upon the ground of their non-exif-
tence ; and even many of the moft able ma-
thematicians have proved that thefe veficular
doctrines were not equal to the explanation of
the phænomena.† Leeuwenhoek, one of the
moft accurate microfcopic obfervers that ever
exifted, in all his reprefentations of the mufcular fibres of different animals, has never
exhibited any fuch veficular appearances.
His figures of the mufcular fibres, as they appear in the microfcope, have the cylindric
form in all the different animals he examined.‡ I can readily account for many fuppofing the fibres to be veficular, from their taking the red veficles of the blood in the veffels
of the mufcles, for the imaginary veficular
fibres.

In all mufcles we may obferve a fibrous
texture. The fibres run parallel to each other,

* Of this opinion was Dr. Hooke, Swammerdam, Cowper,
Baker, Parfons, Le Cat, Muys, Borelli, Bernouilli, and
others.
† See Dr. Pemberton, in his Introduction to the folio
edition of Cowper's Anatomy of the Bones and Mufcles.
‡ Vide Arcana Naturæ Antonii a Leeuwenhoek.

they

they are connected laterally by the reticular
substance, and are disposed in fasciculi, making larger and larger masses ; the whole com-
posing those various and beautiful forms
which we find upon dissection, and by the
action of these organs all our external and internal motions, both voluntary and involuntary, are effected. The muscles contain so
great a quantity of blood as to give them
an intense red colour. The muscles are capable of shortening themselves in such a manner as to produce those various motions before noticed ; and this shortening of the muscles is called muscular motion, action, or
contraction ; these actions or contractions
arise from the application of various stimuli,
such are the nervous energy, electric matter,
heat and cold, sharp points, acids, &c.

This contraction of the muscular fibres we
call irritability.

If any part of an animal body in the living
state is found to contract upon the application of stimuli, we say such parts are irritable or muscular. We assert the contrary, if
the parts do not contract upon such trials.

This contraction depends both upon the
nerves and blood vessels.

If

If the nerves which belong to the muscle are divided, the muscle loses immediately its power of contraction, and it becomes paralytic. If the arteries that supply the muscle with blood are tied or cut, it loses its power of contraction. These facts have often been proved by experiments on living animals. When the phrenic nerves which supply the diaphragm are divided, the action of that muscle ceases. If the recurrent nerves are divided, and some others of the larynx, the voice is lost. When Steno tied the aorta descendens of the dog, the muscles of the lower extremities became paralytic. I must repeat, that a muscle, upon the most accurate examination, consists only of arteries, veins, absorbents, nerves, and reticular substance; this last forming the basis of the others, and connecting them together and loosely to the adjacent parts. These vessels which form such masses lying in the soft reticular substance, and connected in general at their extremities, by those inelastic shining cords called tendons, are the muscles in the aggregate sense. In the abstracted idea, a muscular fibre is nothing more than a blood vessel, viz. an artery with nerves ramifying upon its coats, to carry stimulus

mulus to it, to derive a greater quantity of blood, for its abfolute elongation, and confequent accurtation in the right line, by its becoming tortuous from its lateral connexions with the reticular fubftance. When a mufcle is in its relaxed ftate or not acting, it feels foft and flabby; in action it feels hard, tenfe, and it becomes fixed; it fwells and fhortens itfelf in length, and increafes in breadth. I am likewife of opinion, that there is an abfolute increafe of bulk in the mufcle during its action, which arifes from a derivation of a greater quantity of blood to the mufcle during its active ftate.

It is a fact well known to all practical anatomifts, that the blood veffels, more efpecially the arteries of animal bodies, become tortuous, or ferpentine, in proportion to their diftention by their natural fluid the blood, or by anatomical injections. It is likewife equally certain that their areæ are increafed both in length and diameter, owing to the wellknown law of fluids preffing quaquaverfum on their foft elaftic coats; ftill were the blood veffels not connected to each other by the reticular fubftance laterally; this ferpentine or tortuous effect (upon which the whole of the

P 3   fhortening

shortening of the muscle, and consequently
the motion, depends,) would not take place.
In proportion to the distention of the vessels
is the elongation and the consequent accurtation in the right line of the fibres of the muscles.—There is a passage in Winflow, which
is worth remarking, as it may serve to confirm the truth of what I have afferted. This
remark will be found in vol. I. sect. iii. p. 8,
of the quarto edition of Winflow's Anatomy,
by Dr. G. Douglas : " During the contraction of a muscle, its fibres are bent through
their whole length, or formed into very small
fine folds, in alternately opposite directions,
as may be plainly seen in animals fresh killed,
when the butchers cut their flesh while it
remains warm." That muscles produce
their actions or contractions in this manner, I
have already exemplified in the Iris of the human eye, which membrane is to be considered as an involuntary muscle, different in
the radiation of its fibres, from all other muscles of the body, except the proceffus ciliaris
of the eye, which is another involuntary radiated muscle somewhat similar to the Iris, and
whose office is to move the cryftalline lens,
and by this means to alter the focus of the eye,

in

in order to adapt it to nearer or more diftant
objects. This theory gives us a new ufe of the
arterial fyftem, viz. that of compofing the
mufcles of animals ; and is another reafon for
fuppofing the arterial fyftem an inverted cone,
whofe apex is placed towards the heart. I
have fhewn that this diftention of the blood
veffels depends upon a greater derivation of
blood conveyed to them from the ftimulus of
the nervous energy ; that this takes place in
the blood veffels from nervous ftimuli, the
phænomenon of blufhing is fufficient to prove.
Mechanical and other ftimuli likewife derive
a greater quantity of blood to the veffels, e. g.
If we apply friction to the fkin, we increafe
the derivation of the blood. In digeftion we
know a greater quantity of blood is derived
to the ftomach, and the pylorus or fphincter
mufcle is put into action, which confines the
food for a certain time in the cavity of this
hollow vifcus ; as lefs blood paffes to the veffels of the ftomach, as the procefs of digeftion
diminifhes ; I fee readily how the pylorus becomes relaxed, and the food paffes on to the
firft inteftine, the duodenum. Although I
have fuppofed the diftention owing to a derivation of blood, it is poffible that the nervous

P 4

energy

energy may depend upon a matter fimilar to the electric fluid, and that this fluid may be conveyed by the nerves to the blood ; and by effecting a repulfion of the particles of the blood, probably the red veficles, that the dif_ tention may be produced ; but this remains to be proved, and we are now poffibly near to fuch a difcovery, if we confider that electric matter is found to be collected, and even condenfed, in the torpedo & gymnotus elec_ tricus, as likewife in a fpecies of Ophidion found high up in the Nile, and lately the dif_ coveries made by Galvani in frogs and other animals, feem to fhew that the nervous is fomewhat fimilar to the electric fluid. Before I conclude this effay I may obferve that I made feveral experiments to difcover what motion and fhortening I could produce by injecting different parts of the human body, and other animals. Two of thefe experiments, which are very ftriking, may ferve to illuftrate this theory of Mufcular Motion :——

Experiment the firft.

I injected the funis umbilicalis of a full_ grown human fœtus, both arteries and veins, with

with the common coarſe ceraceous injection; the abſolute elongation produced by the injection, was two thirds of it's length; and the accurtation in the right line one third of the length of the cord.

Experiment the ſecond,

Made THURSDAY, October 27, 1785.

I diſſected the main trunk of the carotid artery from a full-grown horſe, fixed a ligature upon one end, and an injecting pipe in the other; it meaſured fifteen inches in length, in diameter $\frac{3}{8}$ and $\frac{1}{4}$ of $\frac{1}{8}$ in its uninjected ſtate; upon injection with water it became ſerpentine, in proportion to the degree of its diſtention, notwithſtanding it was ſeparated from all contiguous parts. When the water was preſſed out, it was filled with coarſe injection, ſo as to make it very turgid; it then meaſured in length 21 and $\frac{1}{2}$ inches, and in diameter $\frac{5}{8}$ and $\frac{1}{2}$ of $\frac{1}{8}$ of an inch. I may likewiſe obſerve, that it is common for practical anatomiſts to remark, that the arms, legs, fingers, and toes, are put into motion by flexion of theſe parts being produced in injecting our common vaſcular ſubjects, which are

are moft frequently children of different ages ;
the fame thing as often occurs in injecting the
extremities of adult fubjects minutely. This
muft depend upon the diftention of the blo vd
veffels, by the' anatomical injection produc ng
a contraction of the penniform flexor mufcles
of the extremties of fuch fubjects.

J. S.

EXETER, April, 1794.

ON THE

Mythology and Worfhip of the SERPENT.

THE worfhip of the fun and folar fire, is
fo natural in an age of ignorance, that it may
eafily be fuppofed to have exifted in various
and diftant countries, which had no communication with each other. The majeftic fplendour of that luminary, and the benefits it imparted to mankind, could not but excite fentiments of awe and veneration. We need not
therefore have recourfe to a propagation of
opinions from any one part of the world,
either by colonization or conqueft, to account
for a fpecies of adoration, which, while the
creator was unknown, every human bofom
would be prone to pay to the moft glorious
and ufeful of created beings. We need not,
as fome have done, imagine there was ever
any former connection between Afia and America, becaufe nearly fimilar rites were appropriated to the fun in Perfia and Peru.

But,

But, tho the folar worſhip m·ght naturally
ariſe in all parts of the world, what reaſon
ſhall we give for the deification of the ſerpent ? for his being attached to that worſhip ?
and for his being in ſuch a variety of places
confidered either as a malign, or benignant
power ? This ſeems to have been an arbitrary, not a natural fuperſtition ; to have primarily taken place in ſome particular region,
and thence to have been circulated to nations
widely diſtant. Without attempting to an-
ſwer the preceding queſtions, I ſhall, merely
as an entertaining ſubject, give a ſhort ſketch
of the ſerpent worſhip, the origin of which is
loſt in the remoteſt antiquity.

The worſhip of the ſerpent, or of the ſun
and ſerpent, is perhaps among the firſt, if not
the firſt recorded, mode of idolatry. As joined
with the ſun, or under his name of Cneph, in
Egypt, he ſignified the good, as Typhon did
the evil principle. The Phœnicians gave him
a name correſpondent with Agatho-dæmon.
The Egyptians, according to Euſebius, repreſented the univerſe by a ſky-coloured and fiery
circle, in the middle of which was the ſerpent with the head of a hawk, reaching from
one ſide to the other, as if connecting the
whole.

whole. The figure fo drawn, being like the Greek ⊙. Epeis the Egyptian, tranflated into Greek by Arius, calls him, of every ferpent the moft divine, who opening his eyes, fills all things with light in his primogenial refidence, and if he clofes them, total darknefs enfues. This tract, as well as Eufebius's Ethothia, with the theological work of Pherecydes on the ferpent deity and his worfhippers, whom he calls Ophion, and Ophionidæ, are loft, doubtlefs, with much curious information on the fubject.

The high idea entertained of the fame deity by the Perfians, Eufebius fhews by a quotation from Zoroafter Magus on their religious rites: the fame likewife, he fays, is delivered by Oftanes. " The god has the head of a hawk, he is the firft of beings, immortal, eternal, unbegotten, indivifible, indefinable, the giver of every good, immutable, of the holy moft holy, of the wife moft wife, the fource of equity and juftice, felf-taught, natural, perfect, intelligent, and the fole inventor of the facred powers of nature."

Oppofite to Cneph, was Typhon, the former, as I have faid, being the principle of good, the latter of evil, the deftructive ferpent,

pent, the author of darkneſs, of ſtorms, of tempeſts, and confuſion, as the former was of light, of beauty, and order.*

As an emblem of the good principle, the ſerpent ſeems to have been erected by Moſes in the wilderneſs ; to have been placed round the antient figures of the Magi in the ſculptures of Perſia, and on the heads of the prieſts in Egypt. As the good principle, he ſeems, in the Indian mythology, to have ſupported the world on the back of the tortoiſe. To have ſurrounded the ſeven worlds that they might not again be deſtroyed ; and to have attended, and held his head over the infant god Chriſhna, to protect him in the rainy ſeaſon. In the ſame light he was made uſe of by the Genii, being coiled round a huge mountain, with which they churned the ocean to procure the water of immortality, an idea, Titanically ſublime.

The oldeſt reference we have to the ſerpent as the principle of evil, is his tempting

---

* Typhon is at this moment the Aſiatic term for hurricane, and likewiſe, if I miſtake not, for the water-ſpout ; the latter of which, from its ſpiral, and progreſſive motion, terrible appearance, and ſometimes violent effects, was perhaps the origin of the mythological ſerpent, or dragon of the waters, which aroſe from the depth of the ocean, to combat with the ſun, by whoſe power it was vanquiſhed.

Adam

Adam and Eve in Paradife, for which his future punifhment was decreed. As the evil
principle he was fought with and conquered
by various gods. In the Indian mythology
Viftnoo flew the giant or dragon Hirnacks at
the bottom of the fea, and refcued the world,
which he had carried off to his dark recefs.
Chrifhna, after a defperate engagement, conquered and remanded to his den the ferpent
Kellinaeg. In the northern mythology Thor
pulled up the great ferpent of Midgard from
the deep, and bruifed his head with his mace.
The victory of Horus over Typhon is well
known. The Greeks were fo fond of this tale,
as not only to apply it to their Apollo, the van-
quifher of Python, but to their Jupiter, who
flew Typhœus with his thunderbolts, an enormous giant, who had fifty ferpent heads; to
Hercules in various inftances; to Cadmus, to
Jafon, and Belerophon, who flew the Chi-
mæra, one of whofe heads, as well as its tail,
were thofe of a ferpent, the hero's name being
as complex as the figure of the monfter; Bel-
er-oph-on Beli Ignis, Serpens Solis. He was
affifted by Pegafus, whofe name Hefiod derives from πωγαι, the fprings, becaufe he came
from the fprings of Oceanus, which in fact
was

was the Nile. Perfeus, who was an Egyptian
and Eaftern deity, cut off the head of Medufa,
which was covered with fnakes; he likewife
was, in his fubfequent adventures, affifted by
Pegafus. Somewhat analogous to this, is the
white horfe of Chrifhna, which he fent out to
fubdue all nations to his laws.*

From Egypt, the ferpent worfhip was carried into Greece, and in their religious ceremonies, real ferpents were made ufe of by the
priefts in the fame manner.

The Chaldæans feem to have been worfhippers of the fun and ferpent from the time of
Nimrod or Naim-rod, the beauty of the ferpent, the lovely ferpent, or as expreffed by

---

* It is remarkable that a fimilar cuftom exifts at the fprings
of the Nile to this day. For the Abyffinian chief, whofe
authority extended over that country, fent his horfe properly
caparifoned, as a protector before Mr. Bruce, to which, all
who met it, paid homage, as the reprefentative of its owner.
Mr. Bruce may be faid to have vanquifhed the ferpent of the
Nile by means of Pegafus, the horfe of Fafil. Befides the white
horfe of Chrifhna, there is in the Indian mythology another
white horfe with wings, of great virtue and power, being
indeed accounted a transformation of Viftnoo. He refides
in heaven, but at the conclufion of things, will ftrike his
fore-foot with fuch violence on the earth, that the ferpent
will quit his place, and the tortoife, unable to fupport the
world, will caft it into the fea. If any prince prefumed to
ftop the white horfe of Chrifhna, and did not fubmit to his
mafter, he attacked him with an army, and exterminated
both him and his fubjects. In the Revelations, Death rides
on a pale or white horfe, and Hell follows after. In the
more early mythology of Greece, not the eagle, but Pegafus
was the thunder-bearer of Jupiter. Hef. Theogon.

. the

the Greeks Nebrod, viz. On-ab-rod Sol Pater Serpens, down to the time of Daniel, when
Cyrus deſtroyed Bel, and ſlew the Dragon.*

Tho both Cneph and Typhon were ſerpents, they were likewiſe conſidered as having human forms, and it is rather particular
that to Cneph in Egypt, was attributed the
ſame complection, which the Indians gave to
Chriſhna ; Κνηφ, την χροιαν εκ κυανε μελανος εχοντα.
The ſkin of Chriſhna likewiſe, was of a dark
azure colour.†

Con was the name of the Egyptian Hercules,
or the ſun ; Coneph or Cneph, is therefore
the ſolar ſerpent.   From Cneph came cnephod
or ephod, the prophetic garment of the prieſts;
uſed likewiſe by the Iſraelites ; in the breaſt-
plate of which were thoſe precious ſtones,
Urim, the fires, or reſemblances of fire ; and
Thummim or Aith-ommim, lights of the ſun.
The original ephods among the Egyptians

---

* Nimrod was a mighty hunter, ſo was Typhon. He
was hunting by moon-light, when he found the body of
Oſiris, which he tore in pieces.   Orion too, was a mighty
hunter, who was ſlain by Diana for attempting her chaſtity :
as Typhon laid ſnares for Iris in the abſence of Oſiris, which
by her prudence ſhe avoided. Nimrod was ſtiled by the
Gentile writers Orion and Alorus.—Chron. Paſch. p. 28.
Bryant's mythol. vol. 3, p. 17.

† Euſeb. Prœp. Evan. p. 41, 115.   Aſiat. Reſearches, v. 1.

Q   and

and Perſians were probably ſerpents, or girdles in the form of ſerpents. Moſes conſecrated the ephod, tho it was criminally perverted, and applied to the old idolatry by others. For inſtance, by Gideon, when " he ſet up an ephod in Ophrah, (the city of the ſerpent) after which all Iſrael went a whoring, and which was a ſnare to him, and his houſe."

The rod of Moſes was converted into a ſerpent, when he was ſpoken to by the deity of fire from the burning buſh. And afterwards, in preſence of Pharoah, " Aaron caſt forth his rod, and it was turned into a ſerpent. Then Pharoah called for the wiſe men and ſorcerers, and thoſe charmers alſo of Egypt, did in like manner, with their enchantments ; for they caſt down every man his rod, and they were turned into ſerpents ; but Aaron's rod devoured their rods."

The high opinion entertained of the ſerpent as the principle of good by the Perſians, Egyptians, and Phœnicians, we have ſeen ; and likewiſe, that there was a ſerpent of a different character, the principle of evil. From theſe two, ſerpents appear to have been multiplied in different mythologies without number, and without end.

In

In the Indian mythology ferpents abound.
The god Ixora, who, like Ofiris, and the an‑
tient Grecian Jupiter, had an eye in his fore‑
head, wore a robe furrounded by ferpents,
and held one in his hand. An attendant of
his, a figure refembling Silenus, had ferpents
hanging down by their tails from his head,
and a bracelet on his left arm, with two others
about his thighs, made of the fame animals.
Quenavady, the fon of Ixora, had long hair,
tied round with a ferpent.

In one of the antient caverns on the coaft
of Coromandel is a gigantic figure of Viftnoo,
reclining on a coiled ferpent. Viftnoo, in‑
deed, is faid to govern the world repofing on
the ferpent Annatan. This ferpent has five
heads, two of which ferve the god for pil‑
lows, one for a bolfter, and two are under
his hands. But to try the power of Viftnoo,
Annatan once got a fixth head, upon which
Viftnoo got a fixth hand to lay on the head,
and when he generated a feventh, the god
created another hand, and fo on to a thoufand.
This is analogous to Hercules and the Hydra.

Inderfiet, the fon of Rawan, was taught by
Bramha to make ufe of certain words, which
being uttered when he fhot his arrow, con‑

verted

verted it into a ferpent, entangling his adver-
fary. Afterwards, in a fight, taking his ftand
behind *a wheel of the chariot of the fun*, he fhot
one of his arrows, which turning immediately
to a ferpent, fent forth fuch a vaft number
among the apes, compofing the army of Ram,
that they fell in crowds before the giants of
Rawan.*

Near the town of Buddal is ftill remaining
a very antient decapitated pillar, on which,
as appears by a fanfcrit infcription, was placed
Tarkfhya, or Garöör, the foe of ferpents,
who having journeyed, like his fame, to the
extremity of the world, and defcended even
to its foundation, was there exalted with a ferpent in his mouth.

Sir William Jones, from a Perfian tranflation of the Bhagavat, (for he had not then
procured the original) fays, the fovereign of
Patála, or the infernal regions, is called the
king of ferpents.†

In the Revelations, Michael fights with the
devil, that old ferpent, who likewife, as well
as the hydra, had feven heads. The hydra
was not overcome till Hercules applied fire,

* Baldœus, in Churchill's collection.
† Afiatic Refearches, vol. 1.

as

as each head was cut off. Michael, who over-
came Satan, fignifies, the fmiting of the deity
of fire.

To the antient victory over the ferpent of
the Nile, the prophets allude in thefe paffages.

" Awake! awake! put on ftrength, O arm
of the Lord.   Awake, as in the antient days,
in the generations of old.   Art thou not it that
hath cut Rahab ? and wounded the dragon?"

Ifaiab, c. 51.

" Thus .faith the Lord God, I am againft
thee, Pharoah, king of Egypt, the great dragon which lieth in the midft of his rivers.   I
will put hooks in thy jaws ; I will bring thee
up out of the midft of thy rivers." *Ezek. c.* 29.

" In that day the Lord, with his fore and
great and ftrong fword, fhall punifh Leviathan
the piercing ferpent, even Leviathan, that
crooked ferpent, and he fhall flay the dragon
that is in the fea." *Ifaiab, c.* 27.

The Greek legends are replete with ferpents.   To the ftories already mentioned, we
might add that of Tirefias, of Orpheus, of
Efculapius, and others ; likewife of Bacchus,
who paffed through the channels of the rivers
Orontes and Hydafpes, after he had dried
them up by touching them with his rod ;

Q 3   which

which being caft on the ground, began to creep as a ferpent, and wind itfelf round an oak. Nonn. Dionus.

In later times Olympias, the mother of Alexander, was faid to have been impregnated by Jupiter Ammon in the fhape of a ferpent.

> . . . . round her flender waift he curl'd,
> And ftamp'd an image of himfelf, a fovereign of the world.

From the old legends of Cadmus, Hercules, &c. I am inclined to think arofe the hyperbolical ftory of the ferpent which impeded Regulus, and was flain by a formal attack of the army. Our St. George and the Dragon was of Egyptian or eaftern origin ; and the Druidical anguinum, or ferpents' egg, the great ferpent of the north, as well as that by the death of which Ragnar Lodbrach began his acts of chivalry, I have little doubt, had the fame fource.

Even to this day an annual proceffion takes place in Egypt, in which the Pfylli perform the fame part, which probably they did of old. After the different bodies of artizans, the ftandard of Mahomet, and the priefts, I observed,

obferved, fays Monf. Savery, a band of mad-
men with their arms bare, and a wild look,
holding in their hands enormous ferpents,
which were twifted round their bodies, and
endeavouring to make their efcape. Thefe
Pfylli griping them forcibly by the neck,
avoided their bite, and notwithftanding their
hiffing, tore them with their teeth, and ate
them up alive, the blood ftreaming down from
their polluted mouths. Others were ftriving
to tear from them their prey ; it was a ftrug-
gle who fhould devour a ferpent. The populace followed them with amazement, and believed it to be a miracle. They pafs for perfons infpired, and poffeffed by a fpirit who
deftroys the effect of the bite of the ferpent.*

We are affured likewife by Mr. Bruce, that
a fet of men ftill exift in Egypt, who will fuffer themfelves to be bitten, without injury, by
the moft venomous ferpents in that country ;
the wound inflicted by whom would be to
others certain and fpeedy death. He mentions too, the veneration in which fnakes are
held at this time by the natives at the head of
the Nile, where they confult them as oracles

* Savery's Letters on Egypt, vol. 1. p. 71.

Q 4

on every emergency; and by their manner of eating, determine whether good or evil events are likely to succeed.

With refpect to the Pfylli, if they are fo wondered at by the people accuftomed to them, what might not have been their influence in a ftrange country, under the direction of their priefts, and among an ignorant race of men like the primitive Greeks! 'We know when St. Paul fhook off the viper from his hand in the ifland Melita, and felt no harm; the barbarians exclaimed, that he was a god.

Not only this peculiar fpecies of religious worfhip, but every other, with its mythology and facred language, feem to have been imported, at an early æra, into Greece, by the Egyptians. They probably received their religion and knowledge from Chaldæa or Ethiopia. As I have derived Nimrod (perhaps fancifully) from the worfhip of the ferpent, fo, according to Mr. Bryant's Radicals, Ethiopia may be deduced from Aith-ops, Ignis Serpentis; and Cheops, the name of the reputed founder of the firtt pyramid, might originally have been applied to the building it-felf, Cha-ops, Domus vel Templum Serpentis. But nothing is more deceptive than etymology

mology, and without collateral evidence, it is little to be trufted.

While, however, the whole tenor of Grecian hiftory and tradition fhews the power, knowledge, conquefts, and colonization of the Antient Egyptians, fo is this in fome meafure fupported by another moft authentic narration, I mean that of Mofes. Greece, indeed, owed all its arts, as well as religious rites, to Egypt, and was not afhamed to confefs it. It has lately been fafhionable to detract from the merits of the latter country, which in fome future effay I may attempt to eftablifh; and point out the probable time when its great power exifted, and its colonies diffeminated together with religion, agriculture, manufactures, polity, and refinement.

T. V.

To

To the GODS of INDIA,

On the DEPARTURE of SIR JOHN SHORE,
and HUBERT CORNISH, Efq. from *England*,
in the Year 1793.

YE powers ethereal ! who prefide
Where facred GANGES rolls his tide !
Virtues ! or emanating rays
From him, the firft, the laft of days !
Receive for thofe I love my prayer !
Ye myftic powers ! ye virtues, hear !

O GANES, bend thy fapient head,
Deep o'er their hearts thy influence fpread !
So LACHSMI from her plenteous ftore
Bloffoms and fruits fhall round them pour :
At her command CUVE'RA come
From ALACAS' imperial dome.

Or

Or where his radiant car he guides
And thro the sky triumphant rides,
His lap, propitious, to unfold,
And give them pure unsullied gold.

On MERU's hallow'd cliffs which shine
With all the treasures of the mine,
The diamond, and the flaming ore,
Thee mighty IDRA, I adore!
The Genii of the air enchain,
Oh! every sickly blast restrain,
Let clouds and storms thy bounty prove,
And teem with health for those I love!

Thy faces six—thy eyes of pride,
Twelve-handed CARTICEYA, hide!
Or over distant regions wield
Thy javelin sharp, and massy shield!
Urge thy pernicious bird afar,
Nor shock my friends with savage war!

And thou, whose charms the bosom fire
With wanton love, and soft desire,
REMBHA, of frolic mirth the queen,
Entice not those of sober mien!

To

To thoughtlefs youth thy gifts difplay,
Thy rofy bredes, and chaplets gay.
For them in vain thy fongs fhall flow,
In vain thy rubied nectar glow,
Thy Apsaras, fhall breathe perfume,
And from Elyfium fteal it's bloom.

   But thou, O Chrishna, crown'd with flowers
From purer glades, and chafter bowers,
While pearled wreathes thy ancles bind,
With graceful ftep, and fraudlefs mind
Thy modeft nymphs educe to fight,
Infpiring innocent delight !
Sounding the mellow flute advance,
And lead with them the mazy dance !
With afpect bland, and temper meek,
Shew the dark azure of thy cheek ;
Thy generous foul unfold to view,
Thy every thought to pity true,
To mercy, quick, to vengeance, flow,
Yet laying proud oppreffion low :
Raifing the abject from diftrefs,
And fent from heaven the world to blefs.

                            Such,

Such, CHRISHNA, to their eyes appear,
To thee let kindred hearts be dear ;
Thy might, incarnate godhead, prove,
Nor ceafe to favour thofe I love !

A. Y.

ON

ON LITERARY FAME,

AND THE

Hiftorical Characters of *Shakfpeare.*

Nec magis expreffi vultus per a͞nea figna
Quam per vatis opus morea animiq. virorum
Clarorum apparent.

Hor. l. 2, Ep. 1.

THE fame acquired by literary talents, is not only in itfelf of the moft durable and extenfive nature, but the only means of preferving every other fpecies of celebrity. The pyramids of Memphis, and fome ftupendous edifices in India, indeed, exift, after a vaft fucceffion of years; and nothing, in all probability, but an internal convulfion of the globe, will overthrow fuch immenfe piles: yet they have not tranfmitted to pofterity the names of thofe monarchs, through whofe vanity, fuperftition, or munificence, they were erected. The finer defigns of ancient art are

almoft

almoſt totally loſt : the exquiſite performances
of the ſtatuary and the painter are mouldered
into duſt ; but Praxiteles and Zeuxis will always live to fame, though not by their own
efforts ; for the pencil of literature alone,
paints to diſtant ages, and its colours fade not
amidſt the revolutions of time.

> - - - - - - neque
> Si chartæ ſileant, quod bene feceris,
> Mercedem tuleris.
>
> *Hor. l. 4. Od. 3.*

Without the bard or the hiſtorian the monarch builds, and the artiſt deſigns in vain.
Without their aſſiſtance the tribute of applauſe
cannot be levied on poſterity. " Dark, (ſays
Oſſian,) are the deeds of other times, before
the light of the ſong aroſe." And Horace, to
the ſame purport, remarks, that " heroes
exiſted before the Trojan war, but no divine
bard recorded their fame, and their deeds are
concealed in night." L. 4. Od. 9.

Notwithſtanding this obvious truth, the
man of letters is commonly regarded with indifference, poſſibly with contempt, by his
cotemporaries, who act in the more elevated
departments

departments of life. Such, we may suppose, has ever been the case, for the substance of human nature, however the outward form may vary, is still the same. The statesmen and generals of our age, like *most* of their predecessors, (for some exceptions have occurred) little reflect, that whatever character they are to sustain with posterity, will not depend on the adulation of their creatures or the huzzas of the people, not even on the applauses of senates or munificence of kings ; but will, in all probability, be finally established on the credit of some literary man, a silent, but not inattentive spectator ; living unknown, and dying unregarded. Whim, caprice, or fashion, generally govern the world's opinion concerning living authors. The favorites of the day have seldom stood the test of time. The immortal " Paradise lost," was contemptuously said by an author of considerable eminence, " to have been written by *one* Milton, a blind man:" and almost a century elapsed before his merit was properly known. He has been truly compared to a flow, subterraneous stream—it pursues its silent course in darkness, but at length bursts into day, and is adorned with the radiance of heaven. Shakspeare, for a longer
period,

period, obtained but a very moderate degree of eftimation. For a fhort time, indeed, he enjoyed the gale of popular applaufe, and flou_rifhed, in the words of a kindred genius, " like an oak, that pours awhile its green branches to the fun, but is foon enfolded in the fkirts of a ftorm, and clothed on high in mift."

Their fame is now eftablifhed, and cannot, unlefs the world relapfes into barbarifm, fuf_fer a fecond eclipfe. In the days, however, of " the heroWilliam, and the martyrCharles," when Blackmore was knighted, and Quarles penfioned on account of their poetical pre_eminence, the plays of Shakfpeare were fel_dom acted, and Milton was fcarcely known. So flowly does genius emerge beneath the preffure of caprice or ignorance !

A voluminous writer, called Cartwright, who is ftiled by Wood " the moft feraphical preacher of his age—another Tully—and another Virgil," in a poem addreffed to Fletcher, thus familiarly treats his great pre_deceffor :—

Shakfpeare to thee was dull, whofe beft jeft lies
I' th' ladies' queftions, and the fool's replies.

R   Old-

Old-fashioned wit, which walked from town to town

In trunk-hose, which our fathers called the clown:

Whofe wit our *nice times* would obfcenenefs call,

And which made bawdry pafs for comical.

Nature was all his art—thy vein was free

As his, but without his * fcurrility.

Thefe

* What idea could this "feraphical peacher" entertain
of *obfceuenefs* and *fcurrility* (which feems to be here introduced
as fynonimous to *vulgarity,*) in thus complimenting Fletcher
on the nicety of the times? Shakfpeare is not free from licentioufnefs; but, compared to him, exhibits the purity of a
veftal. *His* violations of decency are too grofs for quotation.
Of his fuperlative vulgarity I fhall felect one inftance, and it
would be difficult to find in Shakfpeare, or indeed any author,
an equal quantity in fo fmall a fpace.

Chilax, a veteran officer, is fuppofed to carry on an intrigue with a prieftefs of Venus, in whofe temple he received
a fevere blow from a clap of thunder, which, as he exprefles
it, "gave him on the buttocks a cruel, a huge bang."—
"Had not my intentions been honeft," he adds,

- - - - "I had paid for't elfe too.
" I'm *monftrous* holy now, and *cruel* fearful.
" Oh, 'twas a *plaguy thump*, charged *with a vengeance.*"

The Mad Lover. A. 5.

This paffage is not only remarkable for its vulgarity, but for
its containing, in the fame line, a peculiar phrafe in modern
ufe, both by the great vulgar and the fmall. *Cruel*, among
the Devonfhire peafantry, is fynonimous with *monftrous* in
fafhionable circles. The perfon, whom the latter would
denominate monftrous handfome, monftrous kind, or monftrous good tempered; the other will ftile, with equal propriety, cruel handfome, cruel kind, and cruel good tempered. The word, however, was formerly in more general
ufe to fignify any thing in a fuperlative degree. This meaning is frequently annexed to it in Fletcher's plays; and the
clowns

Thefe encomiums on the fuperior chaftity
and urbanity of Fletcher's mufe, appear fomewhat fingular to us. Pofterity differs in opinion from *Mr. Cartwright; who, notwithftanding his numerous publications, and celc-
brity in his own days, may probably be only
known to futurity hy the ill-grounded cenfure
he has paffed on Shakfpeare, as Zoilus lives
to fame by having depreciated Homer.

If we are to judge from the congratulatory
verfes prefixed to Beaumont's and Fletcher's
plays, we muft conclude that thefe dramatic
bards were confidered as fuccefsful rivals to
Shakfpeare, previous to his death, which happened in his 53d year, A. D. 1616. In the

clowns in "the Midfummer-night's dream," are faid to
"con their parts with cruel pain." But the moft fingular
circumftance relative to the word, is, its having the fame figni-
fication in a foreign language, that it now bears in a pro-
vincial dialect of our own; and its receiving in a tranflation,
not improperly, though it may be prefumed undefignedly,
the correfpondent phrafe of genteel vulgarity. In Andrews'
"Ancient and Modern Anecdotes," a Duchefs of Orleans'
letter is quoted, (p. 391,) in which fhe acknowledges herfelf to be *cruellement laide*, "monftrous ugly." The expreffion is not, however, deftitute of claffical authority to fupport it; for δεινος in Homer, is fometimes introduced as
fynonimous to *valde*.

* He died, according to Wood, at the age of 30, in
1643. Above fifty copies of verfes, written by the moft
eminent wits of Oxford, were prefixed to his plays and
poems, which were publifhed together foon after his death.

R 2   year

year 1642, Shirley, in his prologue to "the
Sisters," laments the neglect shewn to his
performances, and intimates that they were
frequently acted to empty houses. Dryden, in
his "Essay on Dramatic Poetry," published
in 1666, remarks, that Shakspeare's language
was a little obsolete, and that two of Beaumont's and Fletcher's plays were exhibited to
one of his. Shadwell, in the prologue to a
comedy that came out the following year, observes,

" That which the world called wit in Shakspeare's age
" Is *laughed* at, as improper for the stage."

In consequence of which himself and other
wits of the time, generously condescended to
alter many of his plays, and accommodate
them to an audience, grown, we may presume, rather nice and fastidious; having been
for some time in the habit of attending to the
chaste humour and attic elegance of Mrs.
Behn, and Tom Durfey ! In 1707, Shakspeare
was so little known, that Tate published a
tragedy, called " Injured Love, or the Cruel
Husband," and mentioned in the title-page,
that it was written by the author, (meaning
himself,)

himfelf,) of King Lear. He had, indeed, altered it from Shakfpeare, and muft have depended on efcaping detection from the obfcurity of the original; or have fuppofed that it would hide its diminifhed head, and fink into oblivion by means of his fuperior production: he mentions it in his preface as an "obfcure performance commended to his notice by a friend." Steele, in the Tatler, which came out in 1709, gives two quotations, as he fays, from Shakfpeare's Macbeth, (No. 68, 167,) but the paffages there quoted are only to be found in Davenant's alteration of that play. He mentions, likewife, fome ftriking incidents in " Taming the Shrew," as circumftances that occurred in a family, with which he was particularly intimate. (No. 231.) In the firft inftance we are fuprifed that Steele fhould have fo imperfect a knowledge of Shakfpeare; in the fecond, that he fhould truft fo much to the ignorance of his readers.

From this period, however, and chiefly by means of the judicious and elegant affociate of Steele in the Spectator, Shakfpeare as well as Milton, became more generally known to the world. Yet fo late as the year 1750, Dr. Hill, a man not deftitute of tafte, and during

fome

some part of " his many-coloured life," a
theatrical critic by profeſſion, introduces in
" the actor, or a treatiſe on the art of playing" ſome lines, if you will believe him, from
Romeo and Juliet ; " given as the author gives
them ; not as the butcherly hand of a block-
head prompter may have lopped them, or as
the unequal genius of ſome bungling critic
may have attempted to mend them." In
another place he again plumes himſelf on the
peculiar accuracy of his quotation ; and yet no
ſuch lines are to be found in Shakſpeare, they
are copied from Caius Marius, and Otway is
their only juſt proprietor. *He* inſerted, indeed, entire ſcenes into that drama from
Shakſpeare's Romeo and Juliet, for which
he made a very ſlight acknowledgment. Other
critics have been equally unfortunate, and
quoted, as Otway's, ſome beautiful paſſages
which he had ſtolen from *Shakſpeare.

In the Auguſtan age of Charles the 2d, as
it has ſometimes been abſurdly ſtiled, Elkanah
Settle, the city bard, divided theatric fame
with Dryden ; and Sir William Temple, generally reckoned the oracle of taſte in his

* See Johnſon and Steevens's Shakſpeare. Vol. 3, 75. 3d ed.

time,

time, mentions Sir Philip Sidney as " the greateſt poet and the nobleſt genius of any that have left writings behind them, and publiſhed in ours or in any other modern language." He does not condeſcend to name Milton in his Eſſay on Poetry; but evidently alludes to him and Cowley in the following paſſage. " The religion of the Gentiles had been woven into the contexture of all the ancient poetry, with a very agreeable mixture, which made the moderns affect to give that of Chriſtianity a place alſo in their poems : but the true religion was not found to become fiction ſo well as the falſe had done ; and all their attempts of this kind ſeemed rather to debaſe religion than to heighten poetry." Who now can read the inſipid productions of Sidney ? who is not charmed with the ſublime energy of Milton ! but the ſplendour of Sidney's character threw a deluſive glare over his compoſitions, and the gloom of republicaniſm annexed to the idea of Milton, caſt a veil over beauties that could not otherwiſe have eſcaped obſervation.

High rank and temporal grandeur is, however, of no avail towards ſecuring literary immortality. The poems of a Nero, though

lord

lord of " the majeſtic world," periſhed with
him. Thoſe of Homer, an indigent itinerant
bard, are tranſplanted into every poliſhed language, and will live as long as ideas are by
language communicated. The copious works
of the Britiſh Solomon, who " trowed himſelf
to be the oldeſt and the wiſeſt king in Chriſ-
tendom," though bound in purple morocco,
ſtamped with letters of gold, and embelliſhed
with claſps of ſilver, lie worm-eaten and cob-
web-mantled even in the tory's garret ; whilſt
the profane vulgar deem them of little other
uſe than to encloſe the trifling merchandize
of the confectioner or haberdaſher. Sometimes perhaps, ignorantly-flagitious, they kindle their tobacco-charged pipes with thoſe
very pages in which he fulminated againſt the
uſe of it, both as a king and a Chriſtian.

Compare with them the works of the vaga-
bond Shakſpeare ; I fear he ſcarcely deſerved
a better appellation in his youthful days——" the
world was not his friend, nor the world's
law :" they were produced under almoſt every
diſadvantage. But how ſoon did the frigid
beams of royal pedantry ſhed " diſaſtrous
twilight," and ſuffer " dim eclipſe !" whilſt
the flame of genius that inſpired the other,

not

not a fpark of which, poffibly, was noticed in
his native Stratford, and which dimly fhone,
or irregularly blazed (as caprice or envy urged
the gale,) in his own days, kindled as it flew
through the track of time, and now irradicates with permanent luftre the poetic hemif-
phere of Britain! how little did Sir Thomas
Lucy fuppofe, when in the pomp and pleni-
tude of magifterial power, he faw an idle
youth ftand trembling before him, or heard of
his precipitate flight from the terrors of judicial authority, that he fhould be tranfmitted
down to pofterity, by the fame diforderly
youth, under the humiliating appellation of
" Robert Shallow, efq. juftice of peace and
coram !"

It appears, therefore, that genius, whatever
temporary depreffions it may fuffer, is fuperior to all human power, or even " the might
of magic fpell." Kings may dignify difho-
nour, or reward merit; heroes and ftatefmen
may live awhile in the mouths of men; while
the vulgar, like the foliage of the grove, drop
unnoted. Literary genius alone can confer
the unfading wreath of fame on itfelf and
others; can beftow it alike on the prince or
peafant; crown with deathlefs glory, or brand
with

with eternal infamy. Therfites, in the page of Homer, will live as long as the " king of men;" and Hoftefs Quickly will be remembered till the victor of Agincourt is forgotten.

The ideas which I have thrown out, were more particularly fuggefted and impreffed upon my mind by perufing the hiftorical dramas of Shakfpeare. The wonder-working power of the poet's pen is there moft eminently difplayed. " Airy nothings" are embodied ; our anceftors ftart from their tombs, and participate a fecond exiftence. His characters, whether thofe of kings and nobles, of clowns, conftables, or pick-pockets, Cade's licentious mob, or Henry's turbulent barons, are fuch genuine copies from life, that we muft fuppofe the originals acted and fpoke in the manner he reprefents them. Like Homer, and in that refpect he is fingular among our Englifh bards, he has acquired both the credit of an hiftorian, and the celebrity of a poet ; the illufion, at leaft, is fo powerful, that whilft we perufe his account of perfons or events, we cannot eafily difbelieve it. No man of a liberal tafte, defcended from, or related to any of Shakfpeare's favorite hiftoric characters, can avoid feeling, from that very circumftance,

cumftance, additional pleafure in reflecting on them. The natural exiftence of a Hotfpur continued only a few years : the tempeft of war foon quenched that " foul of fire ;" but the pen of Shakfpeare, potent as the magician's wand, has conferred on him an ideal exiftence, which will terminate only with the extinction of the Englifh language, poffibly of the univerfe itfelf.

I fhall, therefore, attempt to inveftigate the caufe or caufes why the characters drawn by our great bard are fo pecularly impreffive, and affect our minds fo differently from what we experience on perufing the productions of any other dramatic writer. The fubject itfelf will, I truft, be interefting ; for what man of tafte is indifferent to any thing that relates to Shakfpeare !

Other dramatic poets deal in *generals,* Shakfpeare in *individuals.* Other poets treat of kings, queens, and heroes, in the *abftract,* he *particularizes* them. Theirs are merely kings, queens, and heroes, all of the fame nature, marked with the fame family features, and " inveterate likeneffes" to each other. But his are Henrys and Richards, Margarets and Catharines, Warwicks and Hotfpurs—all men

and

and women, difcriminated from each other, and infinitely diverfified. This difcrimination is commonly effected by exhibiting fome marking feature, peculiar anecdote, or minute circumftance, appropriate to the character reprefented, in appearance cafually introduced, but which, if I may be allowed the expreffion, identifies and realizes it. When Edward tells the famous Warwick that he would

——— *" Wind his hand about his coal-black hair."*—

Hen. 6, 3d part A. 5. S.

the fable locks of the " proud fetter up and puller down of kings," prefent themfelves immediately to our view. 'Tis faid of Hotfpur, that

— — — — — " by his light

" Did all the Chivalry of England move

" To do brave acts : He was indeed the glafs,

" Wherein the noble youth did drefs themfelves.

" He had no legs that practifed not his gait :

" And, *fpeaking thick, which nature made his blemifh,*

" Became the accents of the valiant."

Hen. 4th, 2d part, A. 2, S. 6.

Who,

Who, after reading thefe lines, can entertain a doubt, but that the gallant Percy had a " twang of that north-country burr," for which the county, from whence he was to have derived his hereditary title, is remarkable to this prefent day.

Such little traits bring the perfonages immediately before our eyes; nor would it be an eafy matter to perfuade us, that the reprefentations were untrue. By fimilar means Homer impreffes on our minds the idea of his heroes' reality. They are not, like a modern regiment, clothed in the fame uniform; nor appear to be of one family, like Virgil's Gyas and Cloanthus; whom he characterifes, with great frugality of diction, by one and the fame epithet; but they are kept diftinct by their appearance, habit, and manners. One is remarkable for height of ftature, another for the breadth of his fhoulders; one for the elegance, another for the rufticity of his apparel; one adopts a peculiar attitude in harranguing a public audience, another ftrikes us with the grace or deformity of his perfon. The colour of the hair, the device of a fhield, or beauty of the creft, and a hundred other minutiæ, mark and diverfify his characters.

He

He refembles our bard likewife in giving, occafionally, fome little characteriftic trait or anecdote, generally communicated in familiar converfation, not always indeed effential to the ftory, but which, from that very circum- ftance, is often more interefting. When Dio- mede ftarts afide from the natural tenor of his difcourfe to boaft of his horfe's pedigree or of his own; or when Neftor as unfeafona- bly expatiates on his former exploits, we, at once, become acquainted with them. In fuch kind of manners-painting converfation (par- ticularly ftriking in the latter part of the Odyf- fey) we lofe fight of the poet. It feems to be the genuine effufion of nature, and its inarti- ficial appearance ftrengthens the deception.

Shakfpeare never ftudied Homer, but was as deeply read as the Grecian bard in the page of nature. In the familiar and confidential converfation occafionally held by his charac- ters, we catch their minds, as if by furprize, in an undrefs; we detect their peculiar habits, and feel, like confidants in an intrigue, a fa- tisfaction in having thofe fecret traits com- municated to us.

Who, for inftance, can doubt that the " proud northern lord Clifford of Cumber- land,"

land," exercifed his baronial privilege of fwearing, uncontrouled, to an eminent de_ gree, when we read Warwick's and Richard's fcoffing addreffes to him as he lay expiring on the field of battle?

WARWICK.

" They mock thee, Clifford, fwear as thou was wont."

RICHARD.

" What, not an oath ! nay, then the world goes hard
" When Clifford cannot fpare his friends an oath——
" I know *by that* he's dead."

Hen. 6th, 3d part, A. 2. S. 9.

If we fuppofe fuch reprefentations are merc_ ly drawn from images, formed in his creative mind, ftill they live to us ; and, through his happy mode of introduction, we become as well acquainted with them as with our own cotemporaries. I am, however, inclined to fufpect, that Shakfpeare, where he does not follow the beaten path of hiftory, drew his characters and incidents from traditionary ftories and family anecdotes ;—fometimes, probably, from preceding dramas in which they were preferved, and other fhort-lived publications that have long fince perifhed in the tide of time.

The

The reflexion thrown out by Surrey to cardinal Wolfey, from its being fo circumftantial in point of time and defcription of perfon,
appears to have been founded on fome well-
known ftory in Shakfpeare's time.

> " I'll ftartle you" [exclaims the intemperate Peer,]
> " Worfe than the *fa ring bell,* when the *brown* wench
> " Lay kiffing in your arms, lord Cardinal."

Hen. 8th, A. 3d, S. 5.

It may be noticed, however, that Wolfey was
particularly odious to the nobility ; and his
cotemporary Skelton, the fafhionable fatyrift
of the day, remarks of him, in a rhyme, to
which Devonfhire-men only can do juftice in
the pronunciation, that

> " He regardeth lords
> " No more than potfherdes."

And the ftory poffibly was invented, or pro-
pagated by means of thofe powerful enemies.
Yet it muft not be difguifed that this " lord
Cardinal" was notorious for his incontinency :
and the laureat, in numbers no lefs fublime
that thofe already cited, and we may fufpect
equally true, ironically obferves, that

" To

> " To kepe his flefhe chafte
> " In Lent for a repafte,
> " He eateth capons ftewed,
> " Fefant and partridge mewed,
> " Hennes, chickens and pigges."

He concludes his invectives with this affecting expoftulation :

> " Spareth neither maide ne wyfe—
> " *Is this a poftle's lyfe ?*"

We cannot but fmile at this wretched doggrel of Skelton; yet there is little doubt, but that it was preferred by our illuftrious defender of the faith, and his obfequious courtiers, to the genuine humour and characteriftic rhymes of Chaucer.

I once thought, likewife, that the more creditable anecdote of Cranmer, given by Hen. 8th, was merely a traditionary ftory.

> " The common voice, I fee, is verified
> " Of thee, which fays thus. *Do my lord of Canterbury*
> " *But one fhrewd turn,* and *he's your friend for ever.*"

A fimilar fpeech, however, is attributed in Strype's Memorials, (B. 3, C. xxx.) not to the king, but to Dr. Hethe, archbifhop of York.

S   We

We have often reason to suppose, that many incidents, now unknown, are alluded to, and some real characters shadowed under fictitious names, not only in Shakspeare's comedies, but also in his historic dramas. The "old lady," for example, in that last quoted, and which may not be improperly stiled an anonymous designation, the friend of Anne Bullen, who tells the turbulent monarch, that his daughter was " as like him as cherry is to cherry, (A. 5. S. 1.) appears to me no ideal personage.

Mr. Walpole has ingeniously observed, that " Leontes and Hermione," in " the Winter's Tale," were the typical representatives of Henry 8th and Anne Bullen ; and the character of Paulina seems to be that of this identical *old lady*, placed in a more conspicuous and advantageous point of view. The same officious zeal to serve her mistress, and the same kind of garrulous intrepidity towards an irascible monarch, is apparent in both characters.—— " The child, says Paulina, is yours,"

" And, might we lay th' old proverb to your charge,
" So like you 'tis the worse. Behold, my lords,
" Altho' the print be little, the whole matter

" And

" And copy of the father : eye, nofe, lip,
" And *trick of his frown*."

A. 2, S. 5.

The conjecture which I am again going to
hazard, may appear, like this, too fanciful.
That Shakfpeare, however, often covertly
alluded to different perfons and tranfactions
in the days of queen Elizabeth, and of her
father, has been clearly fhewn by his commentators in various inftances : but the following paffage in " All's well that ends well,"
has eluded their obfervation, or impofed on
mine. The king fays, that he had prefented
a ring to Helen,

" And bade her, if her fortune ever ftood
" Necefiitated to help, that by *this token*
" *I would relieve her.*"

A. 5. S. 4.

It appears to me, that the romantic ftory of
queen Elizabeth's having delivered a ring to
Effex, with a promife to affift him in any diftrefs on his producing it, gave birth to this incident. Its reality has been queftioned and ridiculed by Voltaire, but it has been fupported
with ability and fuccefs by Walpole. At any
rate it appears to have been a popular ftory ;
of courfe fufficient for Shakfpeare's purpofe,

S 2 and

and for mine.——This opinion, I confefs, cannot be fupported, if we allow thofe dates to
be accurate, which are prefixed to Shakfpeare's dramas by Mr. Malone in Johnfon
and Steevens's edition. He fuppofes that
"All's well that ends well," was reprefented
in 1598. As Effex was not dead at that time;
and as it cannot be imagined, even had he
been fo, that any thing allufive to fuch an
inftance of the queen's partiality for him,
would have been brought forward on the ftage
during her lifetime, we muft either rank this
play among Shakfpeare's latter productions,
or my conjecture muft be given up as deftitute of any foundation. Mr. Malone fuppofes
likewife, that "the Winter's Tale" came out
in *1594; and if fo, it could not have been
intended, according to Mr. Walpole's opinion, as a fequel to Hen. 8, for that drama
appears not to have been written till 1601. I
am, however, unwilling to give up either Mr.
Walpole's conjecture or my own; and it is
obfervable that Mr. Malone, who has fatif-
factorily afcertained the dates of Shakfpeare's

* Since writing the above, I perceive in Mr. Malone's
edition of 1793, that he retracts this idea, and fuppofes it to
have been of much later date. My fubfequent quotation is
from Johnfon and Steevens's 3d ed. p. 286.

other

other plays, expresses some diffidence in regard to " the Winter's Tale" and " All's well that ends well." He observes that, " *if* they did come out in 1594 and 1598, they came out under different titles from those they now bear.—Though supposed to have been early productions, they were not published, it must be acknowledged, in Shakspeare's life-time, but for the dates of them we rely only on conjecture." Again, " the Winter's Tale" was not entered at Stationers' Hall, [neither does it appear that the other comedy was] nor printed till 1623 ; but *probably* is the play mentioned by Meres under the title of " Love's Labour won." These conjectures carry no conviction with them ; and the probability seems to rest on the other side of the question, namely, that we ought to number those plays among the latter productions of Shakspeare ; particularly if the personal allusions are admitted.

I mentioned that several real characters and incidents are alluded to in our poet's comedies. Some have been pointed out, but, doubtless, in respect to the greater part, no clue remains to guide our steps and direct us to the original. I am fully convinced, that

master

mafter Slender fat for his picture to our un-
rivalled portrait-painter, as well as his coufin
Shallow. "His little wee face," "his little
yellow *cain*-coloured beard," his having fought
with a warrener, been intoxicated and robbed
by his knavifh companions, and other exploits, equally memorable, feem to mark a
real character, and to record real facts : circumftances, probably, that excited no little
mirth at the time of reprefentation. But we
are not to wonder at thofe allufions being now
totally loft and forgotten, if we reflect with
what rapidity the perfonal fatire of Foote,
which fo often in our own days "fat the play—
houfe in a roar," is pofting on towards the
oblivious gulf.——The greater part of the firft
fcene in "the Merry Wives of Windfor,"
may have been copied from the life, and have
paffed in fir Thomas Lucy's judicial hall.
Even the breaking open the lodge and kiff-
ing the keeper's daughter, which Falftaff (a
character, it is faid, partly drawn for an inhabitant of Stratford) humoroufly difavows,
may have been charges there ferioufly urged
againft Shakfpeare and his riotous affociates.

As our bard is univerfally allowed to be a
copyift of nature, it induces us to place an
almoft

almoſt unlimited confidence in him. We
cannot but ſuppoſe in his hiſtoric dramas,
even where we are unable to trace him, that
he dwells on real, not imaginary tranſactions ;
and has preſerved many genuine anecdotes,
not of weight ſufficient to have gained admittance into the page of hiſtory, or taken from
authors, whoſe writings ſcarcely ſurvived theiꝛ
own exiſtence.

The following remarkable incident, attending cardinal Beaufort's death, is ſo forcibly
characteriſtic, that we cannot eaſily ſuſpect it
to be invention, though no hiſtory mentions
the circumſtance.

    " Lord Cardinal, if thou think'ſt on heaven's bliſs,
    " *Hold up thy hand, make ſignal of thy hope.*—
    " He dies, and makes no ſign !"

Hen. 6th, 2d part, A. 3. S. 3.

The deſcription of his anguiſh and deſpair
occurs in Hall's chronicle, but the additional
circumſtances thrown in by Shakſpeare, won-
derfully increaſe the horror of the ſcene. The
addreſs to the cardinal may be illuſtrated by
a little devotional book, intitled, " The KEY
of PARADISE opening the gate to eternal ſal-
vation," republiſhed at St. Omer's in 1675,

S 4

but

but when firft printed I know not, in which is the following MEDITATION. "Imagine thyfelf lying in thy death-bed, with a hallowed candle in thy hand, a crucifix on thy breaft, and thy ghoftly father calling on thee, that if thou canft not fpeak, yet at leaft to *hold up thy hand in token* of thy *hope*, and affiance in the mercies of Chrift."

The death of Glofter, in the fame drama, (A. 3. S. 3) though, according to hiftory, its manner was uncertain, is marked with fo many minute and appropriate circumftances, that Shakfpeare moft probably heard it thus particularly defcribed, or took his defcription from actual obfervation, on a fimilar event.

The interview between Henry 5th and Williams the foldier, (Hen. 5th, A. 4. S. 4.) the night preceding the battle of Agincourt, with their interchange of gloves, and the trick in confequence played on Fluellin, appears to have been founded on fome traditionary ftory. Our hearts, at leaft, will not allow it to be a fiction, but feel delighted at fuch an unexpected, though by no means unnatural, recurrence of Hal's original humour.

There

There are many other little incidents, like the foregoing, which we ought not to confider as invention, becaufe we cannot trace them to their fource. Had the ftory of Simpcox of St. Albans, and the combat between the armourer and his apprentice Peter (Hen. 6th, 2d part,) been no where recorded but in Shakfpeare, they would probably have been confidered merely as ludicrous fictions, introduced to put the upper gallery in good humour. Each of thofe incidents, however, is noticed in different chronicles of the times. The numerous circumftances relative to the death of lord Haftings, form a kind of epifode in the tragedy of Richard 3d, and they are adopted from hiftory :——even the compliment which the fubtile tyrant pays to the bifhop of Ely's ftrawberries, and the unimportant errand on which he fends the courtly prelate. Catefby obferves " the king is angry, fee he gnaws his lip :" and Margaret, in her imprecations on him, exclaims,

> " No fleep clofe up that deadly eye of thine,
> " Unlefs it be while fome tormenting dream
> " Affrights thee with a hell of ugly devils."

Rich. 3d, A. 1. S. 3.

We

We are not to confider either of thefe expreffions as cafual, but ftrictly appropriate and
h.ftorically true. Different authors relate,
that " his fleep was (generally) filled with per-
turbations," and particularly that night previous to the engagement in which he perifhed.

When Falftaff ridicules the flender form of
prince Henry, and fays that he would give a
thoufand pounds if he was able to run as faft
as he could, &c. we muft not fuppofe that
thofe words are thrown out accidentally. Hiftorians agree in defcribing him as tall, thin,
and active. Like Achilles he was no lefs confpicuous for fwiftnefs than for perfonal courage. The former is reprefented by Pindar as

$$\text{Κτε-ινοντ' ελαφους ανευ κυ-}$$
$$\text{-νων, δολιαν θ' εγκεων·}$$
$$\text{Ποσσι γαρ κρατισκεν.}$$

Nem. Od. 3.

And we might be almoft tempted to fuppofe
that our old annalift copied from the Grecian
bard, but for the words inclofed in a parenthefis. " He was paffing fwift in running,
infomuch that he (with two other of his lords)
without hounds, bow, or other engine, would
take a wild buck or doe, in a large park."
(Stowe.) " Omnes Coætaneos, fays Thomas
de

de Elmham, *faliendo* præceſſit, curſu veloci
ſimul currentes prævenit." We ſee from
theſe quotations, the propriety of Hotſpur's
ſtyling him "the nimble mad-cap prince of
Wales;" and the peculiar juſtice of the following compariſon, drawn by Vernon, a friend
of Hotſpur's.

> " I ſaw young Harry with his beaver on,
> " His cuiſſes on his thighs, gallantly armed,
> " *Riſe from the ground like feathered Mercury* ;
> " And *vaulted* with ſuch eaſe into his ſeat,
> " As if an angel dropt down from the clouds
> " To turn and wind a fiery Pegaſus,
> " And, witch the world with noble horſemanſhip."

Hen. 4th, 1ſt part. A. 4. S. 1.

A variety of beautiful and happy alluſions
occur likewiſe in the former part of the ſame
ſpeech. An attention to ſuch *minutiæ*, tho'
not hiſtorically true, muſt have a wonderful
effect in realizing the dramatis perſonæ.——
Even in reſpect to animals, as well as men,
Shakſpeare will not deal in *generals*. The tragedy hero of a modern dramatiſt would call
for " his barbed ſteed" or his fiery courſer:"
but a Richard orders his groom to

> " Saddle *white Surrey* for the field to-morrow."—

And

And hiftorians fay, that when he entered the town of Leicefter, " he was mounted on a great *while courfer.*" May we not reafonably fuppofe, that this was the identical Surrey? The gallant earl, whofe name he bore, was warmly attached to Richard, and had probably, as a proof of his regard, beftowed on him this acceptable prefent.

The impetuous Hotfpur impatiently enquires after his "crop-ear Roan," and exclaims, in equeftrian tranfport, " that roan fhall be my throne." His fondnefs for his horfe (of which he appears to be no lefs proud than Diomede, a congenial character, was of the fteeds of Tros,) is one of his marking features, and humouroufly ridiculed by his rival in fame, prince Henry. (Hen. 4th, 1ft part A. 2, S. 8.) When Vernon, therefore, expatiates with more candour than difcretion, in praife of his " noble horfemanfhip," it peculiarly irritates the mind of Hotfpur. His reply, particularly the conclufion, is truly characteriftic.

———— " Come, let me take *my* horfe,
" Who is to bear me, like a thunderbolt,
" Againft the bofom of the prince of Wales.
" Harry to Harry fhall, *and horfe to horfe,*
" Meet, and ne'er part till one drop down a corfe!'"

Hen. 4th, 1ft part, A. 4. S. 2.

Hotfpur

Hotfpur feels himfelf touched in a tender
point. His rival is celebrated for a qualifica-
tion in which he thought himfelf pre-emi-
nent; and his mind reverts with vexation to
the unpleafing idea. The beauty of this natural fally of paffion efcaped the earlier editors
of Shakfpeare; and it has been printed " *not*
horfe to horfe," in every edition but the firft,
till fir Thomas Hanmer reftored the original
reading. Such a little trait diftinguifhes a
mafter's hand more than pages of laboured
declamation.

The mutual antipathy between Hotfpur and
" the fword and buckler prince of Wales," is
finely conceived and admirably executed.
They are * planets in fiery oppofition, contending for fuperiority in the firmament of
glory. We cannot find a fpeech but what
feems dictated by nature itfelf. Their little
ebullitions of paffion, their mutual jealoufy,
which one ftrives to conceal, by treating his
rival with ridicule, and the other by holding
him in affected contempt, familiarize them to
us. We fee, we know them, are privy to the

---

* " Two ftars keep not their motion in one fphere;
" Nor can one England brook a double reign
" Of Harry Percy and the prince of Wales."

Hen. 4th, 1ft part, A. 5. S. 9.

diffipated

diffipated relaxations of the one, and the turbulent thoughts that agitate the mind of the
other. This obfervation may be extended to
almoft every leading character: we contemplate men like ourfelves, endued with the
fame propenfities as thofe that actuate them
in real life, and are confequently interefted in
their fortunes. But our feelings are not excited by the pompous characters in declamatory
tragedy: they are beings of another fpecies,
and we have no concern with them.

If the wonder-working pen of Shakfpeare
induces us to pay more credit to his reprefentation of our hiftoric characters, than hiftorical feverity may fometimes allow, it is a delufion too pleafing to be lightly refigned. We
fee, or feem to fee, realities; and the caufes,
which I have juft explained, operate alfo in
his fictitious dramas. Though he cannot
there build on real facts, yet appropriate and
ftrong-marked defcriptions of perfons and
places, familiar converfation and characteriftic
anecdotes, commonly give an appearance of
truth and confiftency to the moft wild and extravagant fictions.

T. O.

SOME

SOME CURSORY REMARKS

ON THE

Prefent State of Philofophy and Science.

Flits o'er the deep, nor wets his wing.

———

THE hiftory of Antient Philofophy exhibits
fometimes a picture of a lively imagination,
efcaping from the fetters of obfervation ; of
an imagination excentric, ingenious, and occafionally deluded ; fometimes the fublime
fpectacle of the human mind, burfling by its
efforts thro' the furrounding darknefs, glancing at omnipotence, and tracing its finger
thro' the myfterious mazes of human life.
It more frequently difplays only fpeculative
refinements on fubjects, where certainty cannot be obtained, and a fcholaftic fubtilty,
where words hold the place of ideas, and
empty founds are fubftituted for folid information. But of what is now called fcience,
the

the fages of Greece had little knowledge. Pythagoras brought his fyftem from another region: it was taught, commented on, and forgotten. To Mofes much knowledge was attributed; but he feems to have been rather the inftrument of the fupreme agent, to whom the miraculous torments of Pharoah were owing, than a philofopher peculiarly wife, or an obferver fingularly acute. The miracles of Mofes were too ftriking not to have been remembered in the Pagan world; they have been preferved either by hiftory or tradition, and attributed to various fabulous perfonages of remote antiquity. That Mofes fometimes availed himfelf of natural appearances, will be obvious; yet various circumftances may be adduced to fhow, that what appears moft confiftent with the forefight acquired by fcience, muft have been occafioned by fuperior influence, by divine infpiration. Mr. Bruce has fhown, that the eaft wind was calculated to dry up the red fea, and has recorded the appearance of pillars of fire; but the eaft wind has fince prevailed, and the red fea has not been dried; and pillars of fire have appeared, but never, as the Mofaic hiftory records, in the night. Serpents may become immoveable

ble rods in the hands of the Pfylli ; but the great ferpent of the wildernefs, which preys on the reft of its race, has not yet been obedient to their powers. An electrician might infulate an ark, and charge it fo as to ftrike thofe who touched it ; but he could not preferve its virtue; and the beft informed follower of Stahl would not find it eafy, in the wildernefs, to make an impalpable powder of the golden calf. As we cannot draw the line between the works of the Almighty, and the forefight of the legiflator, " fkilled in all the knowledge of the Ægyptians," we are unable to afcertain the fcientific acquifitions of the Ifraelites. We find few traces of fcience in the fubfequent ages down to the periods of Solomon and Daniel. If we except what is faid of Solomon's acquaintance with the vegetable fyftem, and what we know of his political difcernment, the works of the former difplay only the excellent and practical maxims of the moralift ; and in the latter we perceive a fervid unaffected piety, joined with the political acquifitions of a ftatefman. Yet to Solomon has been attributed all that Greece afterwards knew of arts and fciences, all that the Alchemifts boaft of their tranfmuting power; and to

Daniel the whole circle of Ariſtotelian philoſophy.

What the philoſophers of Greece knew,
they knew but imperfectly, if we except only
Ariſtotle. His comprehenſive mind ſurveyed
every thing in its varied lights, and ſaw the
different combinations, which each ſubject
admitted. In the ſcience of natural hiſtory his
knowledge was extenſive; and in phyſics,
particularly in what relates to the air, he
knew, without the aſſiſtance of the air-pump,
what that inſtrument has been ſuppoſed to
have diſcovered. He knew that air was
heavy, and that, from the light, the colour
of plants was derived.

It is ſurpriſing that the philoſophy of Ariſtotle did not receive, in the middle ages, the
attention which was paid to his dialectics. *Theſe*
monopolized the care of the philoſophers, to
whom Ariſtotle, after a long period of ignorance, was firſt known, and ſcience ſoon be-,
came a conteſt of words. It ſunk, to riſe with
ſplendour, in all its varied branches; and if,
as ſome have propheſied, it has paſſed its zenith, and we now admire the mild radiance
of its weſtern rays, without expecting it again
to dazzle with meridian ſplendor, it muſt be

at

at leaft allowed, that its fall is refpectable.
Frivolous purfuits, indeed, employ the attention of fome phïlolophers : indolence has
feized others, from whom much was expected,
while a whole nation, defolated by faction,
appears to behold, with equal indifference,
the ruin of fcience, of elegance, and tafte.
But we need not defpair : we fhall have occafion to fhow, that torpor has not feized every
individual ; anarchy has not diftracted every
nation ; while the difcovery of new regions,
and a more intimate acquaintance with extenfive countries, before imperfectly known, have
enlarged the limits of fcience, and opened the
profpect of new and unexpected acquifitions.

To rife above the topics of the day, the idle
converfation of the frivolous and indolent, was
the object of our inftitution.   It gives me
pleafure to be able to congratulate you on our
fuccefs ; and we may indulge the fatisfaction
of reflecting that our union will be equally
permanent, inftructive, and entertaining.—
From the collifion of varied fentiments, the
moft able may receive information, from the
comparifon of ideas formed under circumftances very different, and with views diffimi-
lar, truth will be often fuccefsfully elicited.

In the philological inveftigations, the mind will be elegantly entertained, its powers augmented by the exercife of critical difcernment, and the judgment ftrengthened by inveftigating the fources of error.

Tho' fecluded in the corner of an ifland, fuch is the force of expanding truth, fo penetrating its rays, and fo generally diffufed its cheering light, that local fituation cannot materially injure us. At this æra, the mind feems eager to expatiate beyond the former confines, the extravagant, and fometimes the erring, fpirit, contribute equally to the diffufion of knowledge by new difcoveries, or by the ruinous refult of fpecious and deluding projects. The philofophers of France long ago raifed an imaginary fabric of fancied excellence. The bubble was blown, and expanded to a promifing fize; but it burft, and threatens to involve in its deftruction, a flourifhing kingdom, arts, fciences, agriculture, and commerce. It is an inftance of the mind fpeculating, without the regulating balance of judgment; eagerly grafping at an apparent good, without weighing the danger which muft refult from the inftruments employed; purfuing with a dangerous violence, what might

might be fafely obtained by a more calm, a more matured, and a flower progrefs. But it is an inftance alfo, that the human mind begins to rife above the trammels of cuftom; that the active fpirit has efcaped from the fhackles of prejudice; that, feeling innate powers, it eagerly preffes forward to exertion.

In other fciences, the progreffive exertions of human reafon afford a more pleafing picture. Tho' fome wanderings have occafionally mifled philofophers; though hypothefis, fancy, and fpeculation have, in a few inftances, deluded them, they have in general preffed with firm and fteady fteps towards the temple of truth. A very few years fince the ultimate analyfes of natural bodies were but at a little diftance from their common forms. At prefent, more is known of the nature of each clafs of bodies, than had been difcovered of all. Air was found to efcape in the various proceffes of decompofition. From this leading fact, Dr. Hales firft ftruck the fpark of future difcoveries; Dr. Black cherifhed and animated it; Dr. Prieftley raifed it into a flame; Kirwan, Cavendifh, Lavoifier, Berthollet, and Fourcroy, have, from this fource, kindled torches, which have illuminated nature in her moft remote receffes. In this pro-

grefs,

grefs, fciences and arts have been materially
affifted. Our dyes have affumed a fuperior
luftre, our linen a more immaculate whitenefs; our glafs vies more fuccefsfully with the
chryftal; iron affumes, in the mould, forms
more delicate than the hammer can beftow;
ftuccos become little inferior to the marble
which they emulate, and our porcelain equals
in fubftance, and in form excels, the rival manufactures of China.

In philofophy our acquifitions have taught
us to guard againft the thunderbolt, to counteract, by the fuperior power of fteam, the
moft copious fountains of fubterraneous water,
to bring the heavenly bodies more completely
within our view; and, when we fee that the
apparently uncompounded element, water,
may become air, and again by a procefs certainly fimple, tho' not fully underftood, re-
gain its more material form, we begin to difcover the real caufes of thofe common changes
in the atmofphere, which philofophers have
hitherto imperfectly comprehended.

An obfcure fubject has lately been illuminated
by a flight ray, which leads to vaft and extenfive profpects. But the whole is yet little more
than fpeculation, tho', in fuch a queftionable
shape,

shape, that it may be allowable to notice what has hitherto been done. The torpedo and the electrical eel from Surinam, are known to produce shocks of the electrical kind, and it is equally well known, that the organs which produce the effect, have a very large and an unusual proportion of nerves. By an accident, Cotunnio of Bologna found a similar effect from dissecting a living mouse. Galvani has pursued the subject; Valli, Fowler, and Monro followed it farther. Little more has, however, been discovered than that the nervous fluid seems to be electrical, that muscular exertions depend on the sudden and violent influx of this fluid, which various medicines and applications will render less mobile, and which may be conveyed by metallic conductors.—— Much indeed, is required in addition and explanation of what is known; but when we reflect that the cohesion of animal fibres depends on the principle of life, and that digestion is destroyed by intercepting the nervous influence of the stomach; that heat depends on the living principle, and putrefaction soon comes on, if the nervous influence be interrupted, it will at once appear that this first step may considerably elucidate the nature of

the

the animal œconomy, and greatly influence every department of philofophy. If, however, by the procefs, the natural electricity of bodies is augmented, and this increafed power only operates on the nerves, in the manner formerly obferved, tho' not explained, all thefe brilliant profpects will be obfcured, all this delufive colouring darkened, and the nature of the nervous power ftill continue among the defiderata of phyfiology.

Fire, the great agent of the chemift, for a while eluded the analyfis of the moft penetrating philofophers, nor could we have heard without the greateft aftonifhment, that it could be transferred from one body to another, with as much eafe as any other ingredient. It is now difcovered to be a principle, more fubtile, probably, than any other, and perhaps never feen wholly feparate ; for in the pureft flame it is combined with light, with the exhalations of the burning body, and with water. The moft aftonifhing exertions of the mind, in an æra, diftinguifhed by furprizing difcoveries, joined with fingular ingenuity, have detected fire in an aerial form, without its fenfible qualities, and in a ftate, probably, the leaft com-
poundęd.

pounded. It is found, where it would be leaſt expected, in the pureſt, and, as it has been ſtiled, without any reference to theory, *empyreal* air. Vital air contains 87 times more heat, in a given bulk, than the pureſt ſpirit of wine, and 870 times more than the fineſt oil.* I may juſt add, among the diſcoveries which have occurred within a few years, the means of meaſuring heat. Mr. Wedgwood's thermometer of contracting clay, has each degree equal to 130° of Farenheit; in other words, the greateſt difference we experience from the ſevereſt winter to the moſt fervent ſummer, amounts but to half a degree of this comprehenſive inſtrument; and it is capable of meaſuring heat equal to what would raiſe Farenheit's thermometer, if the ſubſtances would admit of the experiment, 32,277°.

The other kinds of air, one only excepted, appear to be well known ſubſtances in a new form; and it is among the lateſt diſcoveries, completed at leaſt by the Engliſh chemiſts, that fixed air is only charcoal in this expanded ſtate. Charcoal affords this air, and in affording it almoſt diſappears; the air may be again

* Bergman and Lavoiſer's tables.

brought

brought to affume the appearances and properties of charcoal unchanged, and undimi-
nifhed. The only exception above alluded
to, is the inflammable air, of which we know
little, except that it is, in general, the antagonizing principle of vital air. In folid bodies,
they ufually expel each other : in fluid ones,
they exift together, for the refult of their
union is now very generally agreed to be water.

This doctrine has begun to influence
the explanation of different phænomena of
the animal œconomy. In the compofition of
the fluids, the various gaffes muft have confiderable influence; and, in difeafes, much will
depend on the proportion of fome, and the
abfence of others. If not forbidden by our
rules to be profeffional, I could *not* enlarge
much on this head, for the application of the
doctrine is yet by no means clear. Dr. Bed-
does has lately contributed to retard the progrefs of this kind of inveftgation, by carrying
it farther than obfervation will fupport him.
But we may add, that, in cancers, fea fcurvy,
phthifis pulmonalis, and fome cutaneous com-
plaints, the doctrines of air will be chiefly
ufeful ; in thefe too, if applicable as remedies,
the different gaffes will be found moft falutary.

Thus

Thus extended are the limits of natural knowledge, and the confequences we have already noticed. They are numerous, fplendid, and important; the advantages derived by the manufacturer and artift, are equally valuable. Thefe it is impoffible wholly to explain: the practical application of many of the late difcoveries is purchafed by the manufacturers, fecured by patent, and explained only by a delufive, but plaufible fpecification.

In geography, within nearly the fame period, the difcoveries have been almoft as numerous. The energy of mind, which led Columbus to explore the oppofite fhores of the Atlantic, have, at this period, led the philofopher to the iflands of the Pacific, to deftroy the vifionary phantom of a fouthern continent; and to afcertain the vicinity of the two known continents on the north-eaftern fide of Europe. Science has greatly profited by thefe attempts: humanity and benevolence may rejoice that their caufe has been equally affifted. The difeafes, fuppofed to be effentially connected with navigation, have been averted by the exertions of common prudence, and plain but penetrating good fenfe; nor can the annals of the world equal the late defign of tranf-

porting

porting a vegetable, effentially ufeful to life, in a ftove, conftructed in a fhip, over ten thoufand miles of ocean, thro' climates dangerous from ftorms, and effentially varying in degrees of heat.

The voyages of our countrymen, at this æra, have greatly added to the ftock of natural hiftory. Numerous new vegetables, many of them highly ufeful, have been difcovered; and the 20,000 fpecies, which Linnæus once faid, by a pretty certain calculation,—"calculo fatis certo," would probably limit our vegetable riches have been already nearly doubled. Our territorial acquifitions in India have greatly augmented the fcience of botany. The various new plants from this country have enriched our confervatories, and added to our botanical knowledge. We may be allowed to hope, that the plan of forming a complete fyftematic treatife of the plants of India, fuggefted by Sir William Jones, will not be forgotten. Many elucidations of the antient authors, who fpeak of the plants of India, will probably occur, of which we have one fpecimen in the Afiatic Refearches. The fpikenard of the antients appears to be a fpecies of valerian, for a plant, refembling, in all its

properties,

properties, what Arrian and others have recorded of the fpikenard, is found to belong to this well-known genus, and probably it is not very diftant from the other fpecies of valerian, in its medical properties.

The vegetables riches of New South Wales appear not, at prefent, very interefting. Time may inform us of the qualities of the vegetable fubftances already difcovered, or add to the catalogue; but, at prefent, we know not that the peppermint tree is preferrable to the European fhrub, the red rezin to the kino of Africa, or the yellow, to the balfam of Tolu.

In the animal kingdom, we now are acquainted with the pangolin, a fingular creature, which, like the mole, refides in the earth, and which, from the cartilaginous and mufcular ftructure of its ftomach, unites the quadrupeds with the birds. No animal or vegetable fubftance has been found in its ftomach, and it has been fuppofed, that it may be nourifhed by mineral fubftances. The obfervation does not, however, fupport the conclufion; for, like the falmon, in whofe ftomach nothing is ufually difcovered, the digeftion may be peculiarly rapid; or, like other animals, living without light or air, it

may

may be able to bear a long interval between
the hours of feeding. An animal, who seems
not to possess the faculty of vision in a degree
peculiarly acute, or a sense of smell so nice,
as to distinguish accurately its proper food,
would probably require a stomach which could
receive no injury from substances unsuitable
to its constitution. If the pangolin fed on
worms, with them it might take in the cal-
carious, and probably the flinty particles of
the soil where it lives, which in a stomach so
carefully constructed, can do no injury. This
final cause is supported by what has been observed of the gallinaceous tribe, for Spalanzani
has renderd it uncertain, whether they swallow the fragments of gravel by accident, or
from instinct, for the purpose of triturating
their food; and from the dissection of stone-
eaters, the coats of whose stomachs have been
found indurated and cartilaginous.

It was not easy in this sketch of the present
state of science, to pass over an animal so singular as the pangolin, without a more particular attention than can be bestowed on individuals, whose connection with the more general doctrines of natural history is less strik-
ing. Tho', therefore, our acquisitions in the
order

order of birds and of infects, are numerous, it is impoffible to mention them diftinctly. Among the birds, where we find few species peculiarly docile and intelligent, one may deferve notice. The Indian grofs-beak builds its neft with a care and an extent of judgment feemingly fuperior to inftinct, fcarcely fhort, indeed, of reafon. It is fufpended over water to be fecure from ferpents, its entrance is narrow, and from below, to avoid the depredations of birds of prey. Many fuppofe that it illuminates its neft with fire flies, which it fixes on the fides with cow dung: it is, at leaft, allowed, that fire flies are found in this fituation, tho' uncertain whether defigned for food or for convenience. Thefe marks of judgment and forefight are not, probably, accidental, for the bird is peculiarly docile and obedient; and, when we add, that the grofs-beak is of the fparrow kind, thefe marks of intellect will appear more fingular.

Minerals have alfo been difcovered within thefe few years, poffeffing new and ufeful properties. Scotland has been found to produce a new earth. New South Wales a clay feemingly different from the other fpecies of the argillaceous kind. From the jargon of Ceylon

an

an earth of a particular kind, not hitherto known, has been feparated; and from the Eaft Indies we have procured a fpar equalling in hardnefs the diamond, and called, in confequence of this property, adamantine.

While Scotland has afforded the new earth to which the name of Stronthian has, from the place where it was difcovered, been given by Mr. Kirwan, our neigbouring county has afforded a new metal. The menackanite of Cornwall appears to poffefs very peculiar properties, which have not yet been found united in any one fubftance of the metallic kind; and tho' its appearance, and in fome meafure its properties, feem to refemble thofe of iron, yet they differ fo much from iron, as may probably render it ufeful in many arts. The effects of the acid of phofphorus in diftinguifhing many bodies, and rendering them capable of refifting the moft powerful agents, muft always be kept in view by the cautious mineralogift. In its combination with iron, it for a time eluded the moft accurate analyfes, and the beft chemifts fuppofed they had difcovered a new metal, which, from its connection with iron, they called Siderite. Before, therefore, the Cornifh metal can be
ftyled

ſtyled new, it muſt be again examined with a ſuſpicious caution. But, tho' not new, it may be uſeful and important; tho' a combination, it may be extenſively applicable. The barytes, for inſtance, an earth diſcovered ſome years ſince, in many reſpects reſembles lime, yet it affords a ſalutary medicine, poſſeſſes powers, found in no combination of calcareous earth, and is a re-agent of peculiar utility, becauſe in its union with vitriolic acid, it is almoſt inſoluble. If the aerated barytes, deſcribed by Dr. Withering, be ever met with in extenſive ſtrata, it may be ſingularly uſeful, as affording an eaſy method of preſerving water from putrefaction in long voyages.* The ſtronthian earth alſo, if it ſhould appear to be a new form only of a ſubſtance formerly known, may, from its eaſy fuſibility in particular circumſtances, afford a valuable reſource for enamellers. The manganeſe, which abounds in peculiar perfection in this county, was long ſuppoſed to be a magnetic ore of iron; but even conſidered in this light, the glaſs manufacturer found it

* A ſmall proportion of vitriolic acid, added to water, will prevent it from putrifying; and this acid may be compleatly precipitated by the aerated barytes, which is inſoluble, when united with the acid.

U   more

more useful than any other ferrugineous substance; and its valuable qualities have since
been extended to the potteries and the bleach-
field, in which it is now an indispensible material.

I have engaged in this short digression, to
oppose objections often repeated ; to obviate
cavilling often heard from those who do not
distinguish between the name and the properties, who lessen the value of a discovery,
because its basis appears from investigation to
have been before known. Many similar facts
might have been added, which would have
rendered this part of the sketch both tedious
and disproportioned.

When I formerly mentioned the improvements in the porcelain, it was not the place
to add the causes of its excellence. The materials which occasion its peculiar value are
chiefly found in this and the neighbouring
county. Indeed Devonshire wants only to be
examined by an able mineralogist. Its clays
are excellent ; its manganese of a very supe-
rior quality ; and its marbles, in their beauty
and variety, emulate those of Italy.

Europe has seen, with astonishment, the
enterprizes of the English in the east. They
have

have feen a body of merchants, extending
their power over the territory of Aurengzeb,
exercifing fupreme dominion over countries
more extenfive than Europe, forming an im-
perium in imperio unknown to hiftory, which
the politician views with aftonifhment and
dread ; the philofopher with an anxious impa-
tient curiofity. It is not my bufinefs to efti-
mate the effects of the wealth of Hindoftan,
tranfported to this country, the difproportioned magnitude of the appendage of a fmall
but powerful nation, or the confequence which
the influence of the eaft may have on the political fyftem of the weft. To literature, our
extended empire in the eaft has greatly contributed, and whatever opinion be formed of
Mr. Haftings, as a politician or governor, he
muft be confidered as the greateft benefactor
learning ever had. It is not eafy to believe
that the man, to whom the mild, blamelefs
Bramin opened the facred vedas, to whofe influence it is owing that we have traced philofophy to her cradle, and examined her, while
advancing with unequal fteps, to a vigorous
manhood, could have been a cruel tyrant.

The Arabians, in the middle ages, kept
alive the fparks of learning ; and it was for
this reafon that their language became an effential

fential part of a learned education. Thus
feebly cherished, and almoft neglected, it
was foon cultivated with another view; and
the language of Arabia, the parent of the Perfian, and of the Hindû, was an object of attention to every eaftern adventurer. To this
neceffary acquifition was foon added another
more ufeful to the philofophical enquirer, viz.
the Sanfcrit, the religious language of Indoftan, the facred repofitory of their myfteries, their religion and their philofophy.——
With thefe keys the holy cabinet has been un-
locked, and we have·glanced at the facred
treafures, with an eager defire to examine
them more fully, to poffefs them more completely. I wifh only at prefent to point out
the very great and extenfive influence of what
we·have difcovered in this repofitory, on what
we formerly knew. It is amongft the moft
brilliant difcoveries of this æra.

The hiftories of the Grecian philofophy in
our language, have rather been the lives of
men, than a connected fyftem of opinions.
If the latter had been the object of the different hiftorians, Pythagoras would have been
the firft object. His fyftem, whatever it really
was, feems to have been the foundation of
Socrates' ethics, of Plato's fplendid fancies, of
the

the more fober fyftem of the Porch, and the
more accommodating, more fpecious, doctrines of Ariftippus. Pythagoras, it is faid,
travelled to Ægypt, and there attained his
mathematical and aftronomical knowledge;
his religious and his metaphyficial fyftems.——
The idea is abfurd, for his fyftem is not Ægyptian. He taught that the foul was rational,
immaterial and immortal. Of thefe tenets
the Ægyptians had no idea. He inculcated
the pure principles of liberty: the Ægyptians
were at that time the fervile inftruments of a
defpot. He told his difciples that there was
one god—one, indivifible, and immutable,
while the Ægyptians devoured the leeks and
onions, which they had adored. The tranf-
migration of fouls, and the confequent doctrine of avoiding animal food, was equally.
unknown to thofe who drank of the Nile. If
then thefe tenets are inconfiftent with the fyftem of the Ægyptians, and confonant to thofe
of the Bramins, we can have little doubt of
the fource of the Grecian philofophy. Their
mythology has been already fhown to be nearly
connected with the fables of the Hindoos, by
Sir William Jones, and the connection between Ægypt and India fully proved by Lieut.
Wilford.

U 3 The

The life of Pythagoras, as it has reached us, is only calculated to amuſe and aſtoniſh. That he went to Ægypt is certain ; and, in Æthiopia, might have met with the Gymno-ſophiſts, the naked philoſophers of the Nile, the degenerated diſciples of Bramha. He ſeems, however, to have gone farther ; for Diogenes Laertius ſpeaks of his travelling among the Chaldæans, and the Magi; Cicero mentions his acquaintance with the Magi of Perſia, and Pliny his travels into Perſia, Ara-bia, and Æthiopia. Dr. Prideaux has endea-voured, with ſome ſucceſs, to prove that he was a ſcholar of Zoroaſter ; I mean the ſecond of the name who drew his doctrines, if we can judge from the ſtriking reſemblance between the Zend-aveſta and the ſyſtem of the fol-lowers of Bramha, from the Bramins.

Among theſe reſemblances, nothing is more ſtriking than the triple mithra of Perſia, and the divine triad of Brahma, Veeſhna, and Seeva ; from either of which the Ægyptian trinity of the Globe, the Wing, and the Ser-pent, may have been formed, and the vari-ous alluſions of this kind in Plato and his fol-lowers derived. There is no more ſtriking diſſimilitude, than between this Trinity, the ſacred Oom of the Bramins or the holy Om of
the

the Ægyptians, and the Quaternion of Pytha-
garas. Yet he probably accommodated himfelf to the languages more ufually known;
and, as the facred name of the deity in the
languages generally underftood, were words
of four letters, he might have thought his
Quaternion would be better underftood, than
when comprifed in a word fabricated from
the initials of the three principal attributes of
Bramha.

From the late difcoveries, and thofe points,
at prefent the fubjects of inveftigation, we
fhall probably find, that the mythology and the
philofophy of Greece is Indian; that the myfteries of the groves of Perfia and Hindoftan
were carried by the northern Scythians, bor-
dering on India, to Scandinavia and Britain,
where with unimpaired veneration, the Druids
and their bloody rites were conveyed; that the
great antiquity of the Hindoos is in its more
extraordinary outlines, mifreprefented, for
the Yougs were probably the Magni Anni of
the Sybils, the periods terminated by planetary revolutions, and the laft only the real hiftory of mankind; that the wars of the Giants
or the Titans, taken from the battles of the
Indian Soors and Afoors, good and evil genii,
are only the contefts of the fons of Shem and

Ham

Ham for the empire of the infant world; and that the early divinities of Greece are to be looked for in the earth, in the sun, and the air; in fire, and in water. Whether Chaldæa or India was firft peopled; whether the Hebrew or the Sanfcrit was the original language; whether Hindoftan and its records efcaped the Mofaic deluge, is uncertain. Yet perhaps it will appear that to Chaldæa India was indebted for its firft inhabitants, who, in return, peopled the eaft; and if the Hebrew be the moft antient, the Sanfcrit, probably the parent of the Greek, has been more extenfively diffufed. In fhort, in this enlightened æra, every thing might have been expected, had not the fatal fcourge of war been brandifhed, and devaftation taken place of peace and order, of cultivation and happinefs. May her triumph be of fhort duration; and diftant from fcenes of turbulence and confufion, may we be fenfible of that peculiarly happy fituation, which enables us, uninterrupted, and in full fecurity, to enjoy our literary amufements, to catch, at leaft, occafional fparks from the irradiations of fcience, from the fplendors which we admire at a diftance.

S. I. S.

Aug. 22*d*, 1793.

Of SEPULTURE in GENERAL,

AND

SEPULCHRAL SINGLE STONES ERECT.

THE firſt part of this ſubject I ſhall notice only curforily, and as an introduction to the latter. It is a beaten track, and cannot be ſuppoſed to afford much novelty, tho' I ſhall endeavour to render it not unentertaining.

In the early ſtate of ſociety there ſeems to have been but one common cuſtom, the moſt natural and ſimple, that of committing the body of the deceaſed to the earth, whence it was believed to have been taken. That it was conformable to the courſe of nature for all things to return to their original principles, was an antient opinion ; the ſpirit to the air, the body to the earth: alluding to which, Euripides, in his ſupplicants, introduces Theſeus thus ſpeaking :

" Εασατ

" Εασατ 'ηδη γη καλυφθηναι νεκρυς.

" Οθεν δ'εκαςον εις το σωμ' αφικείο

" Ενταυθ' απηλθε, πνευμα μεν προς αιθερα,

" Το σωμα δ'εις γην."

" Now they are dead, permit them in the earth
" To reft concealed. For whence at firft proceeds
" Each portion of our frame, thither again
" Muft it return, the fpirit flys aloft,
" And, with its native æther, claims alliance.
" The body mingles with the duft below.

In this manner were Abraham and the Patriarchs buried.   In the perfons of Jacob and
Jofeph, however, this rite underwent a change,
for they were embalmed according to the cuftom of the Egyptians ; either to do them honour in the eyes of the natives ; to compliment a people who had given them a moft
hofpitable and generous reception ; or to preferve their bodies till they could be carried into
the land of Canaan, the one at a fooner, the
other at a later period. For though only the
bones of Jofeph are mentioned, we are told
that "they embalmed him, and put him in a
cheft in Egypt." It was a doctrine, held by
the Egyptians, " that fo long as the body was
prevented from falling into a ftate of corruption, fo long did the foul continue with it."
They

They took, therefore, the utmoft care for the prefervation of the one, embalming it with the moft precious odours, that they might preclude it from the defertion of the other; and they then placed it in their chambers, or depofited it in the public catacombs—to which ufage and fuperftition there is the happieft allufion, in an ode by the author of the Pleafures of Memory.

" Proud land, what eye can trace thy myftic lore,
" Lock'd up in characters as dark as night!
" What eye thofe long, long labyrinths dare explore,
" To which the parted foul oft wings her flight.
     " Again to vifit her cold cell of clay,
" Charm'd with perennial fweets, and fmiling at decay."

This mode of preferving the bodies of the deceafed, appears to have been confined to the land of Egypt; for I know not that we difcover traces of it among any other nation; the Greeks, who borrowed almoft all their knowledge, and many of their cuftoms, from the Egyptians, had no acquaintance with, or were averfe from this practice. Their notion of the ftate of the foul after its difunion from the body, was in the higheft degree repugnant to it. To have been deprived of funeral obfequies, was efteemed the heavieft misfortune
tune

tune that could befall them ; the very idea was
worfe than death!   An inftance of this we
meet with in the Spartan foldiers, who were
not even to be animated to the battle by the
infpiriting war-fongs of Tyrtæus, till he had
guarded againft an event, which to them was
of the moft dreadful nature, that chilled their
fouls, and   enervated their bodies.   And
among the Athenians, a people the moft refined and unprejudiced, we learn from Ælian,
that there was an exprefs law for this very
purpofe.

" Νομ℗. δε ην ατ'λιχος, ος αν αταφω περιτυχη σωματι
ανθρωπω, παντως επιβαλλειν γην αυτω."

The fentiments of the Romans were fimilar, and probably derived from the Greeks ;
nor can we wonder at their minds being thus
influenced, when we learn that they in common fuppofed, that while the body of a deceafed perfon remained unburied, fo long did
the foul continue to wander reftlefs and difturbed.

In the fixth Æneid of Virgil, to the queftion put by Æneas, what was the meaning of
the vaft concourfe of fpirits that he beheld
wandering

wandering about the banks of the Styx, the
Sybil makes this reply :

" Hæc omnis, quam cernis, Inops inhumataque turba eſt
" Portitor ille Charon : Hi quos vehit unda, Sepulti.
" Nec ripas datur horrendas et ranca fluenta
" Tranſportare prius quam ſedibus oſſa quiêrunt :
" Centum errant annos : volitantque hæc littora circum
" Tum demum admiſſi ſtagna exoptata reviſunt."

Again. How pathetically do we find Æneas
intreated by the ſpirit of his old companion
Palinurus to perform theſe funeral rites, that
his manes might paſs the lake and reſt in
peace.

" Quod te, per cœli jucundum lumen, et auras
" Per Genitorem, oro ; per ſpem ſurgentis Juli
" Eripe me his invicte malis aut, tu mihi terram
" Injice."

He concludes his adjuration with the motive that urged him to the petition :

" Sedibus ut ſaltem placidis in morte quieſcam."

It may, however, be remarked, that there
were among the ſtoic philoſophers, ſome who
aſſerted that it was a matter of little conſequence what became of the body after death.
Thus we find in Lucan,

" Tabeſne

——— " Tabefne cadavera folvat
" An rogus haud refert, placido natura receptat
" Cuncta finu : finemquo fui fibi corpora debent."

And again:

" Cœlo tegitur qui non habet urnam."

Such alfo were the fentiments of the Cynic Diogenes, who, on being told by his friends, that if his body fhould be expofed as he ordered, it would be devoured by birds of prey and wild beafts, replied to them, " Minime vero, fed bacillum propter me, quo abigam ponitote. Qui poteris? Illi, non enim fenties." To which he laconically anfwered, " Quid igitur mihi ferarum laniatus oberit nihil fentienti ?"—Cic. Tufcul. I. 43.

But it was not only the cuftom of many of the antients to bury their dead, they had likewife the practice of burning them. Such was the ufage of the Greeks, the Romans, and others ; and the caufe that inftigated one nation, may without doubt be affigned to them all. This we learn from Pliny, who, in his natural hiftory, fpeaking of the Romans, obferves, " ipfum cremare apud Romanos non fuit veteris inftituti, terrâ condebantur; at

poftquam

poſtquam longinquis bellis obrutos *erui* cog-
novere, tunc inſtitutum. Et tamen multæ
familiæ priſcos ſervavere ritus ; ſicut in Cor-
neliâ, nemo ante Syllam Dictatorem traditur
crematus." He gives a very good reaſon why
be was thus particular, " idque voluiſſe veri-
tum talionem, eruto Caii Marii cadavere."

In conſequence of a law made by Odin,
we find that the Saxons, Danes, and other
northern nations, adopted this cuſtom. When
a chieftain fell glorioufly in battle, his funeral obſequies were honoured with all poſſible
magnificence ; his arms, his gold and ſilver,
his war-horfe, his domeſtic attendants, and
whatever elſe he held moſt dear, were placed
with him on the pile. And this was done on
the idea, that in a future ſtate the deceaſed
hero was again to enjoy theſe treaſures. In
the preſent life they anticipated the glory
that was to crown them in the next. Their
imaginations dwelt on the honours that were
to attend them, when with all the magnificence of a triumph they ſhould enter the hall
of Odin, accompanied by a numerous train
of flaves, of friends and horſes, and arrayed
in their moſt ſumptuous apparel. In conformity to this notion, we are told by Monſ.
Maillet,

Maillet, that " the armour, and the bones of the horfe on which Chilperic the Firft, fuppofed he fhould be prefented to this ' God of Warriors, have been found in his tomb."

Let us now confider the monuments that have been erected over the dead. Mankind (at every period, and in every clime) whether favage or refined, have had one common fenfation with refpect to the rendering a tribute of honour to a deceafed hero ; and (as far as a monument would effect it) immortalizing his name. In confequence of this, we fee, tranfmitted to us from ruder periods, the barrow, the crom-léch, and the fingle unhewn pillar. While we trace the progrefs of the arts and civilization, in the erection of pyramids, obelifks, and monuments of magnificence, on which were engraven infcriptions, capable, as was thought, to refift the depredations of time, and endure to eternity. But thofe of humble birth, or unacquired fame, were not equally honoured. The cromléch, the pyramid, the pillar or the tumulus, commemorated only the hero flain in battle, or fome prince of the people.

" Regum cineres extructo monte quiefcunt."

Such

Such was the monument that covered the remains of Achilles and his beloved Patroclus: it was the united effort of an army; it was erected on an elevated shore; it was to exist to the latest period of the world.

" Τοις, οἱ νυν γεγαάσι, κι' οἱ μετοπισθεν εσσιλαι."

Or as we have the passage translated by Pope;

" High on the shore the growing hill we raise,
" That wide the extended Hellespont surveys;
" Where all, from age to age, who pass the coast,
" May point Achilles tomb, and hail the mighty ghost."

That it had this wished-for effect, we find from the repeated and successive testimonies of Pliny, Strabo, and some other antient writers; and in the present day, from that of Monf. Chevalier, in his tour to the Troad; who says, " that on the shores of the Hellespont were distinctly to be seen the tumuli of these Grecian warriors." Such, also, with the more appropriate ornament of the pillar (to which I shall now confine my observations) was the monument raised by Cyrus over the body of Abradates and his faithful Panthea.

" και επι μεν (says Xenophon, speaking of the
" μνημα) τη ανω στηλη τε ανδρος και της γυναικος
" επιγεγραφθαι, φασι τα ονοματα Συρια γραμματα."

X   Homer,

Homer, the faithful recorder of manners and cuftoms, tells us, that the body of Sarpedon was ordered by Jupiter to be fent home from the plains of Troy, where he had been flain in battle, to his relations and native country, there to be honoured.

" Τυμβω τε ςηλη τι." For he remarks,

——— " το γαρ γερας εςι θανονίων."

From Eufebius we learn, that the firft temples were built over, or near, the burial places of eminent perfons; and that thefe burial places, in antient times, were diftinguifhed by a pillar or tall ftone, erected over the place of their interment, as appears in the inftance of the pillar which was raifed by Jacob on the burial place of Rebecca.

Hence, probably, may be derived the origin of obelifks in Egypt, which, as the country abounded with fine quarries, gave the Egyptians an opportunity of raifing ftones of the largeft fize to the honour of eminent perfons deceafed. Thus the pillar at Alexandria, erected to the memory of Pompey; the Trajan, and Antonine columns, (all fepulchral memorials) are to be regarded merely as imitations of this antient ufage. ✳ The magnificence of
after

after ages (fays an ingenious writer) ufurping the place of antient fimplicity, and altering the conftruction of thefe monuments, without rejecting or totally obfcuring the cuftom of their predeceffors."

It is a matter of curiofity to confider how uniformly in every region of the globe, in the lefs cultivated ftates of fociety, different nations are actuated by the fame principles, and adapt correfpondent images to fimilar conceptions.

Thus, we find not only in the countries which we have long known, or with which we are more immediately connected, the mount, and rude fepulchral pillar, but the fame were obferved by Captain Cooke in Le-Fooga, one of the Friendly Iflands. He fays, " near the fouth end of the ifland we met with an artificial mount, from the fize of fome trees that were growing on it, and from other appearances, I gueffed that it had been raifed in remote times : I judged it to be 40 feet high, and the diameter of the fummit meafured 50 feet. At the bottom of this mount ftood a ftone, which muft have been hewn out of coral rock ; it was 4 feet broad, 2 and half thick, and 14 high ; and we were

told

told by the natives prefent, that not above
half its length appeared above ground—they
called it *Tangata Arekee*, (the former of which
words fignifies *man*—the latter, *king*;) and
they added, that it had been fet up, and the
mount raifed by their forefathers, in *memory*
of one of their kings."

In the fongs of Offian we meet with the
moft poetical allufions to this antient ufage!
in them it is repeatedly called " the Stone of
Fame."

" If I muft fall in the field (fays Shilric)
raife high my grave Vinvela! the *grey ftone*,
and heaped up earth, fhall mark me to future
times: when the hunter fhall fit by the mound
and produce his food at noon, fome warrior
refts here! (he will fay,) and my fame fhall
live in his praife! remember me Vinvela,
when low on earth I lie."

" Raife Ofcar (cries the intrepid Offian)
raife my tomb! I will not yield the war to
thee. The firft and bloodieft in the ftrife,
my arm fhall teach thee how to fight! but
remember, my fon, to place this fword, this
bow, the horn of my deer, within that dark
and narrow houfe, whofe mark is *one grey ftone*!
Thofe

Thofe days are long paft; the memory,
however, of Offian, ftill furvives, not only in
the fong, but in the rude monument, the *grey
ftone*, fuppofed to have been erected on his
his grave. "In that awful part of Glen Almon, (to quote the words of our countryman
Mr. Newte) whofe lofty and impending cliffs,
on either hand, make a folemn and almoft
perpetual gloom, is found ' Clachan Offian,'
or the monumental ftone of Offian. It is of
uncommon fize, meafuring feven feet and half
in length, and five feet in breadth. About fifty
years ago, certain foldiers employed under
general Wade, in making the military road
from Stirling to Invernefs, through the Highlands, raifed the ftone by large engines, and
difcovered under it a coffin full of burnt bones.
This coffin confifted of four grey ftones, which
ftill remain; fuch as are mentioned in Offian's
poems. Offian's ftone, with the four grey
ftones in which his bones are faid to have been
depofited, are furrounded by a circular dyke,
200 feet in circumference, and three feet in
height. The military road paffes through its
centre." He proceeds to inform us, that it
was intended thefe bones fhould remain in
their place, till general Wade could fee them,

or

or his mind be known on the subject. But that the people of the country round, assembled with one consent, and, venerating the memory of the bard, carried them off, with bag-pipes playing, &c. and interred them with much solemnity on a lofty rock of difficult access, where they might never more be disturbed, in the wild recesses of the Western Glen Almon.

In Devonshire we have many similar remains—at Pilton, near Barnstaple, I have seen a pyramidal stone erect, 10 feet high; and another, of nearly the same height, standing on a common a few miles distant. The tradition of the country runs, that they were erected by giants, which idea corresponds with that recorded by Olaus, who says, "Obelisci, seu sublimia saxa viribus Gigantum ac Pugilum erecta, in biviis seu triviis conspiciuntur." At this place were cross roads, but whether these massy columns were thus presented to the eye of the traveller as memorials of a battle having been there fought and won; or, in honor of eminent persons slain, and intumulated, cannot now be ascertained. On the opposite shore, however, of the river Taw, we have not any tradition, but historical records

cords to identify the appropriation of an immenfe ftone to the purpofe in queftion.

At Appledore there yet appears a barrow,
and of late, if not to this day extant, a large
block of ftone erect on it, raifed to perpetuate
the memory of Hubba, the Dane, who was
there flain in the year 879.

"Dani (fays an antient hiftorian) Cadaver
Hubbæ inter occifos invenientes, illud cum
clamore maximo fepelierunt, cumulum appo-
nentes, Hubbe-lowe vocaverunt!" The termination "lowe," as I find it in Plott's Staf-
fordfhire, being fynonimous to burrow or tumulus; tho' I do not recollect to have heard
the word ufed in Devon. On this tumulus a
vaft ftone was alfo erected: and tho' we are
informed that it was almoft an invariable
practice with the northern nations to engrave
on the ftone the name, dignity, and famous
actions of the deceafed; yet it is to be prefumed, the dangerous ftate of thefe invaders
from their defeat, and the enemy ftill hover-
ing round them, would not allow the time
neceffary for the completion of their defign.

I fhall add but one inftance more, before
the conclufion of my fubject.

In

In a tour made some time since into Scotland, on the grounds of Belmont, a fine seat belonging to the hon. Stuart Mackenzie, not far from Dundee, I visited a vast monument of one rude stone, said to have been erected over the body of the young hero Siward, slain by Macbeth. After the death of the tyrant, it had been raised to his memory, perhaps by his friend Macduff, or by the prince Malcolm, whom, to re-instate in his kingdom, he had accompanied his father " with ten thousand warlike men from England." This stone is nearly 12 feet high, 18 and half in circumference, and computed to weigh about twenty tons : and yet though so high above ground, it was two feet eight inches below the earth.

The circumstance of this young warrior's death is strikingly painted by Shakspeare, who, doubtless, (as a member of the society, has rightly observed) though from lapse of time, we cannot always adduce his authority, stamped a reality on his characters by those minute, but expressive traits, which brought them immediately before the eye, distinguished them from every other, and for which he was often justified by tradition, or by written records then existing. Whether
he

J Serves del.   J Alken fecit.

Monument erected by young Si ....

he had any such authority for this circumstance or not, the behaviour of the father, on
his son's death being announced, he probably
adopted from *Brompton*, who thus describes it.
" A famous captain, a Dane, (other authors,
however, make him Earl of Northumberland,
and brother to Duncan, King of Scots, whom
Macbeth had murdered) named Siward (who
had sent his son to attack a province in Scotland) asked, with great coolness, those who
brought the news of his death, whether he
had received his wounds *before* or behind:
the messenger telling him " that he was
wounded *before*," the father cries out, " then
I have only cause to rejoice; for any *other*
death would have been unworthy of me and
my son." The spirited dialogue of the dramatic bard is as follows:

SIWARD.

" Had he his hurts *before?*

ROSSI.

" Ay, on his very front.

SIWARD.

" Why then, heavens' soldier be he!
" Had I as many sons as I have hairs,
" I would not wish them to a fairer death.
" And so his knell is knoll'd."

Perhaps

Perhaps Addifon took the hint from this paf_
fage in Shakfpeare, when on a fimilar occa_
fion he makes his Cato exclaim,

" Thanks to the Gods, my boy hath done his duty."

Another inftance of the fame kind I fhall
beg leave to quote from the Anthologa.

Ταν πιταιαν Θρασυβυλ⊙ επ' ασπιδος ηλυθεν απνυς
Επ˜α προς Αργιιων τραυματα δεξαμεν⊙.
Δεικνυς προσθια παντα τ'αιματοεντα, δ'ο πρεσβυς
Παιδ' επι πυρκαιης τυνιχος, ειπε, τιθεις
ω Δειλοι κλαιεσθωσαν! εγω δε σε τεκνον αδακρυς
" Θαψω τ' κι εμον, κ˜ Λακεδαιμονιον."

Young Thrafybulus from the Argive field,
Pierced with feven wounds, was carried on his fhield.
Viewing them *all in front*, as o'er the pyre
He bent, in rapture thus exclaim'd his fire.
" Let cowards weep! thefe rites no tear allow,
" I bury *mine*, and *Sparta*'s offspring now."

N. E.

ON

O N

BENEVOLENCE and FRIENDSHIP,

As oppofed to PRINCIPLE.

THAT every man fhould contribute, as far as he is able, to the general welfare, feems to be implied by the condition of focial beings: fince the enjoyments of an individual cannot be difconnected from thofe of his fellow-creatures; his happinefs is interwoven with that of the community. Our prefervation and fecurity arife from a coalition of interefts, and depend on mutual exertion.

If then, a recapitulation of kind offices be neceffary to the exiftence of fociety, a difpofition to do good muft be natural to man. It is an inftinct originally implanted in the human heart. Reafon, indeed, might fuggeft the expediency of performing the relative and focial duties; but reafon exerts too cold an influence

influence for action. The paffions, therefore, are an effential part of the conftitution of man, particularly the *benevolent* and *tender* affections. In the mean time, it is of confequence of obferve, that the benevolent and tender affections are not poffeft by all in an equal degree. One perfon has ftronger or finer feelings than another, and is more readily difpofed to rejoice with the happy, and mourn with the afflicted. And the man of a warmer temperament very naturally conciliates our regard : we view him with favourable prepoffeffions—generofity awakens pleafure! and there is fomething peculiarly interefting in fenfibility! peculiarly attractive in benevolence! But left we fhould indulge too far an agreeable delufion, we ought to confider the whole of that character, to which we are thus attached : and, perhaps, we fhall difcover that the qualities which attracted our efteem, have little connexion with virtue.

The *open-hearted Man*, and the *Man of Feeling*, have been often contrafted with the fly Diffembler and the fanctimonious Hypocrite; and this oppofition invariably tends to raife the former above their real value.
But,

But, perhaps, we shall begin to suspect an improper partiality for those characters, if we contrast them with the *Man of Principle*. We shall see the mere *open-hearted Man* continually actuated by passion : we shall observe the *Man of Principle* governed by reason. The conduct of the one will appear wild and impetuous ; of the other, cool and deliberate. Whilst the latter acts upon a uniform plan, the former is generally determined by the impulse of the moment.

The passions of *Benevolus* were ardent; they had never been checked in their career; and as they often impelled him to actions that his heart applauded, the frequency with which they hurried him into the most licentious excesses, had excited only a flight alarm—a transitory suspicion of error. Born to affluence, and nursed in the lap of indulgence and luxury, *Benevolus* experienced little restraint ; yet nature had gifted him with a large portion of the milk of human kindness, and the more generous propensities were predominant in his constitution. Scarcely did he accede to the possession of a very large inheritance, before he began to distribute his bounties with a spirit that might be termed the frenzy, and a

profusion

profusion that might be called the torrent of extravagance. Though his intelligence was quick, yet his judgement was feeble; the heat of inordinate paffion, indeed, muft always weaken the judgement. He was elated beyond meafure at any circumftance of good fortune; and depreft to the loweft ftate of dejection at the mifcarriage of his moft trivial purfuits. If he beheld an unhappy object, he fincerely pitied its diftrefs, and haftened to its relief: but, from his want of difcernment, he was often deceived by the artifice of impoftors. Thus, while his heart melted at the tale of fictitious calamity, he frequently lavifhed his wealth on the moft infamous wretches.

Notwithftanding this inftinctive generofity, he had a very faint idea of the moral virtues. Seldom did he look up with gratitude to the great fource of all that he poffeffed or enjoyed. Fond of convivial meetings, he indulged, often, with his companions, in the riotous debauch; and without an effort to refift temptation, fuffered himfelf to be carried down the ftream of pleafure. Senfual gratification hath always a tendency to render us felfifh. His voluptuoufnefs, therefore, was
gradually

gradually operating to the suppreffion of that native benignity, for which the world had given him ample credit. Yet he retained his character of " the open-hearted Man ;"—and " he has a good heart,"—was ftill pleaded, in extenuation of the groffeft enormities.

Phronimus was formed of a very different contexture. He was a man of a referved difpofition ; and, from a fettled habit of thinking much and faying little, his countenance had contracted an appearance of morofenefs ; yet he poffeffed an even temper : his mind was ferene, and his behaviour unembarraffed. His converfation was not greatly courted, as the charms of affability or graceful negligence by no means recommended it. His acquaintance, however, conferred on him the flattering diftinction of afking his advice on every important occafion: and, by the continued exertions of his judgement, he had acquired an almoft infallible certainty in his decifions. But this was not all. To ftrengthen his reafon, and regulate his conduct, he had called religion to his aid. To pleafe the deity was the motive of all his actions. He judged of men with candour ; and every attack on the character of another, he was ready to repel.

He

He feldom dropped a tear at the fufferings of a fellow-creature, but he often threw himfelf in the way of the unfortunate, with a view of offering them confolation. He vifited the folitary mourner, he frequented the abodes of want and ficknefs; but he acted from a fenfe of duty, not from *feeling :* in fhort, he was, ftrictly fpeaking, a *Man of Principle.*

Neither *Benevolus* nor *Phronimus* are characters that we fhould wifh to exhibit in our own perfons, fince the former is tainted by vice, and the latter has fome repulfive traits which render it unamiable. Yet the more virtuous part of mankind muft, on the whole, approve the one, whilft they proteft againft the too general practice in countenancing the other.

This propenfity to carefs the *kind-hearted* or the *generous* without the fmalleft regard to correctnefs of conduct, hath been too much encouraged by fome of our moft admired writers. They, whofe genius fhould have given energy to virtue, have been greatly inftrumental, I fear, in relaxing its ties. The productions of *Fielding,* if they have not injured the caufe of morality, have never contributed to its fupport or advancement. From the character of *Jones,* as contrafted with that

of

of *Blifil*, we cannot withhold our applause: Detesting the affectation of virtue, we love unprincipled generosity. The admired *Charles*, in the School for Scandal, shedding the glowing tints of the rainbow on prodigality, and degrading honesty into a " poor vulgar thing," serves only to disturb our notions of moral rectitude. The hero, indeed, of *Sheridan* is but the counterpart of *Tom Jones*. The great rival of *Fielding* is not entirely blameless as a moralist, though I own there are respectable authorities that strongly recommend him to attention and applause. I have heard more than one female reader confess, in the frankness of her heart, that she was almost enamoured with *Lovelace*. Yet *Lovelace* is totally unprincipled ; he is a rake and a villain. His address, however, is charming; it is his gracefulness, his insinuating manners, his intrepidity, his eloquence, that gloss over his vices, and give a lustre to corruption : and, indeed, it will be found in real life, that the wildest and most irregular, if possessing a polished exterior, are often admired by the female sex, and preferred to a man of unexceptionable morals. Nor is this preference confined within the circles of youthful levity ;

Y   it

it extends far beyond the amufements of the
prefent hour. Not only as an affociate in the
dance, but as a companion for life, has a
Lovelace been received with open arms! Expanded, therefore, on the canvas of *Richardfon*,
a picture, fo beautifully coloured, muft produce a pernicious effect on the female mind.
Nourifhing the prejudices of women in favor
of diffipated gayety, it muft render feriouf-
nefs and fobriety diftafteful, and thus imper-
ceptibly detach them from virtue. I have
heard an author, however, of eminence, repeatedly obferve, amidft his enthufiaftic
praifes of *Clariffa Harlowe*, that it is a work
which fhould be almoft ever in our hands;
and that, once a year at leaft, it fhould be
read by the female fex, if only for their moral improvement. Dr. Johnfon remarks, that,
fimilar to that of *Lovelace* is the character of
Lotbario, in the *Fair Penitent* of *Rowe*. It is true
there is a ftrong refemblance between the libertine of the novel and of the play; but we do not
love or admire *Lotbario*, and the reafon feems
to be, that his villainy in debauching *Califta*,
appears at once in glaring colors: we deteft
his libertinifm, before we become acquainted
with his agreeable qualities. The artifices by
which

which he effected the ruin of *Califta*, are fo
far from conciliating regard, that they rather
excite an abhorrence of gilded vicioufnefs;
an abhorrence that mixes with indignation,
as we obferve his brutal triumph over the poor
abandoned woman. It is far otherwife with
Lovelace; he is exhibited to us in various fituations. We are delighted with his manners,
we admire his ingenuity, and we are continually drawn off from the contemplation of his
immoralities, by fome intervening qualities
that irrefiftibly allure; qualities that win our
affection, and fteal us, by a foft attraction, to
the fide of vice, before we perceive the flighteft change in our fentiments or feelings.

But we fometimes meet with a much more
dangerous character than the *open-hearted
Rake*, both in real life, and in the writings of
thofe, who profefs to copy it. *Benevolus*,
whom I juft now defcribed, is evidently
marked by vices, which, in the moments of
fober reflexion, no one can attempt to palliate; and the imaginary perfonages of *Fielding* and *Sheridan*, of *Richardfon* and *Rowe*, are
fo clearly exceptionable in point of morality,
that to propofe them as examples worthy
imitation, would be a palpable abfurdity; an

infult

infult to common fenfe. Contrafted with a *Phronimus*, or the *Man of Principle*, the refined Sentimentalift of the prefent day, or the *Man of Feeling*, whofe vices are impofed upon the world for virtues; and which, through the deceitfulnefs of felf-love, appear amiable in his own eyes, fuch a character might have a portentous influence on the more romantic part of our fpecies. Of this defcription is *Tremellus*, a being whom I contemplate with apprehenfion, as there is a fpecioufnefs in his whole deportment, that is ftrangely delufive. In converfation, his infinuating accents feem to glide into the heart, and take even reafon captive : the delicacy of his tafte is exquifite; and, for his feelings, no language can exprefs them : his ideas of virtue are elevated beyond the conception of vulgar mortals ; and yet, with all this fuperior refinement, *Tremellus* is by no means averfe to thofe gallantries that are fanctioned by fafhion.

Nothing, indeed, is more eafy to the Man of Feeling, than to initiate himfelf into the myfteries of intrigue: " trembling alive all over," he breathes out his foul at the feet of his fair-one, and her gentle nature is fubdued, for fhe fancies his fenfibility is virtue !—Soon,
however,

however, fhe awakes from this delirium of the
fenfes, and the dream of happinefs vanifhes
for ever. Yet there is no doubt but perfons
of this complexion have, not unfrequently,
good intentions—deceiving themfelves, more
grofsly than they deceive the world. They
imagine that they have not in the leaft deviated from the paths of rectitude, at the very
time when the weaknefs of their hearts hath
betrayed them into exceffes: they even indulge a notion of excellence unattainable by
their fellow-mortals; and have ever before
their eyes the flying phantoms of perfection;
their " vifual nerve is purged with euphrafy,"
and they can fee æthereal worlds and fubtle
intelligencies, far other than this earthly
creation, to which we gravitate, from the
weight of matter oppreffing the divine particle within us.

But, in the prefent ftate of fociety, delicate
fenfibility, and refined ideas, are more frequently pretended than real: they are, every
day, affumed, as the pretext for fome criminal defign; and to impofe on the unfufpecting fentimentalift by an affectation of
feeling, requires very little artifice. Perfectly
converfant in all the obliquities of fimulation,

Y 3   many

many there are, who call forth the foft emotion at a moment's bidding, who fhed with
much adroitnefs the tear of fictitious tendernefs, apparently commiferating a fellow-
creature in affliction; though his ftory is too
tedious to be heard, unlefs, indeed, it contains fomething of adventure to gratify curiofity. It is thus that they charm the unwary
with ideas of their fuperior benevolence, and
cover, perhaps, the bafeft of intrigues under
the mafque of virtue. The young and unex-
perienced are commonly the dupes of fuch
impofture; but before they have an opportunity of converfing with the world, their minds
are often fo debilitated by a familiarity with
improper books, that they fall eafy victims to
the tempter, even on his firft infidious attack:
pre-difpofed for infection, they inftantly imbibe the poifon.

After having drawn the lines of contraft
between the *open-hearted Man* and the *Man of
Principle*, I remarked that our predilection
for the former is greatly encouraged by the
falfe lights, with which fuch a character has
been too often invefted, by novelifts and dra-
matifts. This mode of exalting mere natural
propenfities with virtues, is certainly injudi-
cious;

cious; but it need scarcely alarm us, when compared with the mischiefs of sentimental-ism. By writers of a romantic imagination, so beautiful a radiance hath been shed on the *Man of Feeling*, as "like distant lightnings, charms the eye, but proves, on too near ap-proach, a shaft of death." Such, in truth, is the weakness of the heart, and the seduc-tion of the senses, that even they, whose judge-ments are matured by years, are not always on their guard against the contagion of sen-timent. We generally read with avidity, the works that are recommended by taste and ge-nius, notwithstanding their tendency to in-flame the passions.

That writings of the sentimental cast have been admitted, much less scrupulously, as companions of the toilette, than might be ex-pected from the character of parents or guar-dians, is an undoubted fact. If we advert to a few of those productions of the fancy, which are chosen out of a mass of inanity and corruption, for the amusement of females, it will probaby appear strange that such writ-ings should have gained the sanction even of the old and the grave, who severely de-cide upon the common morals, and to pre-

Y 4　　　　　　　vent

vent an indifcriminate perufal of new publications, prohibit a too frequent intercourfe
with the circulating library.

The Tales of *Marmontel* are very commonly put into the hands of young people ;
but they have, furely, a very bad tendency.
Not a fingle ftory, perhaps, is fpotlefs—not
one is untainted by fome indelicate allufion,
fuch as a young lady, poffeffing the genuine
modefty of her fex, could read without a blufh.
The difciples, indeed, of Mrs. Woolftonecraft,
might boldly challenge us to point out the
flighteft impropriety in the moft indecent of
the tales in queftion ; but they who have been
yet untaught " to mention *every part* of the
human frame with the fame indifference as
we notice our heads and our hands," muft
often, in perufing Marmontel, difcover an
emotion " by the cheek's foft crimfoning."
Next to " the Shepherdefs of the Alps,"
(which is full of romantic improbabilities)
perhaps no production of Marmontel is more
impreffive than that of " Annette and Lubin."
Speaking, indeed, as a critic, I confider it a
perfect piece. It is drawn from nature ; the
outline is fine ; the colouring is delicious ;
yet, as a moralift, I muft condemn it. I have
frequently

frequently heard it mentioned by women as a tale exquifitely well told. What is it, however, but an infidious appeal of nature to our appetites and paffions, in favor of the unreftrained indulgence of love? what is it but a fpecious apology for criminal intercourfe? does it not throw the veil of innocence over the features of vice? does it not lend a new charm to amorous voluptuoufnes, as it diffipates the blufhes of guilt? Who can blame either Lubin or Annette? and what fimple girl, too fond in love, might not unwittingly follow the example of her heroine? The author's aim is, doubtlefs, to perfuade us, that the free commerce of the fexes is right, becaufe it is natural; and that all our ideas to the contrary, originate in nothing elfe but inftitution or habit; the policy of ftates, or the refinements of fociety. By fuch inclinations, the fancy is eafily induced to become the partizan of error, and even the judgement trembles in fufpence; yet it would require very little acumen to detect the fallacy of plain reafoning to the fame purpofe. In "*the Sentimental Journey*," which few ladies hefitate to quote in converfation, there are many exceptionable parts. The "*Triftram Shandy*" of Sterne

Sterne is, in my opinion, much lefs dangerous. But the letters of Eliza are all dipt in
the deadlieft poifon ; they have a direct tendency to deftroy the only genuine happinefs
this life affords us, to fcatter the domeftic
pleafures into air, to annihilate every comfort
that fprings from the deareft union upon
earth. As we bend over the bofom-foothing
page, are we not infenfibly attached to the
gentle Eliza, whilft far above the fcenes of
common life, fhe foars amidft the regions of
fentiment, and defpifes the vulgar notions of
conjugal affection ?

Rather than be lax in morals, let us be too
feverely fcrupulous. On the virtue of the female fex our welfare depends. I would keep
even the beft novels at an immeafureable diftance from my daughters, rather than they
fhould incur the danger of contracting a tafte
for works of mere fancy or paffion. Productions
of this fort enervate the mind : continually
acting on the fancy, they permit the judgement to lie torpid : hence the former acquires
an elafticity that is dangerous, whilft the latter lofes its tone. Accordingly we find, that
thofe who have paid an habitual attention to
the leaft exceptionable novels (fuch as the vo-
lumes

lumes of Mifs Burney or Mrs. Smith) generally betray a difrelifh for hiftory or philofophy. I know not, indeed, whether the moft
admired of Mrs. Smith's productions, *Ethelinde*, be quite clear from the blemifhes that I
have juft fpecified. The character of Sir Edward Newenden is, undoubtedly fuch, as, on
the whole, we muft approve. It is fuch, as
we muft efteem and reverence : nor, in the
perufal of the ftory, are we able to detect him
in one fituation, where we can greatly cenfure
his conduct. Irritating as her behaviour is,
he ftill treats his lady with refpect. In her
beft moments, the moments of cafual civili-
ties, her manner, though fufficiently cold, is
repaid by a warmth that feems to fpeak his
gratitude. The farther we advance in the
piece, indeed, the more amiable he appears :
and where his fweet coufin is introduced, a
foil to Lady Newenden, as readily excufe his
moft affectionate attentions to the former,
even anticipating the baronet in his ardors, and
fo ftrongly prepoffeffed with his feelings, as
to overlook every little impropriety, we fhould
otherwife have marked, in his converfations
with Ethelinde. Thus prejudiced in favor of
a fentimental (which is often, but an adulter-
ous)

ous) connexion of the heart, we are fcarcely difpofed to felicitate Ethelinde, on her poffeffing a real lover in Montgomery. After the deceafe of Lady Newenden, we rejoice on the removal of one great obftacle to Sir Edward's happinefs. We are pleafed with his addreffes to Ethelinde in the abfence, and on the fuppofed death of Montgomery; we ardently wifh the baronet's fuccefs: and, in one of the moft interefting fcenes that ever was prefented to imagination, where Sir Edward is pleading his paffion amidft a romantic folitude, we are fhocked at the intrufion of Montgomery, and thus lay down the book with a difagreeable impreffion in confequence of Sir Edward's perturbation and bitter difappointment. This feems the natural procefs of our opinions and feelings: but, on coolly reviewing Sir Edward's conduct, we muft perceive our error. Dazzled by the glittering illufion, we find that we have purfued a rainbow: we had encouraged a married man in the indulgence of a paffion, which ought never to have been admitted into his bofom. If it be alledged that we cannot, in a fingle inftance, accufe Sir Edward of any great mifconduct—that we can fcarcely ftop fhort,

and

and point out an impropriety in his behavior, we ought to ſhudder at ſuch an apology: for if this be true, how difficult is it to diſtinguiſh the line that is the boundary between virtue and vice! how ſoft is the gradation of tints that ſeem to mingle there! That our feelings receive a ſevere check at the termination of the novel, has been pleaded in favor of its morality; but thoſe feelings ought never to have been excited—much leſs indulged: and indeed we deem the baronet amiable, in proportion as he is unhappy. Sympathiſing with our hero in his dejected ſtate, we ſurvey his whole character with a more favourable eye, than if he had actually arrived at the ſummit of his wiſhes.

Commenting in this manner, on books which even graver moraliſts have not ſcrupled to recommend to the female ſex, I need not expreſs my opinion of ſuch productions as " *the New Eloiſa*" or " *the Sorrows of Werter.*"

But enough!—I have done with animadverſions on the creatures of ſentiment, whether they write or read, or talk or ſigh!—All I would add upon this topic is, that we are apt to view life through a deceitful medium, from a long familiarity with the works of imagination;

gination; and that, although our morality remain untainted, we often overlook or neglect the genuine happiness which providence has placed within our reach, from our expectations of visionary felicity. Dull are the realities of life to him whose mind is ever occupied by chimerical pursuits; and he who is perpetually agitated by selfish anxieties, that spring only from fancy, can have little regard for the real welfare of his fellow-creatures; and, as he looks on the ordinary comforts of life with an indifferent eye, he must, consequently undervalue the common evils that, every day, meet his observation. Such a character must be ill-qualified for those kind offices which are recommended by the benevolence of a man, and enforced by the charity of a Christian.

Thus the very end of *benevolence* and *feeling* is absolutely defeated, from their want of connexion with *principle*. That little merit can be allowed to the benevolent or feeling man, merely as such, may appear from the following observations. With regard to those acquisitions, which are the effect of our own exertions or industry, our conduct may deserve praise; but we cannot, in justice, be

either

either blamed or commended for any poffeffion that we enjoy without our own efforts or
will. Now benevolence, as the property of
the many, and feeling, as that of a few, are
not artificial attainments; they are the gifts
of nature : the feeds of both were fown in our
hearts without any co-operation of ours ; we
have no greater claim to merit, therefore,
from the poffeffion of benevolence or feeling,
than from that of wit or beauty, or any other
attribute of the body or mind.

If then, benevolence or feeling have nothing praifeworthy in themfelves, the acts
which cafually flow from them can never be
efteemed meritorious. To relieve a diftant
object from a fudden impulfe—from a rapid
fuggeftion of the heart (abftracted from every
other motive) deferves no great applaufe.—
What excited our warmeft pity, may be regarded with little feeling by another, whofe
heart is lefs fufceptible : but is he cenfureable
becaufe nature hath not endued him with fen-
fibilities fo delicate as our own ? perhaps his
fenfe of duty, both as a man and as a Chriftian, may prompt him to feek out the houfe
of mourning, which we have only vifited by
accident—to fupport the helplefs, and to
cheer the drooping with affiduities that gradually

dually effect his purpofe ; whilft our affiftance, arifing from caprice, is a mere inef-
ficacious effort.

To do good, in fhort, from temper or in-
clination, merely, is not charity. The kind
propenfities of man are fo fluctuating in their
nature, and fo various in their tendency, that,
undirected by religion, they often feduce us
into the mazes of error and of vice, whilft we
fondly deem ourfelves fecure in the ways of
virtue. But virtue only exifts where the mind
is fubjected to known duties ; and charity is
a fteady uniform virtue, not fpringing from
paffion, but originating in reafon and truth.

M. N.

SONNETS in BLANK VERSE, 1793.

SONNET I.

STAY, wild unbridled Licence, on the fhore
Which owns thy birth! roll thy malignant eye,
And fcowl acrofs our guardian waves in vain!
Oh! ever may our pure, enlightened minds
Deteſt that frantic form, thy parent dire,
Philofophy, the Monſter! which prefumes
With worfe than rage Titanic to affault
The throne of Heaven, to banifh from the earth
Morality, and Virtue, focial love,
Honour, and intellectual worth! to plunge
In Stygian darknefs, order, nature, truth:
While human Fiends remorfelefs brandifh high
The affaffin ſteel, with impious orgies hail
Grim maffacre, and feaſt on Royal Blood.

SONNET

SONNET II.

TO A FRIEND.

WHAT virtue, or what talents e'er escaped
Pernicious Malice ? she, with Falshood join'd,
And low, mean Cunning, at the purest heart
Directs her aim. The vulgar crew around
Well-pleased the fancied injury survey ;
And, now (they cry) this bird of stronger wing
Which soar'd through Æther, like ourselves descends,
And flutters in the dust. But *their* weak sight
Beholds not conscious Honour, to the stroke
Her guardian shield opposing—nor the form
Of steady Friendship, from her smiling eye
Infusing confidence—nor where prepared
Impartial Judgment stands, who, soon or late,
Breaks every poison'd arrow shot at Truth.

———————

SONNET III.

SHALL I repine because Ambition wears
The blood-stain'd wreathe of fame ? or cast a look

Invidious

Invidious on the toys which beam around
The flare of gold crime-purchased ? be it mine
Now in the glen, while high above my head
The mountain ash waves his fantastic limbs,
To mark between each quivering shade, which plays
Upon the rifted rock, the sparkling wave
Wild dashing down; or on the bank beneath
Recline ; deep fostering in my secret breast
The strains which nature teaches ; soothing strains,
Caught from her lip purpureal, when she sings
To the charm'd ear of Solitude ; whose form,
Glowing with beauty, wealth and power disdain.

SONNET IV.

THE storm is past ; the drifted rain no more
His course-impeding, lo ! the traveller hastes
To quit his shelter, and with joy pursues
His meditated way. The ploughman leaves
His friendly elm, unyokes the dripping steers,
And whistles t'ward his home. For now the sun

E'er

E'er he retires beneath the weſtern main,
Cheers the whole landſcape ; gilds the barren rock,
And diſtant ſpire, and hamlets, groves, and ſtreams.
The clouds diſparted wave their thinner folds
Skirted with ſplendor.   Every copſe reſounds
With warbled melody.   While over head,
Like Envy ſickening at another's weal,
The pale moon gleams with unavailing ray.

SONNET V.

EVENING retires ; and gathering fold on fold,
Darkneſs at length o'er Nature's paſſive frame
Caſts her thick veil ; the ſilent hours move on
Obedient to her ſway ; Sleep's charmed rod
Seals up each eye-lid ; Philomel is mute.
Now the light crew of dreams on ſilken wing
Glide by, or flutter till the morning dawn ;
Fancy's gay daughters, nurſed in Fairy-land,
And by their mother taught in antic ſhapes
To vie with Proteus ; ſhe their ſports beholds

Well-

Well-pleafed; affifts in every mimic change;
And fmiles at Reafon, ftarting oft in vain,
Oft ftruggling to break through their cobweb wreathes,
Which oft the tittering Pigmies clofer draw.

A. Y.

An ESSAY *on the* ARAMICK LANGUAGE.

— — — Ουδ 'ια γηςυς,
Αλλ γλωςς' Εμεμικτ.'   Hom.

THE name of Συριοι or Συροι, was formerly of great extent, and comprehended the Babylonians, Medes, Perfians, &c. as we learn from Herodotus, Strabo, and Suidas, though in after-ages it became confined to the inhabitants on this fide of Euphrates. The name of Arameans, or Aramites, has had the fame fate ; it was the name of nations inhabiting on this fide of Euphrates, on the other fide of Tigris, and between the two rivers. Mefopotamia was Aram-Raharajim ; Padan-Aram, or Sede-Aram, was the more cultivated part of it. Aram Dammefek was Syria Damafcena, and fo other parts were diftinguifhed by different additional names. Strabo tells us, that the Aramites were Syrians, and that the Syrians were thofe who eftablifhed their kingdom in Babylon and in Nineveh. It feems, then, that the Chaldeans or Chafdim, were but one people, or a part of the Aramites, receiving

ceiving their name after the time of Abraham
from his nephew Chefed. (Gen. xxii. 22.).
But, though the feveral people were thus dif_
tinguifhed by different names, yet the common language of them all retained its original
name of Aramick : thus the ambaffadors of
the King of Affyria fpoke the Aramick lan-
language, (2 Kings xviii. 26.) And the
Chaldeans of Babylon fpoke the fame. (Dan.
ii. 4.) It is therefore evident that this
was the Chaldean language in the time of the
captivity. The Hebrew is called the lan_
guage of Canaan. (Ifaiah xix. 18.) and was
much the fame with the Phenician.

If we examine the nature and form of the
Hebrew character, we fhall be induced by
various confiderations, to conclude that it was
the old Samaritan. It appears, 1ft. that the
Samaritans received the pentateuch from the
Jews before the captivity, and confequently in
the character then ufed. 2d. That the old
fhekels coined at Jerufalem, have Hebrew infcriptions in Samaritan characters. When
the Jews were difperfed in captivity, it is
natural to fuppofe that they would forget their
own language, and learn the language of the
people with whom they were daily conver-

fant

fant; and after their return from captivity,
their frequent intercourfe with their friends
who ftayed behind in thofe countries, muft have
contributed to preferve among them that new
language and character which they had
learned; and therefore when they changed the
character of their fcriptures, (of which fact
Jerome and Origen affure us, as well as the
Jewifh doctors) what character were they more
likely to have taken than that to which they had
been accuftomed in their captivity, and in
their epiftolary commerce with their friends
who remained behind them? The invention
of a new character would have been attended
with great difficulties, and yet have anfwered
no end. Hence it feems probable, that the
prefent character is the Aramick character
ufed at Babylon; and the fimilitude of it beyond that of the Syrian to the old Hebrew,
Samaritan, or Phenician, is an argument of
its antiquity. After the deftruction of the
Perfian empire, when the feveral countries,
compofing it, were divided from each other
in intereft and in government, and the intercourfe between them was interrupted, we
may well fuppofe that their language was
changed, and that out of one common tongue ·
called

called the Aramick, several different dialects
arose.

If it be enquired which of these various
dialects was most likely to preserve the Aramick tongue and character in its purity, it
must be at once obvious, that the Chaldeans,
who were famed for literature, and had records both historical and aftronomical, long
before the time of Nabonaffor, and even down
to the time of Alexander, would beft eftablifh
their claims. Thefe records were extant
in the time of Ptolemy, *i. e.* the fecond century of our æra, and therefore there could
be no doubt about the Chaldee language in
that age. The age of the Targums is uncertain ; but what in the opinion of many authors renders them fufpicious, is to me an
argument of their antiquity, for after the
coming of Chrift, a Jewifh writer would
not have made fo many conceffions, and
have given fo many interpretations, favourable to Chriftianity ; and if the author had
been a converted Jew, or a Chriftian, the
other Jews would not have received thofe
books, and have holden them in fuch efteem.
Let the age of thefe, however, be what they
will, yet the books of Tobit and Judith were
certainly

certainly ancient, and Jerome tranflated them from the Chaldee, which muft have enabled him to judge of that language in Ezra and Daniel. Now as the old Aramick language was preferved in its purity among the Chaldeans only, fo it took the name of the Chaldee language, whilft the new dialect introduced among the inhabitants on this fide Euphrates, took the old name of Syrian or Aramick, becaufe the inhabitants had now engroffed that name, and appropriated it to themfelves, exclufively of thofe who lived beyond the river.

Thus I make the Syrian or Aramick tongue, mentioned in the fcriptures, to be different from the Syrian tongue of later ages : and I cannot doubt that what *we* call the Syrian character, was invented upon the introduction of literature among the Syrians under the Seleucidæ at fooneft ; others, perhaps, will think it ftill later ; for I dont know any thing to be written in that character earlier than the Syriack verfion, and that is not allowed to be fo ancient as fome have pretended.

I fuppofe that the book of Ezra was written in the old Hebrew character, for there
appears

appears no fufficient authority for attributing
the change of character to Ezra, and then
the epiftle to Artaxerxes (chap. 4th) was
a thing written in a different character and
different language, *i. e.* the Chaldee. The
hiftorian, therefore, to introduce this piece
(which was an extract from fome Chaldee
record) prefaces it thus; and the writing of
the letter written in Aramick, *i. e.* in the Aramick character, and *expreffed* in Aramick, *i.e.*
in Aramick words. Womthurgam is rendered by the Septuagint Και ερμηνευμενον and Le
Clerk fays it fignifies conceptum, and not
verfum or tranflatum; but I think I have
given the fenfe of it in the word expreffed,
and fo I apprehend the 70 underftood it; for
Ερμηνεια is elocutio or enunciatio; and Ερμηνευω
is to exprefs. Thus Pericles in Thucydides,
fays of himfelf, that he was inferior to none,
γνωναι τε τα δεοντα, Και ερμηνευσαι ταυτα, both to conceive things proper to the occafion, and to
exprefs or deliver his conceptions. And Dionyfius Hal. criticifing a fentence of his fpeech,
fays it was ηρμηνευμενον δαιμονιως, happily expreffed; to which I might add many other inftances. This is the true natural import of
the word, and it has the fenfe of interpreting
or

or tranflating only by accident, *i. e.* when a thing delivered in one language is expreffed or explained into another. The letter mentioned v. 7. (ch. 4.) I fuppofe to be the very fame letter with that mentioned v. 8, 9, &c. and that the writers of this letter were called Methridath and Tabeel among the Jews, but Rehum and Shimfhai, among their countrymen, juft as Daniel was called Beltefhazzar among the Chaldeans ; and Zerubbabel was called Shefhbazzar. In v. 7. therefore, the Hebrew hiftorian tells us, that Mithridath and Tabeel wrote to Artaxerxes, and the writing of the letter written in Syriack, *(i. e.* Aramick,) and expreffed in Syriack, was " Rehum, the chancellor, and Shimfhai," &c. Thefe words, v. 8. " Rehum, the chancellor," &c. I fuppofe to be the beginning of the Chaldee extract inferted by the Hebrew hiftorian for explaining to us, *who* Mithridath and Tabeel were ; and I take the whole verfe to be the preface of the Chaldee writer.

The next verfe I take to be the fuperfcription of the letter itfelf, it being ufual at that time to fet the name of the writer at the top, inftead of fubfcribing it at bottom. The words v. 11th. " This is the copy

of

" of the letter that they fent unto him," I take to be the words of the Chaldee writer, included in a parenthefis ; and then follows the letter " Unto Artaxerxes the King. Thy " Servants," &c. I underftand Bifhlam, v. 7th with the LXX to be *ν ειρηνη. The word v. 10, 11, 17, Cheheneth, I underftand with Le Clerk to be a form of abbreviation, Και τα εξης, et cetera. Jofephus mentions but *one* letter written by Rehum (Ralhumus) and Shimfhai (Semellius) ; the apocryphal Efdras makes all four Mithridath, Tabeel, Ralhumus, and Semellius, join in the fame letter. Berruyer, the Jefuite, fuppofes that the two firft wrote one letter in Syriack, and the two laft another letter in Chaldee. Junius and Tremellius, and Le Clerc, fuppofe them two letters, and that Rehum and Shimfhai, the officers, wrote at the requeft of the Toparchs, Mithridath and Tabeel. But to what purpofe did the author tell us that the letter was written in " Syriack," if he did not give us the letter itfelf ? and why was it neceffary to mention the language of this, more than the language of the letter to Ahafuerus ? If however it is underftood, as I have attempted to explain it, then the words will have their ufe, and
serve

ferve as an introduction to a paragraph quoted
in another language. In the fame manner, I
think you will find all the Chaldee paffages in
Ezra and Daniel to be not the words of the
hiftorians, but quotations made verbatim from
Chaldee or Aramick records, or from writings
made in Aram or Chaldee.

N. R.

REFLECTIONS

REFLECTIONS

ON THE

COMPOSITION and DECOMPOSITION
of the ATMOSPHERE,

As influencing METEOROLOGICAL PHÆNOMENA.

Non ufitata nec tenui ferar
Pennâ —— per liquidum Æthera.

HORAT.

IF Syftems have been fometimes rafhly and
haftily conftructed, without a due attention to
the Phænomena, and their refpective relations,
we have equal reafon, at other periods, to
lament that facts have been accumulated, without adverting to the confequences, which may
be drawn from them, when collected with
care and compared with attention. From the
unfufpected coincidence of various obfervations, fcattered in works not generally known,
I mean, in the prefent Effay, to draw conclufions, which may perhaps elucidate fome important

portant parts of Natural Philofophy. At leaft, I fhall bring together, what is now widely difperfed; and, though the refults may appear, in fome inftances, incorrect, the facts themfelves are curious, and, in other hands, may lead to important confequences.

Rain is one of thofe Phænomena which has engaged, hitherto unfuccefsfully, the attention of Philofophers. The attempts to explain its caufe were unfuccefsful, becaufe Water and Air were confidered as unchangeable elements; and the philofophical enquirers of the laft century, if we except only Niewentyt, found the tafk of deftroying former fyftems, and conftructing others equally vifionary, not very difficult.

Dr. Franklin, Dr. Hamilton, Lord Kaims, and M. Le Roy, about the fame period, the middle of the prefent century, fuggefted a new fyftem, and contended for the priority, with a zeal ufually infpired by the undifputed difcovery of an important truth. This doctrine of the folution of Water in Air, and fubfequent depofition in Rain, was firft hinted at by a late refpectable philofopher, Dr. Halley: yet, in this period of fcience, when the doctrine was again revived, it lay fo

near

near the furface, that a flight penetration might have difcovered it, and each author may have deferved all the merit, which the difcovery ever could beftow ; but I leave the arguments and explanations in the different modern fyftems to be examined at leifure. The whole is recommended by its fimplicity, its perfpicuity, and the eafe with which it feems applicable to the moft important phænomena.

It was foon however found, that evaporation would go on in an exhaufted receiver ; that, during the procefs, heat difappeared, and was again fenfible when the water recovered its firft form ; and evaporation feemed alfo to take place from ice, when the air was below the freezing point. As heat is now known to be a peculiar fubftance, and not a modification of matter only, when it is loft in the evaporation, it muft become either an intermede, affifting the folution, or an ingredient in the new compofition. Something muft therefore be added to the fyftem, the fimplicity of which was fo obvious, and appearance fo feductive. The phænomena of dew feem to admit of the moft eafy explanation on this fyftem ; but if this very frequent appearance requires

A a   an

an additional. and a very different agent, it
will be obvious, that the folution of water in
air, though indifputable as a fact, is limited
in its operation and powers.

Thus far went M. de Luc, a laborious and
ingenious philofopher, hinting indeed at more,
often without explaining what his additional
views were; and this is the lateft author who
has aimed at novelty, for Dr. Hutton has only
attempted to elucidate and enlarge the theory
originally derived from Halley.

The foundation of all the errors, the fource
of all the difficulties on this fubject, confift in
the common prejudice, that air and water are
unchangeable elements. We *now* know that
water may be formed from the union of two
kinds of air, and may again be feparated into
its conftituent parts : in fact, that water and
air are convertible, in various natural procefles, into each other. Why then may not
thefe procefles go on alfo in the atmofphere ?
Why may not the atmofphere differ at times
in it's real absolute quantity, as well as in its
denfity and elafticity? Why may not rain
and dew, be air converted into water ? Thefe
are queftions, which may be ftarted as fubjects of inveftigation and enquiry ; to fharpen
the

the mental powers by the difcovery of new relations, which may give a certainty to what at firft ftarts forward in a queftionable fhape, or deftroy a phantom, whofe appearance is fpecious but delufive. I fhall attempt to fhow that thefe are not fuppofitions only ; that meteorological phænomena really fupport this variation of the quantity and ftate of the atmofphere ; this change of water into air and the contrary : that, in all thefe changes, there are concomitant appearances, which point out fome of the agents, by which they are probably produced.

The variation of the actual weight of the atmofphere may be fuppofed fufficiently clear from the different heights of the mercurial column in the barometer. I cannot however take this as fatisfactory evidence, for, in general, the barometer is an inftrument of a very complicated kind. Its height is not only a mark of the weight of the atmofphere, but of its elafticity alfo, which, in meafuring the heights of mountains, is corrected, partly, by the temperature. If, however, we look at the more extraordinary commotions in the atmofphere, we fhall fee decifive evidence of the variation of the quantity of air. In the defcription of

A a 2 hurricanes

hurricanes, the wind is always faid to rufh
from every quarter at the fame moment, and
the barometer to have been peculiarly low,
fome time preceding. It requires no argument to fhow, that this cannot be the cafe,
unlefs there is a comparative vacuum on the
fpot; and we fhall fee great reafon to fuppofe, that the quantity of air may, at any
time, be fuddenly diminifhed. The whirl-
wind and the water-fpout are appearances of
the fame kind, and differ only from the hurricane by the vacuum taking place in a fpot
ftill more confined. The examination of
thefe meteors firft led me to the explanations I fhall fuggeft. No reafon could be
given for the appearances of the water-
fpout, if a vacuum did not exift. Suppofing
a vacuum to have taken place in that part of
the air only, the water would be impelled
upwards by the weight of the neighbouring
air, and it would be impelled exactly in the
manner ufually defcribed, from the refiftance
of the atmofphere around. Thus water
paffing through the neck of a funnel, is feen
to affume this fpiral motion; a bullet driven
from a gun, moves, in the fame manner, thro'
the whole of the barrel; and it is mathema-
tically

tically demonstrable, that it must assume this kind of motion from the composition and resolution of forces. Winds are seemingly owing to a local vacuum in a less degree.— High winds are preceded by a falling of the barometer, while the elasticity of the air remains the same. If they consisted only in the restoration of the æquilibrium of the air, rarefied by heat, every wind should feel sharply cold, for, added to the coldness of the atmosphere which gave it density enough to supply the place of heated air, the percussion would render it more peculiarly piercing. The coldness we feel is from the force, with which the heated atmosphere is driven from the surface of our bodies, for wind often makes no change in the state of the thermometer, when we feel it unpleasantly sharp.

Though facts oblige me to disclaim the sinking of the mercurial column as a mark of the diminished weight of the atmosphere, without some restrictions, it is undoubtedly in many cases a proof of the diminution. If air assume the form of water, without any other change, we may presume the whole should continue equally heavy, or become more so; but we know that the water remains suspended. On the

contrary,

contrary, when the ſtate of the air changes, the vapour in the clouds ought not to be heavier in the form of air, than it was in that of water. In-both inſtances, the diminiſhed and increaſed elaſticity of the air have ſome effect; but, in the latter, there ſeems to be really an increaſe in the height of the atmoſphere. Evaporation begins immediately to take place on the ceſſation of rain; and, when comparative obſervations on hills, and in the vallies beneath, have been made, the rain in the vallies has always been found heavieſt at the beginning of a ſhower, and lighteſt at its end.

In determining this queſtion, the evidence of our feelings is equally equivocal; yet, like the changes in the barometer, they may come in aid of other arguments. The oppreſſion we often feel when the barometer is low, may be connected with the ſtate of vapour in the air, the want of its uſual elaſticity, ſince in ſuch circumſtances the air is remarkably inelaſtic, or to other cauſes. But, when we find that this extreme languor is felt on high mountains, where the preſſure of the air is greatly diminiſhed, we ſhall be inclined to attribute it in part to this cauſe. Some philoſophers have

lately

lately contended, that no languor is felt on the fummits of the higheft mountains; but Sauffure found this oppreffion very confiderable on Mount Blanc, 2450 toifes, little lefs than three miles above the level of the fea; indeed fo great, that fome of the guides, ufed to elevated fpots, could not fupport the fudden and violent change.

The obfervations felected, fhow that the quantity of air over given fpots is probably at different times very different, from caufes not yet explained. It is therefore neceffary to adduce the evidence that renders the mutual converfion of water and air, in atmofpherical phænomena highly probable.

If the doctrine of the folubility of water in air, and its fubfequent decompofition were univerfally applicable to the theory of evaporation and rain, the diminution of heat muft, in every circumftance, be attended with the depofition of water; and on the contrary, the depofition fhould be always connected with cold. In a certain degree, the former is true; but the latter fcarcely obfervable in any inftance. Indeed the oppofite change is fo confiderable, that rain muft always, if this fyftem be adopted, counteract its own caufe, for

while

while evaporation is attended with cold, and the depofition fuffers the heat to efcape, the temperature, during rain, fhould conftantly increafe, fo that the air muft be enabled to retain an excefs of moifture. In one inftance it is generally fuppofed that water is depofited by cooling the air. No one doubts, that dew falls in the evening, from this caufe. Yet dew is not a conftant phænomenon : it is not moft copious in the coldeft evenings, or after the hotteft days. Some other caufe muft therefore concur; and, tho' more than feventy years have elapfed fince Mufchenbroeck, De Fay, and Gerften, made experiments on this fubject, they have been little attended to.

Dew is of three kinds, either the condenfed perfpiration of plants, the condenfed evaporation from the earth, and what has been confidered as water depofited in the evening, that had been diffolved in the air during the day. The two latter appearances I mean chiefly to notice, and, if thefe are not merely depofitions, from an alteration in temperature, there will be more reafon for fuppofing, that water and air are mutually convertible. The afcending dew is found to rife to the height of 31 feet at leaft ; the defcending dew has

no

no peculiar region: Sauffure perceived it on the top of Mount Blanc, and where unconfined air is found, dew is occafionally obferved. It is not however depofited, on all fubftances, equally, for Mufchenbroeck remarks, as a fingular fact, that, on a *leaden* gutter, dew con- denfed on every kind of fubftance ; on a table in the garden, it condenfed equally on bodies of very different kinds. Yet, in Germany, Gerften obferved that it did not condenfe on metals. At Utrecht, it falls on glafs, china, polifhed and *varnifhed* wood, and does not fall on metals of any kind. This appeared " con- " fufion worfe confounded" to the Dutch philofopher, who made many other experi- ments, lefs conclufive. To us, the clue is not difficult. Du Fay obferves, that, at Paris, he put two glaffes, like thofe that cover the dials of watches, to receive the dew ; the one placed on a metal, the other on a china difh. The laft collected fix times the quantity of the for- mer ; and this glafs, which had a metal ring round its edge, was dry near half an inch in the circumference next the ring. Dr. Wat- fon found in fimilar circumftances the afcen- ding dew affected in the fame manner. Even a red wafer appeared to repel it to a confider-

able

able diftance. Cold therefore is not the only caufe of the condenfation. The change of vapour from its veficular ftate to that of water, is connected with electrical principle, and all the variety depends on the pofitive or negative ftate of the electricity of the air. At leaft fo much neceffarily follows from the facts particularly afcertained.

Mifts are generally fuppofed to be the condenfed fluid, which has been diffolved in air; but thefe are lefs connected with cold than dew. The water of the mift, like that of dew, is in the ftate of veficles, and fuch is its hygrometrical affinity, that it carries the index of the hygrometer farther to the point of humidity, than even immerfion in water. Yet it feldom falls in rain, and is depofited very fparingly on the earth, unlefs on bodies adapted by their nature, or their furface, to receive it. On animal and vegetable fibres, it is depofited copioufly, and, by this, is meant the hygrometical affinity fo often noticed, with fo little attention to the claffes of bodies diftinguifhed by this elective attraction. On metals, it is never depofited, but the intermediate claffes are not afcertained with that precifion, which enables us to determine,

termine, whether the conducting or non-
conducting nature of the fubftance is connected with the event. From the fimilarity of
the phænomena of dew and mift, there is
much reafon to fuppofe that the caufes, which
influence the depofition, are not very different. But to this may be added fome
pofitive facts of importance. During the
prevalence of mifts, the cork balls diverge
confiderably : the air is highly electrical, and
the electricity generally pofitive. While
mifts rife on the fide of the hills in mountainous countries, they are attracted and repelled alternately, bounding, like white maffes, from and towards the mountain. Thefe
appearances Sauffure obferved on Mount
Rofe; Reynier often remarks them in his
alpine excurfions, and I have more than once
feen them near the high hills of this neighbourhood.

If, in phænomena fo frequent and apparently fo fimple, the depofition of water does
not depend wholly on the change of temperature, the diminution of heat muft have lefs
effect in producing rain. The fouth wind,
which in this country ufually produces rain,
is always warm; and the appearances are not
thofe which prove that humid air is wafted

from

from a rainy region. Rain often comes on in a ftill atmofphere : clouds collect without motion : diftant hills, inftead of being feen in a blue glowing light, affume a darker hue, and neighbouring objects appear much more dif_tinct : the atmofphere becomes wet : fmall drops are fcattered, till they appear more collected, and of a larger bulk : the elec-trometer fhows a confiderable variation in the ftate of the electrical fluid, and the barometer, that the quantity, the weight, or the elafticity of the air, is greatly diminifhed. Thefe ef-fects cannot depend on the wind, for the moifture of the air is perceived by hygrome-trical changes, in the moft confined room with large fire, or in the clofeft drawer. In either place, alkaline falts will diffolve ; and the barometer will fink, with whatever care it is fhut up. Thefe facts can only meet in one point, that air is at times converted into water, and that the electrical fluid is an agent either immediately, or remotely, connected with the change. The remarkable tranfparency of the air, previous to rain, has not hitherto been noticed or explained. In that ftate of the air, the water does not affume the veficular form, nor does it yet appear like water. The rays of

light

light thus pafs through a medium more uniform, and of courfe, experience fewer refractions; befides that, in a compound men-
ftruum, various faline, and other bodies which
float in dry air, and difturb the paffage of the
rays of light, by innumerable reflections, are
diffolved. Thefe reafons are fupported by
various analogies. Thus in air, almoft wholly
deprived of moifture, and attracting it from
all bodies, during the prevalence of the Har-
mattan on the Coaft of Africa, the haze is very
confiderable : in the dry haze in this country
in 1780, the hygrometer continued immove-
ably at the dryeft point ; and hydrophanous
ftones, become tranfparent on being wetted.
But, from every view, the following circumftances are uncontrovertible. The moifture is
brought by no wind : the change takes place
at the fame time, in every part of the atmofphere, and moifture is formed, at once
feemingly in every minute portion of air.

While this change of air into water explains,
very fatisfactorily, the various phænomena,
we muft not affent implicitly without enquiring, whether, in other experiments, it is
found to take place. We have obferved that
water may be produced from air, and air again
from

from water. In the procefs of vegetation, this change is peculiarly confpicuous, for plants affording copious ftreams of pure air, may be nourifhed by the pureft diftilled water. Water, expofed to the fun, will produce air without limitation, and it has even been analyzed into air by chemical experiments, particularly in the æolopile. Analogy would therefore lead us to conclude, that the change was highly probable ; and, had no other kind of proof exifted, the various circumftances of thefe experiments, might have been brought together in fo connected a form, as to have juftified the conclufion according to the moft rigorous rules of analogical reafoning. This however is unneceffary. There are decifive experiments, that a permanent, elaftic, aereal fluid may be produced from water, in the common procefs of evaporation.

Few are ignorant that all fluids evaporate fafter when the preffure of the air is removed. Some bodies, indeed, evaporate only in the moft perfect vacuum : quickfilver itfelf will evaporate in the upper part of the toricellian tube, and be condenfed at its top, where the mercury in its afcent has never reached. In high mountains, evaporation goes on rapidly ;

and,

and, when proper allowances are made, the
air on mountains is dryer than on plains. We
may add to this, that, on the moſt accurate
calculations, the quantity of water diſcoverable
in a cubic inch of air by hygrometical affinities, is very inconſiderable. Where then is
the water raiſed from the earth by evaporation? What are its receptacles, or how can
it be again recovered? Some experiments
made by Sauſſure, with a different view, and
from which he drew different concluſions,
will illuſtrate this ſubjeét. He found, that
water during its evaporation augmented the
volume of air, and that this vapour was permanent, elaſtic, (Eſſais ſur l'Hygrometrie,
§. 190) and in particular circumſtances, tranſparent (§. 217). It is produced from ice; and,
in the moment of congelation, its proportion
is increaſed,* leſſening afterwards according
to the degree of cold. This elaſtic vapour
is more copious in rarefied, than in open air;†
and M. Sauſſure found that, when Farenheit's
thermometer was at 66, the elaſticity of the
air increaſed $\frac{1}{4}$ while the hygrometer went
from extreme dryneſs through ¾ of its ſcale,
towards

* Wallerius in Aét. Suecicis. † Aét. Suecic. An. 1738.

towards moifture (§. 110). When thefe experiments were purfued farther, it appeared
that every grain of water became an elaftic
fluid, capable of fupporting nearly half an
inch of mercury (§. 114. 118.) The immediate conclufion from thefe laft experiments,
feems to be in favour of the fuperior elafticity
of moift air; a conclufion apparently fupported by the experiments of the Chevalier
Andriani, who found the elafticity of the air, in
which alkaline falts had deliquefced, greatly
leffened. Yet, from the whole, it is more
probable that in evaporation, a permanent
elaftic air is really formed. It is at leaft permanent in every trial, which has been made;
and, as it is formed at a lower temperature,
than that of freezing water, is certainly not to
be condenfed by cold of that degree.

It is remarkable, that when air is rarefied
by the pump, it appears peculiarly dry.
Moifture is attracted from all fides, and even
the water, depofited on the internal furface
of the receiver, foon difappears, while the
index of the hygrometer haftens to the dryeft
point. The elaftic fluid, thus formed, foon
influences the manometer, and we find an
elaftic gas produced from water, not by means
of

of air, but from its deficiency. In the open
air the production of this vapour is not equally
rapid, and it foon efcapes; for, as it is
lighter than atmofpheric air in the proportion
of 3 to 4, it rifes to the higher regions. This
newly formed, dry, aereal, fluid was found by
Sauffure on Mount Blanc, by M. de Luc on
the Glacier de Buet, and other mountains ;
and fo powerful is its attraction for humidity
in thefe elevated regions, that after the tor-
rents of rain, which ufually fall there with
violence, the hygrometer immediately haftens
towards the dryeft point.   Each obferver
found alfo the moifture leffen during the
night, while the cold was exceffive, when, if
evaporation depended on folution, it ought
to have been again depofited.

If then it be admitted, that water may
fometimes difappear, in confequence of folution in air, it is highly probable, from the
facts already ftated, that it may alfo become
a permanent gas, unchangeable, like other
compounds, except by an elective attraction
fuperior to that which unites its ingredients.
Sauffure's and De Luc's experiments fhow
that water in either ftate does not affect the
hygrometer, and this inftrument feems capa-

B b   ble

ble of meafuring only the water beginning to
form, or beginning to feparate, and to point
out the firft change from the aerial to the
humid ftate. The term hygrometical affinity
therefore, as it is connected with the depofition of the water, may perhaps be greatly
influenced by the nature of the body employed, a circumftance which has not yet
obtained the degree of attention, which it
deferves.

Water, in air, affumes alfo the form of
mift ; and this has been called its veficular
ftate. If the progrefs of evaporation be diftinctly obferved, it will appear, that the form
of veficles is probably in every circumftance,
the firft ftage of the procefs. It is evidently
feen on the furface of rivers in a warm day,
by travellers on the Alps, and on the fteam
of boiling water, which, in Sauffure's experiments, afterwards affumed the form of a
pure, permanent, elaftic gas. The bulk of
each veficle, in both inftances, is calculated
to be the 3600th part of an inch ; and, as the
veficles are fpecifically heavier than air, they
muft be fupported in the atmofphere by the
repulfive power already noticed.

The

The ftriking appearances of electrical influence in the depofition of dew, and the repulfive power of mift, would immediately
fuggeft the probability of electricity having
a confiderable fhare in the different meteorological phænomena. Innumerable authors have,
on various occafions, hinted at this caufe, but
without afcertaining the principle on which
it operates, or means by which the feveral
changes are produced. M. de Luc, whofe induftry is perfevering and whofe obfervation is
acute, could not have failed in applying the
facts before him, had he not been mifled by a
theoretical explanation, which he feems to
have adopted early and trufted implicitly. He
fuppofed, that every fluid is compofed of a
groffer, and a more yielding ingredient; that
its denfity confifts in the proportion of thefe
component parts, and confequently that the
electrical fluid would be found among thofe of
the rareft kind. In his difpute with M. Libes
(Journal de Rozier) he mentions the opinion
I now offer, but thinks it is not to be fupported by facts; in reality, every fact mili-
tates againft the doctrine, if his theorem, which
however is purely hypothetical, be admitted.

What

What authors have called atmofpherical electricity is apparently the uncombined fluid, which floats in the atmofphere, and, while the air is in a dry, non-conducting ftate, does not reach the earth. In thefe circumftances, it is conftantly pofitive : in fteady rain it is the fame ; but, in ftormy weather, it frequently changes from pofitive to negative often with fingular rapidity, while at intervals, no electricity is obfervable. In fhort, if the electrometer be obferved during a ftorm, it feems to point out the various fucceffive changes of two fportive contending fluids, changes which may be almoft ftyled the alternate victories and defeats of the fpirits of the air. If the atmofphere be examined during a ftorm, alternations equally fudden are obfervable ; fqualls and momentary calms ; winds fhifting ; rain changing in its direction, its violence and its appearance. Obfervation has not yet fhown, that the variations of the electrical fluid always accompany thefe changes, though various facts appear to point out their coincidence.

Whatever opinion be formed of the relation or oppofition of pofitive and negative electricity, the appearance of the former in the atmofphere has been confidered a problem, difficult

of

of folution, and of fufficient importance to require particular attention. That the electrical
fluid may afcend in dew and in the perfpiration of plants, will be readily admitted ; but
thefe conveyances can only eftablifh an equilibrium between the air and the earth, while
the problem to be folved is by what means a
fuperabundant quantity of electricity is carried
into the higher regions of the atmofphere, and
from what fource the conftant fupply is derived. It appears to me highly probable, that
the pofitive electricity of the air, which is its
moft conftant and apparently its natural ftate,
is owing to the decompofition of water, which
in its change into air, fuffers the electrical
fluid, feemingly one of its component parts,
to efcape. But this opinion muft not reft on
fufpicion only.

It has been long fince obferved, that the
fteam of boiling water is electrified negatively,
while the vapour of water, poured on a hot
iron, poffeffes an electricity of the oppofite .
kind. Thefe facts ftill appear unaccountable,
and have not hitherto I believe been connected
with two others, that inflamable air is conftantly produced by water paffing through an
intenfely heated gun barrel, filled with iron

filings,

filings, and that the air proceeds from the decompofition of the water. If then the electricity muft proceed from a conductor or an electric per fe, there can be little doubt of its fource. The inflamable air may be procured alfo, if copper be employed, but in lefs quantity; and fometimes even through porcelain though imperfectly, and apparently, in confequence of the bifcuit containing fome iron. With this clue let us examine M. Sauffure's experiments particularly.

When a little water falls on iron intenfely heated, it does not immediately evaporate: like the drop of water on the cabbage leaf, the reflection fhows, that it is not in contact with the iron, but kept by a repulfive power, at fome diftance. When the water is dropped into a crucible, it remains a little longer, and difappears only after feveral feconds. The electricity is then pofitive. When the heat is lefs, the evaporation is quicker, and the electricity lefs powerful: when ftill lefs, fo as to occafion a hiffing noife, the electricity is negative. In porcelain veffels, it is generally negative, and in veffels of pure filver always fo.

M. Sauffure, who relates thefe experiments, has involved the fubject by confidering the disappearance

difappearance of the water as, in every inftance, owing to its evaporation. If, as we
now know, water be decompofed, while in contact with hot iron, all the intricacy will be
removed ; nor can we fpeak, with our author, of ' thefe unconnected facts, as with
difficulty reconciled to the common fyftems,
and as feeming to fhrink from principles
hitherto known.' The time he obferves,
when water difappears moft flowly, is that
when the crucible ceafes to fhine. This circumftance would be a priori probable, if the
difappearance of the water proceeded from its,
decompofition, for it is the loweft degree of heat
in which the feparation of the ingredients takes
place, a procefs always connected with light.
At a lower degree, the water forms only veficular vapour, and, as it is ftill a watery fluid no
change of electricity is obferved, or from
caufes, which it is unneceffary to explain, the
electricity becomes negative. Silver does not,
in any refpect, contribute to the decompofition of water, and conducts more readily,
when warmed, the electricity, which the water
might have poffeffed. In an iron or copper
veffel, with a narrow orifice, the water difappears more quickly and the electricity is pofi-

B b 4   tive,

tive, as might have been expected from the additional heat, which the water was subjected to. In the æolopile, water feems to be conftantly decompofed, for it makes fire burn, with an enlarged and more brilliant flame, a proof of the prefence of a pure elaftic fluid, whofe exiftence and whofe fource has not hitherto been fufpected.

M. Sauffure is equally perplexed by the refult of other experiments, which the fame explanation will reconcile. He was greatly fur_ prized to find electricity only in boiling liquors, not in burning bodies. It is well known, that after the moft careful diftillation, the whole of the water cannot be recovered, and it is equally certain, that fome water is formed during the burning of every vegetable fubftance. The electricity therefore efcapes, in the firft inftance, on the decompofition of the water, and is combined with the water in the fecond.

It is now admitted that water is decompofed in the procefs of vegetation, and in various inftances we have difcovered marks of the efcape of the electrical fluid. The motions of the mimofa are known to depend on electricity, various plants have been found to

fparkle

fparkle with electricity, and the colour of vegetables, fuppofed to be owing immediately to
light, is now difcovered to proceed from the inflammable air of the decompofed water, for the
light acts only as the irritating principle or as a
component part in the flourifhing plant. Without light the mimofa no longer fhrinks from
the touch, the calendula furnifhes no fparks, and
the hedifarum gyrans is ftill. The inflammable
air alone is rendered fenfible in our chemical
decompofition of vegetables, but this aereal
fluid united with light is intimately connected
with electricity. Kirwan, Prieftley, Lavoifier, and Sauffure, feem to think the electrical
fluid compofed of thefe only, for the electrical
fpark, frequently paffed through common air,
greatly diminifhes its bulk, and renders it inflammable, while light alone efcapes. In this
experiment, the electricity is loft, and in long
circuits, particularly, if various junctures require numerous minute explofions, the electricity difappears (Prieftley & L'Epinaffe Phi-
lof. Tranf. v. 57. p. 186). In the fhocks received by the human body, when on an infu-
lated ftool, the electricity is loft or deftroyed ;
nor when a highly charged cloud burfts on fome
elevated part of the earth, and reftores the relative

lative æquilibrium, is it certain, that the bal-
lance is owing to the earths having acquired
more electricity, rather than to the clouds having loft its fuperabundant proportion.

In atmofpherical phænomena, we find various proofs of electricity proceeding from the
decompofition of water, and again difap-
pearing on its formation. Signors Volta and
Beccaria found the foggy vapours, which arife
in the morning without any marks of electricity; but when they began to difappear,
the electricity was very fenfible, and became
pofitive. When clouds form in a ferene fky
Beccaria found the electricity diminifhed; and
it became fenfible again, when the clouds
difappeared. This laft change appeared fo
ftriking that he calls it electricita di raffere-
namento. M. Lullin made a very fingular and
curious remark. A pole was fixed in the fide
of a mountain, extending beyond it: when light
clouds arofe to the height of its extremity and
difappeared, the pole was electrified, but
when they remained in maffes and enveloped
the mountain, no electricity was obferved.

Though the air on mountains is dry and
highly electrical, the formation of fteam is
flow, and the time required to bring fluids to
a boiling ftate longer, notwithftanding the
temperature

temperature neceffary for ebullition is lower. It feems as if fluids, in thefe fituations, more readily affumed the form of air than of fteam, to which the heat, neceffary to form veficular vapour, readily contributes. In elevated fpots fire does not burn with rapidity, for the air is greatly contaminated with the hydrogen from the water, and is alfo very rare. To this ftate the debility felt on very high mountains may in a great degree contribute.

Modern philofophers have endeavoured to afcertain the altitude, moft conducive to health, and have fixed it, for reafons not fully explained, at 2400 feet above the level of the fea. It has been determined, with more certainty, that the moifteft region of the atmofphere, or the height to which vapours, either not diffolved or not converted into air, moft commonly rife, is about 1600 feet above the fame level. But when we fee water converted into air rifing from its levity to the higher regions, a levity eafily accounted for by the proportion of inflammable joined to the vital air, and find the upper regions chiefly contaminated by the former, we fhall with greater probability fix the moft healthy region below, or a very little above that of the watery clouds.

If

If we examine the progreffive ftate of atmofpherical electricity, we fhall find it intimately connected with the ftate of water in the
air. Aerial electricity has its diurnal and its
annual revolution. It daily ebbs and flows,
like the tide, following, in fome degree, the
courfe of the fun. In fummer, when the ground
is dry, and the air ferene, the electricity increafes from 4 in the morning, or more nearly
the rifing of the fun, till 3 or 4 in the afternoon : it then diminifhes gradually till the
falling of the dew, when it increafes, again to
diminifh, and to become almoft infenfible, at
4 the next morning. This is the progrefs it
would have, if connected with the decompofition of water : thus we find the hygrometer
little affected at 4 in the afternoon, and the
moifture greateft from 8 or 9 in the evening,
to 4 in the morning. When the earth is wet,
its progrefs is very different, and that this
difference depends on the moifture is certain ;
for, when fine weather, in fummer, fucceeds
continued rain, the electrical variations are in
the fame order as in winter. It is then greateft
at 9 in the morning, and diminifhes gradually
till 6 : it increafes till 8, and diminifhes till
6 o'clock the next morning. This is not eafily
                                        explicable

explicable without the hygrometer, which follows, at thefe periods, nearly the inverfe ratio, for it points to the greatest moifture, when the electricity is leaft, and the contrary.

The annual variation equally confirms the fyftem. Electricity decreafes from November to March: it increafes gradually from March to September. It decreafes in the dampeft period, and increafes as the air is drier.

The diurnal variations of the barometer on the mountains, are equally decifive, and I felect the obfervations on thefe, as, in the valleys, various exhalations may contribute to raife the mercury. We there find the mercury loweft at 8 in the morning, the period at which the newly formed air can fcarcely be expected to have afcended; and higheft at 2 when the evaporation has had its fulleft effect.

Thefe remarkable coincidences between the appearance or difappearance of electricity, and ferene or rainy weather lead me to conclude, that the electrical fluid is an important agent in the feveral changes. From thefe alfo it appears probable that the electricity is combined with the water, and confequently all the difficulties, that have embarraffed M. M. Sauffure and De Luc are avoided. I aimed at no more
                                                            than

than to connect the facts; for to explain all the appearances which may result from them, would require a volume; to point out the means by which the union and separation are effected, demands a much more extensive knowledge of the properties of these subtle fluids, than we at present possess.

Rain however occurs in particular circumstances, where the usual causes can have no influence, where the connections already assigned seem not to exist. When the wind blows from any point of the east, the rain, which accompanies it, is essentially different, in its appearance, from what has been already described. Instead of a sky, uniformly dark and gloomy, low black clouds, interrupted with brighter spots, give the delusive promise of fairer weather. In these circumstances, the rain often comes on unexpectedly thick and heavy; while, at other times, tho' the clouds are apparently lower, and the sky more uniformly gloomy, rain does not fall. The barometer is seldom affected; and every common sign of impending rain is either not observed or fails in the event; the hygrometer points to its dryest point, the electrical machine acts imperfectly, and there is little uncombined
electricity

electricity in the higher regions of the atmosphere. The dryness of the air renders it capable of abforbing the moisture of the earth, yet during cafterly winds evaporation is neither general nor rapid. In other respects, it is unfavourable to vegetation, injurious to health, and unpleasing from the feelings it imparts, as it is sharply and uncomfortably cold.

The fufpicions offered to your notice in this effay, will contribute to explain some of thefe peculiarities. The air, loaded with water, has abforbed the uncombined electricity of the atmosphere, and the vesicular maffes of clouds appear to be repelled from the earth, occasioning the appearance of more radiant spots, till the furcharged cloud again approaches, and is again repelled. I have not been able to explain, what occasions the formation of water in the air to admit of its falling in rain at any time, and have confequently not aimed at giving the theory in a more fatisfactory form. It is no difgrace therefore to leave what has appeared to all meteorologifts the moft finglar anomaly, in its former obfcurity.

The

The drynefs of the eafterly wind feems to arife from the hygrometrical affinity of the earth, for it is not favourable to evaporation in general; effects by no means contradictory, fince from evaporation, the uncombined electricity would be fupplied. Excefs or defect of this fluid, in the air, appears equally injurious to animal life, for previous to hurricanes in the Weft Indies, when the air is highly electrical, the health of the inhabitants is greatly injured; and Swinburne remarks, that during and after the fatal earthquake in Calabria, fcarcely an inftance of mifcarriage occurred, an event otherwife very ufual in that country.

Though, in this way, we approach nearer to the explanation of a problem ufually confidered as infoluble, I cannot help adding, that I think thefe fuggeftions very unfatisfactory; and, while the electrical fluid performs feemingly fo important an office in meteorological phænomena, it muft be remembered, that it is a compound, and that the union of its ingredients may be deftroyed; but this is untrodden ground, and I have carefully avoided the flowery but delufive paths of conjecture. The compofition of the electrical fluid is not yet properly afcertained: it is not

yet

known whether it is ever loft in its circuit. Whether its activity contributes to its deftruction, or whether the light, which it difplays, is an effential ingredient in the compofition.

When we contemplate the ebbs and flows of agents fo powerful and active, a fufpicion will naturally arife, and we may be tempted to afk, whether other periodical phænomena may not have a fimilar origin. The caufe of the regular fwell of the fea is generally fuppofed to be the attraction of the fun and moon, and it is commonly admitted, that this attraction, acts immediately on the waters of the ocean. The opinion was firft fuggefted by Kepler, and explained fhortly and comprehenfively in the earlieft edition of the Principia. Newton was followed by Euler, Daniel Bernouilli, Maclaurin and Clairaut, who were competitors for the prize offered by the French academy on this fubject. Maclaurin demonftrated, that a fluid fphere acted on by powers, proportional to the diftance from the axis, would affume the figure of an elliptic fpheroid; and and Clairaut extended the propofition to a fphere not homogeneous. Yet each fuppofed the fphere compofed of parts moving on each other; and, in this enquiry, as well as the in-

C c   veftigation

veftigation of the caufe of the fpheroidal form
of the earth, the body muft be capable of admitting a change of figure in all its parts : the
change muft alfo be gradual and progreffive.
Thofe authors, who fuppofed the change of
figure in both thefe inftances as a fimilar effect, feem to have overlooked an effential diftinction. Attraction is a fimple power acting
in ftrait lines, or from the effect of different
forces in a diagonal line. The direction of
the centrifugal force is in the tangent of a
fphere and it is, in reality, communicated motion, in a direction different from that of the
body which impells.

This defect in the firft ftep of the proof, is
not lefs confpicuous, than a difficulty in its
progrefs. If, as the Cartefians have already
remarked, the fea is raifed by attraction, why
fhould the waters rife on the oppofite fide,
where the attraction is confeffedly diminifhed ?
The reply has been that when the waters are
raifed by the attraction, the centre of the earth
is drawn alfo nearer to that fide, and the waters of the antipodes, now at a greater diftance
from the centre, rife from a deficiency of the
ufual attracting power. The explanation is however only applicable to a fphere whofe parts
move

move freely on each other, and, if the authors
had faid 'centre of gravity,' it would have been
more confiftent with the properties of a denfe
planet. But, if centre of gravity were fubftituted, it would not contribute to the explanation, fince no caufe is affigned why the
balance between the different parts of this
globe fhould be preferved by this, rather than
any other mode. To which may be added,
that the denfity of the earth at its centre, will
occafion very little difference in the fituation
of the centre of gravity from the partial and
unequal rife of a fluid fo light as water on its
furface. If, as has been afferted, the attraction of the fun and moon acting in an oppofite
direction to that of the earth, and leffening
the attractive power of its centre, fhould caufe
the waters to fwell in the zenith, they would
fwell alfo in the nadir, from the deficiency of
attraction. In that cafe, the rife of the waters
would be only in the ratio of the difference of
attraction ; and the calculations of the abfolute force of the attraction, muft fail.

The calculations are not however fupported by facts, nor are the facts confiftent
with the general theory. From calculation, the
fea ought to rife, where not impeded by ob-

ftacles,

ftacles, eight feet; but in the Atlantic and Pacific Oceans, it fcarcely rifes three feet. Near the fhore, the tides are higher, and thefe are accounted for by the refiftance the earth gives to the expanfion. The reafon might be admitted, if the fea, when uncontrouled, rofe to its proper height; but the fact requiring an explanation is, why the tides do not anfwer to the calculation, when no obftacle is oppofed.

The Mediterranean, a large expanfe of water does not rife or fall, or fwells only in a very inconfiderable degree. M. de la Lande has indeed demonftrated a propofition of Bernouilli, that the height of the tides in feas is proportional to their longitude; but the propofition does not apply to the Mediterranean, which is continued in longitude with the Atlantic by the Straits, nor does the degree in which the tides really rife correfpond with its own extent in longitude, when the various local obftacles are alfo taken into the confideration. At the Straits, the tides are confpicuous: they are confcious alfo at the bottom of the Adriatic, perhaps influenced in part by the current, but thefe various anomalies are not eafily reconciled to the caufe, almoft exclufively affigned for tides, the attraction of the fun and moon.

To

To have enlarged on the infufficiency of former theories, without being able to fuggeft a more fatisfactory explanation, will require fome apology. But I fhould not have engaged in the enquiry, were it not to hint, that, tho' the fun and moon feem certainly to occafion the alternate ebbs and flows of the fea, yet the more immediate caufe appears to be a variation in the height, and confequently in the pref-fure of the atmofpere. It muft be remembered, that the greateft height of the tides is fucceeded by the loweft ebbs ; that the greateft fwell is not in the moment, when the power of attraction is greateft, that high winds, which certainly proceed from partial vacua in the air, will greatly increafe the height of the tides. If the earth, furrounded by its amofphere, be for a moment confidered as a fpheroid of which the terrene part is an immoveable nucleus, the whole theory of attraction, as applied to the parts furrounding the nucleus, will be en-cumbered with fewer difficulties. Yet thofe which remain will be numerous and will not probably be folved, till the phænomena of tides be more accurately inveftigated. Their caufe has been fuppofed well known, and the circumftances accurately underftood, fo that

enquiry

enquiry has been for many years at an end, and obfervers have been inattentive.

A few reflections, in conclufion, may not be unfuitable.——To many philofophers, diftinguifhed for the extent of their knowledge, and penetration of their judgment, the molaic account of the deluge has appeared a correct and philofophical narrative of the progrefs of this planet from a ftate of chaos to its prefent harmony. Every late difcovery confirms this opinion; and, if air and water be mutually convertible into each other, a deluge whether univerfal or local will not be a problem fo difficult as has been generally fuppofed. If the quantity of air over any one fpot were converted into water: if the air which covers the ocean were equally changed, the one would deluge the earth, and the other burft its cearments. "The fountains of the great deep" would be feemingly "broken up," and the water would cover the higheft mountains, while thofe who were preferved would only feel the changes which every traveller who has afcended the higheft mountains muft have experienced. If the fubject be examined in its full extent, fome confiderable general convulfion will appear effentially neceffary in the

progrefs

progress from chaos, to harmony, to order, and that balance in the series of cause and effect, which can only ensure a permanent arrangement.

If the ideas, which I have endeavoured to support, in this essay, be true, they will contribute to explain the different circumstances, which occasion the rise and fall of the barometer. Little has been said of former systems in this essay, and of course, the various and discordant opinions of philosophers on the subject need not be repeated.—The latest explanations are those of De Luc and Pignotti, but these are perplexed with difficulties; and I hazard little in adding, that neither system is supported by observation or experience. The barometer, I have already observed, is a complicated instrument. It in some measure, points out the elasticity of the air, but, in the higher regions, chiefly its weight. As a *mano*meter, it must be corrected by the temperature of the atmosphere, and, from this circumstance arise the various ambiguities, in its predictions of the weather. Like the oracles of antiquity, it is sometimes mysterious, and sometimes deceitful. As a *baro*meter, showing the actual weight of the air, it is influenced by

C c 4   the

the changes mentioned ; for, when rain is impending, the elaftic vapour is affuming the form of water, and the real height of the atmofphere greatly diminifhed. The height of the clouds is various : they are bodies of vefïcular vapour, and, from a calculation of their comparative denfity, are capable of rifing occafionally to the height of 13500 toifes, exceeding 16 miles.

This fyftem alone explains, why high winds fhould affect this inftrument. Winds can never occur but to reftore the equilibrium of the air, and the equilibrium cannot be deftroyed, but by caufes diminifhing the weight of the atmofphere, at one place. This was the chief difficulty in the theory of winds. Rarefaction, by heat, could effect it but flowly, and the return muft be gentle and gradual, fuch as we find the recurrence of the fea breezes, in the iflands between the tropics. The caufe was however inadequate to the explanation of violent ftorms, and no other has been fuggefted. But, if air be decompofed, and, if the decompofition be fudden, we can have little difficulty in explaining the caufe of the violence with which the air around reftores the equibrium, or the reafon of the barometer
suddenly

fuddenly finking. I remember, about the time when the earthquake happened on Calabria and Sicily, which defolated that fertile, but devoted country, I was in the habit of examining the barometer to adjuft the fcale of one, which I had made. I faw the mercury fink very rapidly, far below the point to which it commonly falls in this country. I expected a violent ftorm, and predicted it. But a ruffling wind with a peculiar appearance of the clouds only followed. On examining the journal, this low ftate occurred the day *after* the violent earthquake, and the air rufhing in to fupply the vacuum, even left the other parts of the atmofphere deficient, as the wave which fills the hollow, left by his predeceffor, forms a fimilar vacuity behind it. A fimilar fall of the barometer occurred at Durham, and a gentleman, acquainted with Naples, told Mr. Swinburne that an earthquake had probably happened about this period, in a more fouthern region.

Some other conclufions and reflections might be added ; but thefe are fufficient to enforce the importance of enquiries on the grounds I have ftated and endeavoured to eftablifh. Should the foundation be found unftable,

unftable, I fhall readily refign the fuper-
ftructure, wifhing only to affift the progrefs
of fcience by marking fome relations, which
others might have overlooked, and collecting
facts, which, widely difperfed and hitherto
carelefsly preferved, might have been neglected
or forgotten.

―――――― " fungar vice cotis acutum
Reddere quæ ferrum valet, exors ipfe fecandi."

September 25th, 1794.

S I S.

An APOLOGY

FOR THE

CHARACTER AND CONDUCT

OF

I A G O.

—————— perago loca nullius antè
Trita pede.

LUCRET.

AS I mean nothing ironical in this undertaking, I am aware of incurring fome fufpicion of having tafted

—————— " of the infane root
That takes the reafon prifoner."

It may be urged againft me that the name
of Iago is almoft proverbial for a clofe dif-
fembling villain; that Dr. Johnfon obferves,
" his character is fo conducted, that he is,
from the firft fcene to the laft, hated and defpifed;" that " it is fo monftrous and fatani-
cal,

cal, if we are to credit Lord Kaims, as not to be fufferable in a reprefentation—not even Shakfpeare's mafterly hand can make the picture agreeable :" and, that old Rymer, long before them, obferved, " He was too wicked in all confcience, and had more to anfwer for than any tragedy or furies could inflict upon him :" That, in fhort, he is held, by the world in general, no lefs than by Othello, as the " damned damned Iago."

Permit me, however, firft to obferve, that I do not abfolutely undertake to vindicate him, but to fhew that his conduct admits of much excufe. His character, as I apprehend, is greatly mifunderftood and requires an explanation.* " An honeft man, fays Davy, is able to fpeak for himfelf when a knave is not." Iago, is not indeed, as this acute reafoner affirms of the knavifh VISOR, " my honeft friend ;" yet as he ftands in a fimilar predicament of not being " able to fpeak for himfelf," and never did any of us the flighteft injury, " I befeech your worfhips let him be countenanced."

Some eminent characters in the dramatic line, have publifhed APOLOGIES for their lives.

That

* Hen. 4. 2d part. A. 5.

That their modefty induced them to adopt
this title from the primitive fathers, by whom
it was frequently ufed, I prefume not to fay.
But it is to be feared, that in thefe degenerate
days, not one of them has fo extenfive a circulation as that of Mrs. Bellamy or Colley
Cibber. The latter was often in former times
Iago's theatrical reprefentative; and I do not
fee why the original is not as deferving of an
apology as the copy.

Before I enter more particularly into my
client's defence, I cannot avoid noticing a paffage in Mr. Twining's notes on Ariftotle's
Poetics, in which he compliments Richard the
3d at Iago's expence. "Dr. Johnfon, fays
he, obferves, that there is always danger left
wickednefs conjoined with abilities fhould
fteal upon efteem, though it miffes of approbation; but the character of Iago is fo conducted, that he is, from the firft fcene to the
laft, hated and defpifed. *But not fo*, adds the
learned critic, *Shakfpeare's Richard.*"

Now, with all due fubmiffion to the Tranflator of the Poetic, I conceive that the crimes
of Iago, when fairly compared with thofe of
Richard, will fade, like the new moon over-
powered by meridian fplendor.

To

To the unrelenting cruelty of a Borgia, Richard added more than Pharifaic hypocrify. The only virtue which he poffeffed, if an inborn faculty deferves that name, was courage; but he poffeffed it in common with Iago. The latter, to revengein juries, which I fhall fhew were of no trivial kind, is guilty of murther: and infufficient as this plea may be to exculpate him, not one of fo mitigating a nature can be urged in extenuation of the various murthers committed by Richard. The intended victims of Iago's revenge are three; Othello, Caffio and Defdemona; yet neither feems to have had the leaft claim to his regard.—A hoft on the contrary is facrificed by the fanguinary tyrant. A *wife, a faithful friend, an affectionate brother, two amiable nephews whom he was bound by every facred tie to protect:

    " Who fhould againft their murtherer fhut the door,
    Not bear the knife himfelf."

All thefe, and many other innocent victims, he immolates to his diabolical ambition, without the leaft remorfe or compunction: nor,
till

* Her death by poifon is rather hinted at than directly avowed by Richard. (A. 4. S. 2.) Her fubfequent appearance however with the ghofts of " all thofe whom he had murthered" ferves to confirm it. (A 5. S. 5.)

till he awakens from his horrid dream, does he betray the flighteft feeling of humanity. He then indeed exclaims ;

> " My confcience hath a thoufand feveral tongues,
> And every tongue brings in a feveral tale ;
> And every tale condemns me for a villain.
> Perjury, perjury to the higheft degree ;.
> Murther, ftern murther to the direft degree ;
> All feveral fins, all urged in each degree,
> Throng to the bar, all crying *guilty, guilty !*"

As men are not apt to fee their own conduct in the moft unfavourable point of view, I will reft Richard's character on the account he gives of himfelf, and proceed to that of Iago. The principal charges urged againft him are, his ingratitude and treachery to Othello ; his perfidy to Caffio, and to Defdemona.

Previous to the opening of the drama, we are led to underftand that Iago's character was refpectable both as an officer and a man. His military fervices are often alluded to. He is made known to the gentlemen of Cyprus, by Caffio, as " the bold Iago." Othello reports him to the Duke of Venice as " a man of honefty and truft." In another place he talks of him as

> ———— " of exceeding honefty,
> And knows all qualities with a learned fpirit
> Of human dealings."

other

other speeches of a similar kind shew that
Iago had often acted, by Othello's own con-
fession, in such a manner as to deserve his
favor: yet over this tried and experienced soldier, of whose prowess

> —— " his eyes had seen the proof
> At Rhodes and Cyprus, and on other grounds,
> Christian and heathen,"

He places one,

> " Who never set a squadron in the field,
> Nor the division of a battle knew
> More than a spinster."

Must not this have been a justifiable cause for
resentment, if any can be so, to a brave and
enterprizing soldier? Some critic styles him
‘ a false, dissembling, *ungrateful* rascal.’ Nothing however can be more unjust than the
last epithet. Othello was unkind and ungene-
rous; Iago not ungrateful. The strongest
reason for his resentment to the moor is yet to
be told. He suspected that he had been injured by him in the most tender point; that
he had seduced his wife Æmilia, a suspicion
which does not appear destitute of foundation.
The discourse she holds with Desdemona
amply demonstrates that she was very far from
entertaining any rigid notions of conjugal
fidelity.

fidelity. (A. 4. S. 13.) She tells her mif-
trefs, that fhe would not carry on an intrigue
" for a joint ring, for meafures of lawn, nor
for gowns, petticoats nor caps nor any petty
exhibition. But for all the whole world!
(alluding to what Defdemona had faid) why
who would not make her hufband a cuckold
to make him a monarch?" After again pro-
feffing that fhe and an infinity of other women
would break their matrimonial vow for fome
fignal advantage, fhe adds,

> " I do think it is their hufband's faults
> If wives do fall. Say, that they flack their duties,
> Or pour out treafures into foreign laps;
> Or elfe break out in *peevifh jealoufies*
> Throwing reftraint upon us; or fay they *ftrike us*
> Or fcant our *former havings* in defpight:
> Why we have galls: and though we have fome grace,
> Yet have we fome revenge."

Æmilia here feems to allude to her own fituation. Iago was of a jealous temper, not always continent of his hands toward her; was
reduced to a ftate of indigence, and could not
confequently fupport her in her ufual ftile of
living—" her former havings." In fome fubfequent lines fhe follows up her argument with
equal fpirit and energy; but the lines quoted
are fufficient to fhew that Iago was by no

means

means fortunate in his matrimonial connexion. Warburton suppofes that, when he informs Roderigo in the firft fcene of Caffio's promotion over his head, he afterwards alludes, in an abrupt manner to fome former farcafm from Othello relative to the levity of Æmilia.

——— *" A Florentine's
A fellow almoft damn'd in a fair wife!"

If we allow this interpretation, Othello added infult to injury.

Whatever

* When Caffio fays, " I never knew a Florentine more kind and honeft." (A. 3. S. 1.) He feems evidently to mean Iago. Were the latter a Venetian, as fome commentators fuppofe, can we reconcile it to the common mode of converfation, that when he calls Roderigo, " a poor trafh," he fhould add—" of Venice!" Would an Englifhman, after defcribing a countryman of his as a poor wretch, add—of England? But, did he talk of an Alien in that ftile, he would in all probability, like Iago, particularife the country he belonged to. When Othello fays, liftening to Caffio's converfation, " Do you triumph, Roman? do you triumph?" may we not take him literally, and fuppofe that Caffio was of Rome? His being reprefented as " a bookifh Theorique" certainly does not militate againft the idea. Whether this conjecture be allowed or not, it does not appear that the paffage above has been explained more fatisfactorily by other Commentators than by Warburton. It muft be acknowledged that in the fifth act Iago calls Roderigo his countryman: and it is not improbable that Shakfpeare had forgot what he had faid of him in the firft—not unufual with other eminent delineators of ideal characters. Cervantes, in the firft book of Don Quixot, calls Sancho's wife JOAN GUITEREZ; but fhe is afterwards known by the name of TERESA Panca; and in the fecond part where he takes an opportunity to fatirife the Author of a furreptitious Don Quixot, he is particularly fevere on him for being guilty of fo palpable an error as ftiling her JOAN GUITEREZ: not aware that he himfelf had led him into it by one more ftrange and unaccountable.

Whatever ftrefs may be laid on this circumftance, it certainly required no common
degree of chriftian charity to forgive fuch
treatment as Iago had experienced from the
Moor.

But what excufe it may be faid is there for
his behavior to Caffio? He never perfonally
injured him; nor does it appear that he had
at any time endeavoured to fupplant Iago, tho'
he was fortunately preferred before him.

I cannot however allow that he had no caufe
for refentment againft Caffio. He fufpects
him no lefs than Othello of a criminal intercourfe with Æmilia: (A. 2. S. 8.) And revenge, though contrary to the precepts of the
gofpel, is not fo ftrongly prohibited by the
military code of honor.

Again: though it does not appear that he
had attempted to fupplant Iago, yet the circumftance alone of his undeferved promotion
over him, muft have kindled in his breaft,
unlefs endowed with the apathy of a ftoic or
the meeknefs of a faint, fome fparks of anger
and indignation againft the fuccefsful rival as
well as the unjuft patron. On this point, I believe I might with fafety appeal to the officers
of the Britifh army; to thofe, who like Iago,

have

have fignalifed themfelves in the field, have met with the approbation of their General who witneffed their exploits and honored them with apparent friendfhip. If in fuch circumftances, fome young man, fome meer " bookifh Theorique," was promoted over them, would they feel no difguft, no indignation at the perfon fo promoted ? Can they conceive many circumftances more likely to kindle fuch refentment as might be fatal, or more excufable if attended by fuch effects ?

It would have been certainly much more noble in Iago to have fuppreft his refentment againft Othello and Caffio, and wifer probably to have winked at the frailties of Æmilia ; but many allowances ought furely to be made for the imperfections of human nature, when placed in trying fituations : and why fhould not Iago be entitled to the benefit of this plea as well as more exalted characters ?

I obferved that Iago's military deferts are never queftioned ; and, in the firft fcene, he fpeaks like one, who was no lefs confcious of his own merit, than tremblingly alive to the indignities he had fuffered. " By the faith of man," fays he,

" I know my price, I am worth no worfe a place."

He

He concludes his fpirited fpeech with remarking, that notwithftanding his fervices,
Othello permitted him to

———— " be beleed and calmed
By debtor and creditor."*

This fomewhat foftens an exceptionable
part of his conduct, the " making his fool his
purfe." He had a right to expect promotion.
In confequence of this expectation he had
lived,

---

* Then follow thefe lines.
———— " this *counter-cafter!*
He, in good time muft his Lieutenant be,
And I, God blefs the mark! his Moorfhip's Ancient."

Shakfpeare appears in this drama to have entertained a
very ftrange idea of military fubordination. Othello is
General of the Venetian army, yet the immediate officer,
next to him, is Caffio, his Lieutenant, and then Iago the
Ancient, or Enfign. This arrangement is fuitable to the
officers of a company, but not to thofe belonging to a great
army.
His ideas on this fubject feem no lefs incongruous in other
dramas. We are fo familiarifed to the title of *Ancient* when
applied to PISTOL, that it feems to form part of his name,
and to be almoft infeparable from it ; yet Fluellen talks of
" one Ancient-Lieutenant Piftol uttering prave words at
the pridge ;" and Fluellen is reprefented as exactly converfant in military affairs, or, to adopt his own words, in " the
ceremonies of the wars." We muft fuppofe therefore that
he is not defignedly made to confound thefe diftinct ranks.
In the fame play, Piftol expreffes his hopes of being " futler
unto the camp," a poft probably derogatory to an officer,
even in the time of Hen. 5th. Bardolph is fometimes Falftaff's fervant, his corporal, his lieutenant, and at laft
hanged under the denomination of *a foldier* for ftealing a
" pax of little price." We might almoft fuppofe that thefe
adventurers adopted travelling titles to gain themfelves oc-

D d 3   cafional

lived, it may naturally be concluded, more profusely than he would otherwise have done; had involved himself in difficulties, or as Æmilia expresses it, had " scanted his former havings"—another cause for chagrin and anger against Othello, whose cruel neglect had obliged him, to stoop to meannesses he would otherwise have detested. Instances of faults committed by naturally virtuous characters in reduced circumstances, which they would have abhorred in a state of affluence, every day occur. The proclivity natural to error is too well known to be insisted upon. Not the death of Cassio, but the depriving him of his office was Iago's original design. Had he succeeded to the command he so justly claimed,

we

---

casional credit; yet when Hostess Quickly, endeavouring to mitigate Pistol's fury, calls him " good Captain," and " sweet Captain," her female visitor, who felt no resentment at his having been previously stiled ANCIENT, abuses him in the most virulent terms for assuming a title to which he had no pretensions. (Hen. 4. 2d part. A. 2. S. 10.)

Our old dramatic bards attended possibly less to the *costume* in military affairs than in any other respect. In Beaumont and Fletcher's plays, the Lieutenant and Ancient are generally represented as not very distant from the Commander in Chief: a Colonel indeed sometimes intervenes, as second in command to the Hero of the Drama, whether that Hero be Roman, Greek, or Barbarian. A Lieutenant, by the instigation of his Colonel, exposes his life to the pistol of Demetrius Poliorcetes [*The humorous Lieutenant*]; and a Corporal Judas serves in the Roman legions under Suetonius in Britain (*Bonduca*).

we may conclude, reafoning from probabi-
lities and the common courfe of events, that
he would neither have betrayed Othello, de-
frauded Roderigo, nor acted unkindly to
Caffio, but have continued " honeft, honeft
Iago" to the end of the chapter.

The laft charge, and the fevereft is, his
cruelty to the innocent Defdemona. This is
generally confidered as the very acme of villainy, and it admits indeed of lefs excufe than
the former accufations, for fhe had never
wronged him. Iago however does not behold
her in the fame point of view as a reader or a
fpectator of this tragedy. He is by no means
convinced of her virtue and purity of heart, as
appears from his obfervations on the firft interview between her and Caffio, (A. 2. S. 5.)
from his fubfequent difcourfe with Roderigo,
and the foliloqy which follows.

> " That Caffio loves her, I do well believe it ;
> That fhe loves him, 'tis apt and of great credit."

Other fimilar paffages might be adduced :
and it is not unreafonable to fuppofe, that his
fufpicions of his wife had foured his temper,
and excited in him a general averfion to the
female fex. It appears indeed to have been
of fo violent a nature as even to overcome his

D d 4   policy.

policy. In the firſt ſcene between him and Deſdemona at Cyprus, (A. 2. S. 5.) he betrays a moroſeneſs unſuitable to his ſituation and deſigns ; for had Othello been led to ſuppoſe that he diſliked his wife, or was on unfriendly terms with her, any teſtimony of his to her diſcredit muſt have been weakened in proportion to that idea. This mode of behavior therefore betrays an irritability, and in ſome reſpect an imbecillity of character in Iago, rather than hardened villainy : that, I apprehend, is never accompanied with acute ſenſibility and an unguarded warmth of temper.

On the whole, his conduct to Roderigo, concerning which no accuſation has been preferred, appears to be the leaſt excuſable. To him he was indebted for pecuniary obligations, but for none of any kind to either of the other characters. On the contrary, from the firſt of them he had, moſt decidedly and incontrovertibly, received injuries of the ſevereſt kind. He had no trivial cauſe for his averſion to Caſſio. Deſdemona, as being a woman, was not an object of his regard ; as the friend of Caſſio and Æmilia ſhe appeared to him in a diſguſting light, and more ſo probably conſidered fidered as the wife of Othello. In order to diftrefs *him*, however, not to gratify any averfion towards Defdemona, he contrives her death: fhe is merely an inftrument to effectuate his vengeance: and if vengeance can be vindicated by an accumulation of injuries, Iago's, though exorbitant, was juft.

It appears therefore, notwithftanding the general opinion, that his conduct admits of much palliation ;—this is all I contended for: and I truft, that if you ftill think him a villain, you confider him as one of the lower clafs, " a puny whipfter" in the fchool of iniquity, not to be ranked with Richard the third, Aaron the moor, and others of the higher order, his ufual affociates. Let me add only, that if I have not wholly wafhed the blackamoor white, I truft I have taken a fhade from his colour; I have offered *fome* apology for his " character and conduct."

A VENE-

A VENETIAN STORY.*

NO one, acquainted with the Venetian State, can be a stranger to the excessive jealousy of its Government.—And the secrecy and celerity with which persons (*suspected* only of intermeddling in State Affairs) are punished, have peculiarly marked the judical administration of that famous Republic.

The injustice often occasioned by this mode of proceeding, cannot fail to excite in *our* bosoms the liveliest indignation, and at the same time cause us to reflect with pleasure on being born in a country, where the guilty alone have reason to fear, and innocence is sure of protection and security.

The

---

* The leading incidents of this affecting story are to be found in Mrs. Piozzi's Travels. The author has attempted only to fill up a meagre outline; to add some circumstances and reflections not unsuitable to the scene and the characters introduced.

The History of Albano, a young Nobleman of Venice, who lived about the middle of the 16th century, furnishes an affecting instance of the cruelty arising from the jealousy of the Venetian Government. Endowed with the strictest integrity, and happiest talents, he was beloved and esteemed by the Patricians, and almost idolized by the People. But notwithstanding his rank, his unblemished character, his signal atchievements in defence of his country, and his unwearied exertions for her welfare, Albano incurred the suspicion of concerting measures against the State ;—a suspicion which his too delicate, or rather romantic, sense of honour prevented him from clearing up, and subjected him to a disgrace and punishment more intolerable even than death itself.

It was observed by one of the spies, that, constantly, about the hour of midnight, Albano, muffled up in his cloak, with the most studious care, entered the house of the French Ambassador.——By the rigid laws of Venice, no nobleman is allowed to visit a foreign minister, unless on some well known business, and by the permission of the senate ; so apprehensive are they, lest any innovation should

be

be planned, or any change of the conftitution
be attempted.

The myfterious manner in which Albano
repeatedly vifited the envoy's houfe, could
not, therefore, fail of attracting the moft curious attention of the vigilant fpies of the
Venetian Government; and his conduct was
foon reported to the illuftrious magiftrate, fu-
perintending the police, the intimate, the
bofom friend, as it happened, of Albano.——
Surprized at the relation, and with all the
anxiety which the moft ardent friendfhip could
excite, Friuli hefitated to believe the account,
though minutely and circumftantially delivered; and to be affured of its truth or falfe-
hood, directed a faithful agent of his own to
watch the footfteps of the unfufpecting Albano.
At the expiration of fome days he received a
confirmation of thefe nightly vifits, and of the
fecret and difguifed manner in which they
were always made. Agitated by the moft
painful fenfations for his friend's fituation, but
at the fame time remembering the duties he
owed to the State, the mind of Friuli became
the prey of the deepeft forrow and diftraction.

Still unwilling to believe, that the beloved
companion of his earlieft days, the friend of
whofe

whose honor and patriotism he had ever entertained the most exalted idea, the ornament of
the State, and the idol of the People, could
harbour even a thought inimical to his country, he resolved before the execution of those
laws, he was sworn to maintain, to be himself
a witness of the criminal visits imputed to
Albano.

Too soon was he convinced that the relations he had received were well-founded : for
several successive nights, at the most silent
hour, in the most studied concealment of dress,
did he observe Albano approach the house of
the French resident, and, on a signal given,
admitted into it with the utmost precaution
and secrecy.

The welfare of the Republic, the high sense
of the duties with which he was invested, and
incontrovertible proof he had himself obtained,
would not permit Friuli longer to delay calling
on the transgressor of the laws to answer for
his misconduct, or explain his mysterious behaviour. Friuli's patriotism, glowing and
sincere, impelled him to struggle against those
feelings, which friendship eagerly and anxi-
ously suggested, and severely did he suffer from
this conflict. With the sharpest anguish, he
beheld

beheld his dearest friend exposed to the unrelenting vengeance of the severest laws, and
his soul sickened within him at the dreadful
prospect of the event. Stifling, however, all
sensations which opposed the interests of his
country,* he determined faithfully to dis-
charge the duties of his office.—Having passed
a melancholy and sleepless night, the next
morning his orders were issued for convening
the supreme council, and his warrant for ap-
prehending the unfortunate Albano.

These orders were punctually and speedily
obeyed; and Friuli prepared himself to appear before the council, and disclose the facts
which constituted his accusation.

The council, composed of the noblest, wisest,
and most venerable Venetians, bore on their
countenances the impression of the profoundest
grief, when they understood on whose fate
they were to decide. An awful pause, a silence,
more expressive than eloquence itself, ensued.
The eyes of all spoke most forcibly, but their
tongues were mute.

Friuli,

---

* Neque contra rempublicam, neque contra jusjurandum
ac fidem, amici causâ, vir bonus faciet ; ne si judex quidem erit de ipso amico : ponit enim personam Amici, quum
induit Judicis.   CICERO.

Friuli, his whole frame trembling, his voice half choaked by the rifing tumults of his breaft, broke the fearful filence by addreffing the auguft affembly.

He began by obferving, that he at once perceived the eyes of the whole council turned towards him, expreffive of their aftonifhment and forrow that Albano fhould be accufed, and that he fhould be his accufer. Would to God, exclaimed he in the bitternefs of his foul, that I had perifhed ere I had feen this day. He continued, " that when he looked on that grave and honourable body of men, whom he was then addreffing, he was confident that he beheld in them the zealous and ftedfaft friends of the facred conftitution of Venice; thofe who would not only bravely defend it againft all attacks from an open enemy, but with equal rigour and alacrity repel and punifh every infidious endeavour, fecretly to impair or deftroy it.—In every other refpect, he moft humbly confeffed, he was their inferior; but in the love of his country, in unabated zeal for its profperity, in inflexible rigour againft its enemies, he proudly declared, he could yield to no one; and, whilft the big drops ftarted into his eyes, added, *that*
day

day would confirm what he had afferted, and prove it not the oftentatious language of vanity.

They beheld, he obferved, at their bar, *him* who was once the ornament of the Republic, the brighteft example of all that was excellent or great, the honoured and beloved companion of their councils, not only accufed of having actually violated the laws of Venice, but labouring under a heavy fufpicion of concerting meafures hoftile to her fecurity. And by whom accufed? By one whofe life would have been chearfully devoted to preferve *him* whom he accufes; by one, who, had he liftened only to the voice of friendfhip, muft have fheltered him from the purfuit of juftice, and fhielded him from her uplifted fword; by one, who in vindicating the laws of his country, yielded up at once the peace and happinefs of his future days.——Oh my country! cried the wretched Friuli, what do I not facrifice to thy welfare or to thy fafety? I offer up as a victim, the friend of my bofom, the far better part of myfelf. A purer or brighter flame never burnt on the altar of friendfhip, than that which warms my breaft, but at thy call, my country! I ftifle its influence, and

extinguifh

extinguifh every fenfation, which can interfere with thy fecurity.

He then entreated their pardon for the prefent diftraction of his mind; and endeavouring to reprefs the tumults of his agitated bofom, proceeded to lay before them the *particulars* of the tranfaction which formed the charge.

It was a long time, Friuli added, before he could be induced to give any credit to the information he had received; but the repeated nightly vifits of Albano were too certain. He obferved, that the mere going to the Ambaffador's houfe unauthorifed, was contrary to the eftablifhed laws; but when the unfeafonable *bour*, the ftudious concealment of drefs, and the exceffive caution ufed in the admittance, were confidered, nothing lefs could arife than a moft violent fufpicion of fomething detrimental to the ftate being in agitation. Notwithftanding, however, this unfavourable light in which Albano ftood, Friuli entreated of the council, that in confideration of his friend's former unblemifhed character, and glorious fervices to his country, they would permit him to offer any exculpatory matter, and hear him explain a tranf-

E e   action

action which, at prefent, they could view only in a criminal light.

He hoped the council would allow he had that day difcharged the duty repofed in him by the laws ; and unequivocally evinced that no facrifice was in his eyes too great, when required by the good of the ftate. He again intreated them to bring back to their remembrance the obligations which Venice owed to the accufed, for his exertions in her behalf at home and abroad. He concluded by exhorting them never to forget, that to temper juftice with mercy, was moft pleafing and acceptable in the fight of heaven.

The whole affembly were greatly affected by the addrefs of Friuli, whofe conflict between duty and affection equally excited their pity and admiration. After a fhort interval, Albano was called on to anfwer to the charge which he had heard made againft him, and with a ferene countenance, in a firm tone of voice, with equal modefty, dignity, and grace, Albano began his addrefs to the council.

He affured them, that he *then* felt more for his accufer, whom he was once permitted to call his friend, than he did for himfelf: That the fituation of Friuli *was*, and *muft* be, more
distressing

diftreffing than his own, let the iffue of that
day prove to him ever fo difaftrous.

Of what had been alledged refpecting his
vifits to the ambaffador's houfe he freely admitted the truth; and if in fo doing he had
offended againft any law, even though dor-
mant or obfolete, he, of courfe, was fubject
to its penalty. But, he obferved, that no
guilt had been proved, or could be fixed on
him from the fact, except it were connected
with the fufpicion of his being engaged in
concerting meafures detrimental to the ftate.
It was a hard thing, he faid, to contend with
fufpicions; facts could be anfwered, refuted,
denied or explained; but as to fufpicions, he
knew not how to repel them, otherwife than
by requefting of that affembly, to whom in-
dividually he had long been known, to look
back on the tenor of his whole life, and to
examine moft ftrictly and feverely, whether,
at any period of it, the fmalleft ground could
be difcovered to warrant a fufpicion of
treachery in him. He modeftly reminded them
of his fervices to the Republic, that he had
unremittingly laboured to promote its intereft
and exalt its glory. He invoked heaven to
witnefs that neither in deed or thought, had

he

he ever conceived or formed any one meafure unfriendly to the government, and as pure and immaculate towards his country did he at that moment ftand, as at any period of his life. He denied that a firmer friend to Venice, or a more ftrenuous fupporter of its conftitution than himfelf, exifted.

He felt himfelf, he faid, fo much fupported by his own integrity and innocence, that he moft chearfully fubmitted his caufe, his honor, and his life into the hands of that illuftrious affembly, trufting they would, by their una— nimous decree, efface from his character the blemifh which had that day been caft upon it, by the moft unmerited fufpicions.

After fhortly deliberating with the other members, the prefident informed Albano, that enough had been lain before the council to fatisfy them that he had not only tranf— greffed one of the fundamental laws of Venice, but acted in fo queftionable and myfterious a manner, as to render it indifpenfable for him to account for his conduct, and difclofe its motives; to explain the real caufe of his vifits to the French minifter, and ingenuoufly con— fefs the reafon of his induftrious endeavours to conceal them: that he had incurred very fe-

vere.

vere penalties by the fact, which he had admitted, but that in confideration of his former fervices, they were inclined to relax the rigour of the law, provided he would impart to them the true inducement to his fecret vifits, from which they fhould otherwife conclude that fomething inimical to the government had been intended.

Albano thanked the council for their lenity and proffered favours, at the fame time declaring he could not, with the approbation of his own heart, explain the particular circumftances of his conduct. In the moft animated language, and in the moft folemn manner, he difclaimed any defign againft the well being of his country, and ended with affuring the affembly, that be the iffue what it might, no power on earth fhould wreft from him his motives: on that fubject he would preferve the profoundeft and moft invincible filence.

It is fcarcely poffible to defcribe the grief and aftonifhment of the whole affembly on hearing this declaration; the cool tone and determined manner in which it was made, left them no reafon to hope, that any thing would ever fhake the refolution he had juft expreffed.

Albano

Albano was ordered to withdraw. The council, after examining his conduct in every point of view, discovered in it much to blame, and more to suspect: his refusal to enter into any explanation of it, seemed to confirm the opinion of all, that something very criminal must be attached to it. Whatever their first prepossessions therefore might have been, they did not now hesitate to impute to him the crime of plotting against the safety of the state. The council had already departed widely from the general practice, on similar occasions, and had, in consequence of his virtues and services, displayed a clemency, seldom, if ever, exercised by the Venetian government.

Under that famous square in Venice, known by the name of St. Mark, are dungeons so deeply sunk, as to be considerably below the level of the sea ; through an apartment at the top, the wretched victim of state suspicion is let down, never more to return ; through this, his miserable and scanty food is conveyed, through this alone, the air sluggish and damp from the massive and enormous arches raised over the opening, with difficulty works its way

to

to fupport the hated exiftence of the devoted victim below.

Thus immured, carefully and cruelly prevented from availing themfelves of all means of putting a period to this undefcribable ftate of horror, in total and almoft palpable darknefs, for ever cut off from the world, without the fainteft or moft diftant hope of ever again feeing their friends, their families, their deareft connections, nay of ever more beholding any object on earth, thefe victims of fufpicion endure torments far more agonizing and exquifite than the moft terrific death.

In one of thofe dreary cells, was Albano condemned to pafs the remainder of his days. The decree once paft was irrevocable; the execution of it followed clofe, and without being permitted to bid adieu to his relatives, his expecting family, his anxious friends, without any preparation for fo dreadful an event, was this unhappy nobleman conveyed to thofe fcenes of horror and of darknefs, and in the flower of his age, and the vigorous exercife of the moft brilliant faculties, buried alive, and for ever fhut out from the voice and fight of human kind.

Notwith-

Notwithſtanding the ſecrecy and diſpatch with which this buſineſs was tranſacted, the populace of Venice ſoon felt the abſence of their patron, their benefactor, their friend. Bred up in ſubmiſſion the moſt humble to their rulers, they dared not clamour for, and demand their protector, or even to murmur againſt thoſe, by whoſe means they had the ſtrongeſt reaſons to ſuppoſe they were deprived of him. But their ſorrow was not leſs poignant or ſincere becauſe it was ſilent; the whole city ceaſed not to lament and deplore his fate.

The ſtern patriotiſm even of Friuli, could not ſupport him under the grief excited by this dreadful ſentence. He contemplated with horror the ſituation to which he had reduced his much loved friend. The picture was too ſhocking for him to look on; the emaciated countenance of Albano, wherein were marked the deep lines of hopeleſs expectation, and the traces of approaching diſſolution, conſtantly appeared to Friuli's imagination; the deſpair of his eye, the faint ſweat on his brow, the convulſion of his altered features, and the juſt, though gentle, reproof from his dying lips, all paſſed in terrible review acroſs his agitated mind, and forbad him to enjoy either

either repofe at night, or tranquillity by day.
His health impaired, and his fpirits worn
down by unceafing forrow and remorfe, he
furvived but a fhort time, and by his death
proved that his *friendfhip* equalled in ftrength
and fincerity, his *love and zeal for his country.*

How long the ill-fated Albano dragged out
his miferable exiftence in thefe regions of woe
cannot be known. The moft profound filence
was ever preferved on this occafion, and no
one dared to enquire after the fate of the
prifoner, or ventured even to name him.

Many years had elapfed after the period of
Albano's confinement, when a prieft was called
to adminifter fpiritual confolation to a lady at
Paris, in her laft moments, and perform
thofe offices which her religion taught her to
require. Amongft other matters which the
dying Adelaide difclofed to her Confeffor,
was the following incident; that nearly twenty
years before fhe had refided at Venice in the
houfe of the French ambaffador, accompa-
nying his wife thither, to whom fhe was related, and whofe friendfhip fhe had poffeffed
from her earlieft age; that during her abode
there

there fhe became acquainted with a young
Venetian, of whofe title fhe was ignorant, but
of fuperior birth and quality ; that his perfonal accomplifhments, united with the charms
of his converfation, fubdued her heart ; and
though fhe had unwarily yielded up her honour, yet every fucceeding day feemed to add
to their paffion, and ftrengthen their attachment ; that as he could not unite himfelf to
her by the bonds of marriage, without de-
gradation, the moft private mode of vifiting
her was adopted, and, through the affiftance of a faithful domeftic, he was conftantly
introduced into the houfe at the hour of midnight ; but fuddenly, without any information
whatever, ceafed to come to her ; that diftracted by a thoufand conjectures and fears,
her health began daily and vifibly to decline,
upon which it was thought advifeable that fhe
fhould return to her native country, where fhe,
at length, regained her health, though never
her tranquillity.

  Adelaide, faint and exhaufted by the re-
cital, had fcarcely received the abfolution,
which fhe implored, and by her fincere pe-
nitence feemed to deferve, when fhe breathed
her laft figh.

Hence

Hence it became moſt apparent, that the unfortunate Albano was innocent of every crime againſt his country ; and that his viſits, which were conſtrued as proofs of his machinations againſt the ſtate, were made to a beautiful and beloved miſtreſs. He preferred enduring the miſeries of perpetual confinement in a dungeon, (ſo horrible, that the eye of the humane Howard was not allowed to explore it,) to the riſk of expoſing to the reproachful voice of the world, *her* whom he adored. In the admiration of his honourable ſpirit, his ardent love, his unſhaken fortitude, we may be allowed to forgive the indiſcretions of Albano, or if we blame him for an error, to drop over his aſhes the tear of ſympathy and commiſeration.

C. B.

ODE TO VICTORY.

THOU! whom of yore upon their naval prow
Themiſtocles and Cimon ſaw confeſt,
When Greece made haughty Perſia bow,
  In ſky-bright robes of waving azure dreſt !
    Whoſe voice exulting o'er the main,
    Red with the blood of thouſands ſlain,
  Shouted aloud, " thus ever ſhall the race
    " Of Freedom triumph, when with patriot might
    " They ruſh indignant to the fight,
  " Reſolved with fame to live, or glorious death embrace.'

Ethereal Victory ! Jove's darling child,
  Twin-born with Pallas, when the daring maid
Urged on with rout, and terror wild,
  (The maſſy ſpear high-brandiſh'd o'er her head,)
    That impious crew, whoſe giant pride
    All Heaven's authentic powers defied :

When

When redient from fuccefsful war,

 He bade thee fit near his immortal throne,

 Around thee braced a golden zone,

And wreathed thy head with beams pluck'd from the morn-

  ing ftar.

Ethereal Victory! Oh! Heed my prayer!

 By all thy antient trophies won,

By all thy favourite Britain hath achieved,

 By the deep wounds, which every warrior fon

Of her's, with extafy hath e'er received,

  When liberty and juftice ftrove

  To fire heroic fouls with ardent love,

By thy own dauntlefs mind, O Goddefs, fwear,

  Swear, that " from Calpé to each diftant pole,

  " Wheree'er the glittering billows roll,

" Britannia's progeny fhall ftill furvey

  " Thy guardian form, thy out-ftretch'd arm,

  " Forceful the raging winds to charm,

" Scatter oppofing hofts, and fubjugate the fea."

          She

She fwore the mighty oath ; to Howe was given
    To teach, while thunders fierce he hurl'd,
    The aftonifh'd Gaul, the liftening World,
The oath by Victory fworn, and ratified by Heaven.

A. Y.

Some

Some OBSERVATIONS on

HESIOD and HOMER, and the SHIELDS of HERCULES and ACHILLES.

HESIOD was probably no favourite with Longinus; he quotes the Ασπις Ηρακλιος once, to find fault with a part of the defcription of woe in that poem, and contrafts it with fome lines in Homer.

" Τηs εκ μεν ρινων μυξαι ριον,"
" Hujus quidem ex naribus mucus manabat,"

which he fays is a difguftful image. It is fo. Nice tafte cannot be pleafed with it. In a fine portrait this fingle feature is difproportioned. " Pravus eft nafus, cum nigris oculis nigroque capillo" But how could he pafs over the ftrength and pathos of the laft fentence ?

——— " Πολλη δε κονιs κατενηνοθεν ωμαs Δακρυσι μυδαλεη."

" Multus

"" Multus autem pulvis conftraverat ei humeros
Lachiymis madens.''

Would not the Critics' attachment to Homer
fuffer him to commend a writer who might in
any refpect be called his rival? and whom, if
prior to him in time, he imitated, but did
not excel? How otherwife could fo competent
a judge, in a tract on the fublime, have neglected to mention the battle of the Gods and
Titans, and Jupiter's victory over Typhæus,
in the Theogonia, thofe inftances of more than
Homeric elevation? How could he have paffed
over the defcription of Pandora in the Ɛργα
χ̓ Ημεραι, which agrees with his peculiar notions
of that happy arrangement and texture, con-
ftituting the *fublime*, in, what other critics
would ftile the *beautiful* Ode of Sappho?*

How

* Thus fpoke, and fmiled, the fire of gods and men.
To temper clay with lymph he order'd ftrait
Illuftrious Vulcan; and with human fpeech
And active energy the mafs endow.
Then with a face like heaven's immortal powers,
To deck the living Virgin's beauteous form,
Thrice-amiable. To Pallas gave command
Ingenious works to teach her, and to weave
The gloffy web. And Venus on her head
To pour attractive charms, the foft extreme

Of

How could he have failed to quote the afcent
of Hercules into his chariot, when completely
fheathed in his ponderous armour, and bearing
his immenfe fhield?

———— ———— " Επι δ' ιππεια θορε διφρε
Εικελος αστεροπη πατρος Διος αιγιοχοιο,
Κυφα βιβας."

———— " Equeftrem autem infiliit in currum
Similis fulguri patris Jovis ægida tenentis,
Leviter ingrediens."

This is brief, expreffive and fublime.
Homer applies the fimile to Idomeneus in the

F f   13th

Of paffionate defire, and all the cares
Of ornament and drefs. And Hermes bade
To place within her petulance of foul,
And witcheries fallacious. They obey'd
Saturnian Jove high-reigning. Firft, of clay
Vulcan compofed her like a modeft maid,
Suffufed with blufhes. Pallas with a zone
And fplendid gems adorn'd. Each fifter Grace,
And Eloquence divine, upon her frame
Shower'd golden wreathes. Adding their choiceft gifts,
The fair-hair'd Hours around her temples twined
Bright vernal blooms. Pallas with niceft art
Adapted to her limbs the flowing robe,
And every ornament. But falfhood's fnares,
And witcheries fallacious, in her foul,
And bland feductive accents, Hermes hid,
Such was the will of Jove. And now her name
The herald of the fky announced to all,
Pandora.   (Εργα κ̄ Ημεραι.)

13th book of the Iliad with lefs energy, as he is more diffufe, wifhing at the fame time to exemplify the fpeed of the hero, and the fhining of his armour.

> " Βη δ' ιμεν αστεροπη εναλιγκιος, ητε Κρονιων
> Χειρι λαβων ετιναξεν απ' αιγλημτος Ολυμπυ,
> Δειχνυς σημα βροτοισιν· αριζηλοι δε οι αυγαι·
> Ος τε χαλκος ελαμπε περι στηθεσσι θεοντος."

> " Perrexit ire fulguri fimilis, quod Saturnius
> Manu acceptum miferit ab illuftri Olympo
> Oftendens fignum Hominibus. Præclari autem ejus radii
> Sic Hujus æs fplendebat circa pectora Currentis."

Were there no confufion in this fimile, it fhould not have been ufed for Idomeneus, at leaft not to convey an idea of his fwiftnefs; for foon after he is thus defcribed.

> " Ου γαρ ετ' εμπεδα γυια ποδων ην ορμηθεντι,
> Ουτ' αρ' επαιξαι μεθ' εον βελος, ετ' αλεασθαι·
> Τω ρα θηη εν σταδιη μεν αμυνετο νηλεες ημαρ,
> Τρεσσαι δ'ετι ριμφα ποδες φερον εκ πολεμοιο."

" Non jam firmi artus pedum erant quum impetum faceret, Neque ut irruere poffet ad fuam haftam, nec ut evitaret : Ideoque in ftataria pugnâ quidem arcebat fævum diem, Ad fugam vero non jam facile pedes ferebant ex pugnâ."

Without commenting at prefent on any other paffages of the two poets, I fhall enlarge

on

on the fhields of Hercules and Achilles.
Thefe are the two fineft poetical pictures of
antiquity. The different fcenes are placed
immediately before the eye. The various
figures have life, motion, fenfe, voice, and
progreffive action. It feems ftrange that a
queftion fhould have been ftarted, whether
they could have been really comprehended
within the limits of a fhield, and that Mr.
Pope efpecially, to pleafe others we may fuppofe, not himfelf, fhould have mifpent fo
much time on this fubject. He might furely
have fpared himfelf the trouble of detailing
M. Dacier's reply to the objections of the
critics, and likewife M. Boivin's diftribution
of the fhield. His own effay, in which " the
words of Homer being firft tranflated, an attempt is made to fhew with what exact order
all that he defcribes might enter into the
compofition, according to the rules of painting," is more ingenious than folid. Whether
engraved, expreffed in relievo, or painted,
the miniature fcenes and figures muft have
been either very imperfectly and ludicroufly
reprefented, or have appeared to the fpectator
as ftrange maffes of confufion and diforder.
They were indeed never meant to take a

visible form; they were pourtrayed by the imagination to the imagination. Were the shield containing them four, or even six feet in diameter, a puppet-shew would be exhibited—— what should be great, would be converted into mere farce. Pope's picture of the shield of Achilles, is a burlesque of Homer. But to the eye of fancy all is clear, and the mind easily comprehends the whole imagery of the poet.

None but a divine power could fashion such bucklers, which must for ever remain inimitable by any mortal artist. Tho heaven itself, and the works of heavenly beings are not above the descriptive genius of writers like Hesiod and Homer. The superiority of poetry to painting, and the immense distance to which the latter is thrown by the former, is no where more conspicuously exemplified than in these pieces.

They were in fact neither shields humanly wrought, nor ever meant to be degraded to the standard of human skill. That of Hercules was, as the poet informs us,

" E'en to the eye of heaven's deep-thundring fire
A prodigy of art."

" θαυμα

" θαυμα ιδειν και Ζηνι ϲαρυκτυπω."

The ſhield of Achilles was the work of
Vulcan at the requeſt of Thetis—When
brought to that Hero he is ſtruck with aſto-
niſhment, and exclaims,

" Μητερ εμη, τα μεν οπλα θεος πορεν, οἱ επιεκες
" Εργ' εμεν αθανατων, μηδε Βροτον Ανδρα τελεσσαι"

'" Mater Mea, hæc quidem arma Deus dedit, qualia par
" Opera eſſe immortalium, neque letho-ſubjectum virum
perfeciſſe."

Without entering now into the diſpute
whether Heſiod was more antient than Homer,
or whether the Ασπις Ηρακλεος was written by
him, or ſome ſubſequent author; I ſhall only
obſerve that it is plain, one poet muſt have
determined to try his ſtrength with the other,
or both muſt have had recourſe to a deſcription by ſome previous bard. For beſides
many ſimilar ſcenes and images, ſome verſes
are literally the ſame. This could not have
happened accidentally. It appears indeed to
me from the internal evidence, that Heſiod's
compoſition was the original.—It has a freer,
bolder air. It has more of the terrible graces.
It's colouring is not ſo diſtinct. The circumſtances are more briefly, and rapidly touched
on. It has more ſublimity, but leſs beauty.

F f 3

It

It has not that appearance of care and art ; that laborious and nice arrangement of incidents. It is the " monte decurrens amnis, quem imbres fuper notas aluere ripas ;" while Homer's flows thro' the plain, fmooth, and more uniformly majeftic. It is what Virgil in many places is to Homer, what Sophocles is to Æfchylus.

The Dragon, the Serpents, the Lapithæan War, Perfeus and the Gorgons, the affembled Gods, with Apollo and the Mufes, the Port, the Courfing fcene, the Horfe and Chariot Races, are omitted by Homer, perhaps becaufe he could not vary them with advantage. In the Battle, he fails, and even takes the moft ftriking image, word for word, from Hefiod. In the previous circumftances, the council of the Befiegers, and the ambufh of the Befieged, he is tame on comparifon. Nor, are Pallas and Mars at the head of the citizens, in arms of gold, and of fuperiour ftature like gods, equal to the fame deity, ftanding on his car, " imbathed in blood, as he had ftripp'd the fallen e'er they expired."—Or to Minerva with her fpear, her helmet, and Ægis,

———— ———— " as on fhe moved,
And fought the thickeft ranks of cruel war."

The

The mundane fyftem placed in the fhield of Achilles, is Homer's own, and exceedingly grand and magnificent; but disfigured by

" Αρχτον θ', (ην θ ϗ αμαξαν επικλησιν καλευσιν.")

" Urfamq. (quam et plauftrum vulgo vocant.")

A parenthefis equally exceptionable, though not fo long as that of Horace in his fine Ode Qualem Miniftrum, &c.

Befides this, we have the beautiful rural fketch, where, " fhepherd huts, and fhreds, and fcattered fheep-cotes variegate the fcene."

We have likewife the elegant Cretan dance; and the two lions feizing the bull, which he has fo extremely well managed (though we can difcern a hint for the fubject in the wild Boars and Lions of Hefiod) as to have almoft appropriated it to himfelf.

Homer's long account of the peaceful city, with the trial and decifion in the forum, appears to me fcarcely to equal the more rapid ftrokes of Hefiod; while the two talents in the midft are copied from the golden tripod of the latter. He may indeed here, and in the fcenes which remain unnoticed, be faid to have added many different and pleafing figures, to have ornamented them with new

F f 4   lights

lights and fhades, and to have fuffufed over the whole a perfpicuous varnifh; but the primary defign, the ground-work, and original fketches are Hefiod's. And on examining the two vineyards, I fhall not pretend to judge which is the moft delightful and finifhed picture.

One advantage on the fide of life and fpirit, the fhield of Hercules may claim over that of Achilles. With refpect to the latter, we fee the whole mechanical procefs of it's formation, as it is gradually fhaped by Vulcan; the former is a work already completed, and we pafs in an inftant from fcene to fcene, without the Εν δε ποιησι—Εν δε ποικιλλι—Εν δ'ετιθει, &c. which give a comparative degree of languor, and an imaginary lofs of time.

Hefiod decorates the ocean, which furrounds both the fhields, with fwans and fifh. In my opinion Homer has fhewn his judgment by concluding with greater fimplicity.

After defcribing the fhield of Achilles, Homer tells us, Vulcan formed the other parts of his armour, which he briefly fpecifies; and he is more brief, becaufe he intended to mention them again, when Achilles armed himfelf for battle. The heroes are furnifhed alike,

except

except that Hercules has no fword, Achilles
no arrows. The arrows of Hercules are partly
defcribed by their effects. " They ftrike the
foul with horror. They are the diftributors of
death and filence; for death is on their point,
and they are moiftened with tears. In the
middle they are long and polifhed; above,
they are overfhadowed with the wing of the
black eagle." This is furely fublime painting.

But though we fhould allow that Homer
borrowed one line word for word, for, unlefs
from defign, the coincidence could fcarcely
have happened,

" Δευτερον αυ θωρηκα περι στηθεσσιν εδυνη,"

and to have taken Achilles' facility of motion
from the

———— ———— " επι δ'επτατο θορε διφρω
Εικελος αστεροπη πατρος Διος αιγιοχοιο
Κυρα ΓιΓας"

of Hefiod; he has fo varied the defcription,
fo elevated it by fimilies, and the

" Πειρηθη 'δ εο αυτε εν εντεσι διος Αχιλληυς, &c &c."

is fo much fuperior; that in no place of his
works hath he fo truly exhibited the hand of
a mafter. He not only excels Hefiod in this
paffage, but even himfelf.

Pope

Pope, with the partiality of a tranſlator for his author, ſpeaks with much contempt of the Ασπις Ηρακλεος; I ſhall tranſcribe the note which contains his opinion.

" A field deep-furrow'd, &c." " Here begin the deſcriptions of rural life, in which Homer appears as great a maſter, as in the great and terrible parts of poetry. One would think he did this on purpoſe to rival his contemporary Heſiod on thoſe very ſubjeꞔts to which his genius was particularly bent. Upon this occaſion I muſt take notice of that Greek poem which is commonly aſcribed to Heſiod, under the title of Ασπις Ηρακλεος. Some of the antients mention ſuch a work as Heſiod's; but that amounts to no proof that this is the ſame : which indeed is not an expreſs poem upon the ſhield of Hercules, but a fragment of the ſtory of that Hero. What regards the ſhield is a manifeſt copy from this of Achilles, and conſequently it is not of Heſiod. For if he was not more antient, he was at leaſt contemporary with Homer; and neither of them could be ſuppoſed to borrow ſo ſhameleſsly from the other, not only the plan of entire deſcriptions (as thoſe of the marriage, the harveſt, the vineyard, the ocean round the margin, &c) but

but alfo whole verfes together. Thofe of the *Parca* in the battle are repeated word for word. And indeed half the poem is but a fort of *Cento* compofed out of Homer's verfes. The reader need only caft an eye on thefe two defcriptions, to fee the vaft difference of the original and the copy ; and I dare fay he will readily agree with the fentiment of Monfieur *Dacier* in applying to them that famous verfe of *Sannazarius*

" *Illum Hominem dices, hunc pofuiffe Deum.*"

To fee how they would appear on comparifon in a different language, I have tranflated the fhields of Hercules and Achilles. The fhield of Achilles I thought to have made ufe of from the verfion of Mr. Cooper, but on examination found it too flat and profaic. Mr. Pope's being in rhyme, would not anfwer my purpofe of a comparifon, even if he had not in fome paffages, deviated fo widely from his author. A few lines however I have borrowed from each of thefe writers ; and have been as literal as the genius of our language, the ftructure of the verfe, and a poetical drefs would allow.

If there were no other reafon, the pleafure to be derived from reading the *Tafk*, fhould

forbid

forbid any feverity of criticifm on Mr. Cooper's *Homer*. In the firft he feems to have formed his ftile, on the manner of Shakefpeare and Young; neither has the more familiar and dramatic phrafeology of the former, or the abruptnefs of the latter, a bad effect. But when this ftile is introduced into an epic poem, it is totally out of it's place; and we cannot but afk why inftead of Shakefpeare and Young, had not the ingenious author kept a fteady eye on Milton? When tranflating the fhield of Achilles, I naturally confulted both him and Pope, and in confequence have made a few obfervations on them both, merely as tranflators, regarding the fenfe of their original, and in this paffage only. Pope indeed never undertook to preferve the ftrictnefs of fidelity; Cooper profeffes to have given " the *full* fenfe; to have omitted *nothing*."

Yet, " toiling with fkill divine" does not anfwer to " ιδυιησι πραπιδεσσι," which includes the peculiar feat of the foul, and the employment of its fkill, knowledge, and energy in the work. Pope's " bright image of the mafter mind" raifes, but is nearer to the original. " πολεις μεροπων ανθρωπων," is ill tranflated by " cities, fuch as men build."—Both Pope and Cooper

Cooper neglecting it's mythological origin, apply the masculine pronoun to the bear.

" Σκηπτρα δε κηρυκων εν χερσ' εχον περοφωνων"

Cooper renders " Each with an herald's sceptre in his hand."

The more probable meaning is, that each took, or put his hand on the sceptres of the heralds, to atteft his juftice and impartiality, then rofe and gave his award. The epithet περοφωνων fhews them to have been the fceptres of thofe heralds who attended, and previoufly ftilled the cries of the people. According to Pope—" Alternate each the attefting fceptre took." It is curious however that *he* fhould have admitted fo ludicrous an idea as

" The reverend elders nodded o'er the cafe,"

for which Homer affords not the leaft hint.

" Οι μεν τα προιδοντες επεδραμον, ενθα δ'επειτα
Ταμνοντ' αμφι Βοων αγελας κι πωεα καλα
Αργειων οιων. κτεινον δ' επι μηλοβοτηρας."

There is an obfcurity in this paffage. Who are the Οι προιδοντες? Cooper makes them the fpies. Pope, the troops in ambufh. Moft probably under οι, the poet intended both.

Cooper

Cooper tranflates

" Swift ran the fpies, perceiving their approach,
And intercepting fuddenly the herds,
And flocks of filver fleece, flew alfo thofe
Who fed them."

Pope writes

In arms the glittering fquadron rifing round,
Rufh fudden—hills of flaughter heap the ground.
Whole flocks and herds lie bleeding on the plains,
And all amidft them dead the fhepherd fwains.

This hyperbolical flaughter of herds and
flocks which had only two drivers, is not
Homer's, but Pope's.

Clarke tranflates ταμνοντ', Prædantes-abdu-
cebant, which elucidates the meaning.

—— " Forth rufh'd the glittering bands
To feize their plunder ; hurried on the herds,
And fnow-white flocks, and flew the fhepherd fwains."

I have fome doubt with refpect to " ολοη
Κηρ," which I have tranflated, " A deftructive
Fury." There could have been no objection to
Fate, or Deftiny, (except the violence of the
action) had not the Κηρες of Hefiod been defcribed by him, as diftinct from Clotho,
Lachefis, and Atropos, who only ftand by,
marking their favage deeds, and horrid engagement with each other. They more nearly
refemble the Furies of Æfchylus.

There

There is much confufion in Hefiod's Theogonia with refpect to the Fates.—In the firft
place he fays, fpeaking of Μορος and Κηρ as if
they were different perfonages, and in the
fingular number ;

" Νυξ δ'ετεκε στυγερον τε Μορον, και Κηρα μελαιναν."
" Nox peperit gravem sortem, Parcamque nigram."

A few lines after he tells us of *Night,*

" Και Μοιρας, και Κηρας εγεινατο νηλεοποινους."

" Et Sortes, et Parcas genuit immites." And
as if thefe were fynonimous terms, fpecifies
them and fixes their number

" Κλωθωτε, Λαχεσιντε, και Ατροπον." They are
enumerated among the children of Night,
whom fhe had without a father.

In the latter part of the fame poem he only
calls them by the name of Μοιραι, and gives
them a very different origin.—Jove is their
father, and Themis their mother.—To him
fhe brought forth the Hours,

" Μοιρας θ' ης πλειστην τιμην πορε μητιετα Ζευς
Κλωθωτε, Λαχεσιντε, και Ατροπον."

— — — — " peperit Horas,
Sortefque, quibus maximum honorem dedit prudens Jupiter,
Clothoque, Lachefinque, et Atropon."

Whether

Whether we call " Ολοη Κηρ'' a Fate, or a Fury, the image here is, that " with her right hand, in the eagerneſs of rage, ſhe ſeizes and graſps a warrior juſt wounded, and another unhurt, while with her left hand ſhe drags a third already dead, through the field.''

Cooper miſtakes, confidering it three diſtinct actions.

> — — " She, *now* a chief
> Seized newly wounded, and *now* captive held
> Another yet unhurt, and *now* a third
> Dragg'd breathleſs thro' the battle by his feet.''

Pope, as improperly,' transfers the action of the Fury to the combatants themſelves.

> " One, reared a dagger at a captive's breaſt,
> One, held a living foe that freſhly bled
> With new-made wounds—another dragg'd the dead.''

> " The waving ſilver ſeem'd to bluſh with blood,''

Is a prettineſs of Pope—his idea perhaps was taken from

> Lympha púdica Deum vidit, et erubuit.

In the two laſt lines however, he has raiſed the image like a good poet, and though not a tranſlation, we can ſcarcely wiſh the couplet to be altered.

" And

" And the whole war came out and met the eye,
And each bold figure feem'd to live or die."

" Ομιλευν δ'ωστε ζοι Βροτοι, ηδ' εμαχοντο."

Cooper has it

" Like living men they traverfed and they ftrove."

He has likewife rendered τριπολον, well-till'd, which Pope properly tranflates " the third time laboured."

Οξιας δρεπανας, he has rendered " fharp-tootb'd fickles," which are fimply fharp, or keen.

Βασιλευς, he has tranflated, Mafter, and σκηπτρον εχων——ftaff in hand.

Whereas, this is a portrait of antient manners, when it was not beneath princes and chiefs to overfee their harveft. The heralds in attendance fhew the quality of the perfonage. Ulyffes in Ithaca ploughed his own fields—Laertes worked in his orchard.

Pope too has thought it neceffary to qualify *monarch* with the epithet *ruftic.* " The ruftic monarch of the field." And he has omitted the *heralds,* thinking them probably, of too high rank to drefs a *farmer's* fupper.

" Αταλα φρονοντες" Cooper has tranflated *blithe,* which Pope has omitted, and Clarke

G g   renders

renders " teneris animis." It means tenera cogitantes, with thoughts of innocence and affection adapted to their years.

Pope did not miftake λινον a ftring, for Linus the bard, but he thought it more poetical to allude to him.

Cooper renders " Βοων ορθοκρειραων" very inelegantly " tall Beeves." Bovum, capita alte ferentium.

Λαθυσσιτοι has a more ftrong and comprehenfive meaning than. the Englifh word *lapped*, which applies only to liquids.—If not tranflated with a periphrafis, *ingorged* perhaps might have been ufed, which like the latin *hauriebant*, would anfwer both for fluids and folids.

Cooper fays,

" The lions tore the *hide* of the huge prey,
And *lapp'd* his entrails, and his blood."

Of the dogs fet on by the herdfmen to attack the lions, Homer tells us

" Οι δ' ητοι δακιειν μεν απετρωπωντο λεοντων,
Ιϛαμενοι δε μαλ' εγγυς, υλακτεον, εκ τ' αλεοντο."

— — " The herdfmen ftrove
In vain, in vain their active dogs they cheer'd,
Who the grim monfters fearful to affail,
Yet, clofe-advancing, bay'd, and nimbly fhunn'd."

According

According to Cooper,

— — — " Meantime
The herdſmen troubling them in vain, their hounds
Encouraged; but no tooth for lion's fleſh
Found they, and therefore ſtood aſide and bark'd."

Pope too, deſtroys Homer's picturefque deſcription, of the fear, the ſpirit, and agility
of the dogs; for he makes them ſtand at a
diſtance, though in the original they are μαλ'
εγγυς, admodum propè.

" The dogs oft cheer'd in vain defert the prey,
Dread the grim terrors, and at diſtance bay."

Pope's is a beautiful dance; but it is not
Homer's. He is much more ſimple. The
youths and damſels firſt foot it, holding each
others hands, then dance in a circle, which
he compares to the ſwiftneſs of a potter's
wheel—laſtly in ſtrait lines, changing ſides
alternately.

This is neither expreſſed by Cooper, nor
Pope.

" Αλλοτε δ'αυ θρηξασκον επι ςιχας αλληλοισι."

" Quandoque autem rurſus diſcurrebant per ordines
invicem."

Pope,

Pope, I believe, means to render it thus, and transposes the action, placing it before the formation of the circle.

> — — " Now shape in oblique ways
> Confusedly regular, the moving maze."

Cooper says,

> " They with well-tutor'd step now nimbly ran,
> The circle, swift as when before his wheel
> Seated, the potter turns it with both hands
> For trial of its speed ; now crossing quick,
> They pass'd at once into each other's place."

Εδινεον, exerted themselves, shewed their dexterity, he translates *rolled.*

> ——— " two tumblers *rolled* themselves
> Between the dancers ; singing as they *roll'd.*"

The singing of the tumblers, Pope arbitrarily transfers to all the company.

> " And *general* songs the sprightly revels end."

From Pope's prose translation of the shield of Achilles, we may observe that he often understood his author, yet voluntarily deviated from him in his poetical version.

For instance—" The people of the town rushed upon them, carried off the oxen and sheep, and killed the shepherds."

" There might you see cruel Destiny dragging a dead soldier through the battle ; two
others

others she seized alive, one of which was mortally wounded, the other not yet hurt."

" In the middle of them a youth played on the lyre, and charmed them with his tender voice, as he *sung to the strings*, (or as he sung the song of *Linus*.")

Βασιλευς he translates, the *lord* of the field ; the heralds he stiles, his *officers*. He has likewise the following note.

" *The rustick monarch, &c.* Dacier takes this to be a piece of ground given to a hero in reward of his services. It was in no respect unworthy such a person in those days to see his harvest got in, and to overlook his reapers. It is very conformable to the manners of the antient patriarchs, such as they are described to us in the holy scriptures."

Virgil, whose judgment was at least equal to his imagination, scrupled not to charge the shield of Æneas with a greater profusion of figures, to whom was given more complex and extended action. The miraculous work was Vulcan's ; it could not, he knew, be copied by a human painter, or sculptor, so as to be rendered visible to the eye, while all was distinctly conceived by the mind, without the smallest violation of poetical propriety.

G g 3

Let

Let us turn to the Æneid, and we shall find the poet had no idea of a mechanical division into compartments. Thirty at least must have been appropriated to his description; and on a shield of four feet in diameter the figures must have been reduced " to the smallness of gnats, have been pointed sharp as needles, or melting into air." What would become of the cities, the three triumphs of Augustus, the three hundred temples, the promontories, the ocean, the various nations and people, the ships equal in size to the Cyclades or mountains? The imagination, and the imagination only is so capacious as to hold them all. The imagination has " ample room, and verge enough" on which to *trace* these *characters* of genius and sublimity.

The SHIELD of HERCULES.

From HESIOD.

THEN in his hand he took the various fhield
Ne'er pierced, or injured; wonderful to view.
With filver,* amber, and pure elephant
It fhone; and dazzled with refulgent gold.
Cærulean lines parted the diverfe fcenes.

Fix'd in it's centre was the Dragon, fierce,
Ineffable portent; his eyes afcance

G g 4

Glowing

---

* An apology ought to be made for rendering τιτανος, filver; it
properly means gypfum, a very inadequate material for a fhield;
while filver, though it feems a neceffary article, is omitted. But
we may fay, in the hands of a Deity, no fubftance would be inadequate; and a fimilar objection might be raifed to amber, and ivory.
Confidering the general refemblance of the two defcriptions, Hefiod
probably alludes to the fame material, whatever it might be, to
which Homer applies the epithet μαρμαρεην, and which compofed
the circles of his fhield; not marble perhaps, but fome cement, or
enamel, which might equal it in whitenefs, and polifh.

Glowing with fire. His mouth with snowy fangs
Replete, cruel, insatiable. Above
His dreadful front flew stern and gloomy Strife
Enkindling war ; but every heart and mind
Annihilating, which against the son
Of Jove advanced in fight. Whose souls descend
Beneath the earth to Orcus, while their bones,
The investing skin by torrid suns destroyed,
Rot on the dreary ground. Here was design'd
Onset, and there Retreat ; and Homicide,
Contention, Tumult, Rout, and Terror raged,

There a destructive Fury in her hands
Grasp'd One with wounds half-dead, and One unhurt,
Dragging Another through the ranks of fight
Deprived of life. Around her shoulders hung
A vestment grain'd in blood ; stern was her eye ;
And fierce and loud her shouts resounded. There
Twelve heads of cruel Serpents, whose aspect
Baffled description ; while the Race of Men
They struck with fear, all who the son of Jove
Oppofed in battle. When Amphitryon's Heir

Assail'd

Affail'd his Foes, they gnafh'd their favage teeth,
Dreadfully audible.˙ Thefe wond'rous works
Were all diftinct, while on the azure back
Of every Serpent, fpots, it feem'd, appear'd,
And black was every jaw.—And now a Troop
Of foreft Boars and Lions rufh'd amain,
Threatening on either fide with angry glare:
Thick, with their briftling necks they onward came,
Nor one the other dreaded. On the earth
Lay a huge Lion, and beneath him gafp'd
With necks relax'd two favage Boars in death;
Their black blood floated round, and dyed the plain
The reft with double fpirit glow'd, incenfed,
And prompt to fight, both the wild foreft Boars
And horrid Lions.—Next, appear'd to view
The Lapithæan war ; here Cæneus ftood
Great King of men, Dryas, Pirithous,
Hopleus, Exadius, Mopfus, Phalerus,
Bold Titerefius favourite fon of Mars,
And Thefeus equal to the immortal Gods :
All form'd of filver, and in arms of gold.
The Centaurs were againft them ranged ; there ftood

The

The vaft Petræus, Afbolus the Seer,
Arctus, and Hurius, and with coal-black locks
Mimas, the two Peucidæ, Dryalus,
And Perimedes; all of filver form'd,
And wielding golden pine-trees in their hands.
Each rufh'd to battle, and, as if alive,
Fought hand to hand with pine-trees and with fpears.

Amid them, prominent in gold, were feen
The winged Horfes of terrific Mars;
There too the Spoiler, the deftructive God,
High on his Car; with fhouts he urged them on,
Imbathed in blood, as he had ftripp'd the fallen
Ere they expired. Befide, Alarm, and Fear,
Eager with the conflicting Hofts to join.
There too was Ageleia, Triton-born,
Daughter of Jove, as when fhe wills to ftir
Tumultuous battle; in her hand the fpear,
The golden helmet on her aweful brow,
The Ægis on her fhoulders. On fhe moved,
And fought the thickeft ranks of cruel war.

Near

Near thefe, affembled fat the immortal Powers,
While in the midft Jove's and Latona's Son
Struck his fweet lyre ; Olympus, their high dome
The melody reechoed. There was feen
The feftive Hall, with richnefs, as a zone,
Embraced, refplendent with the wealth of Heaven ;
In which, like Virgin Bands uttering foft airs,
Pieria's Sifter Deities began
Their mazy ftrains, each vying in the fong
Of mutual harmony.—And now, a Port
Of the vaft Main, fafe, eafy of accefs,
And circularly form'd with molten tin
Refembling waves ; the Dolphins here and there
In it's mid entrance, eager for their prey
As if they fwam ; two, near the furface rifen,
Of filver mould, ingorged the finny race,
And fpouted the falt tide. Beneath, the fhoal
With brazen fcales gleam'd trembling. On the bank
A fifher fat obfervant, in his hands
A net, and bending as in act to throw.

Here fair-hair'd Danae's progeny was feen,
Steed-loving Perfeus, with his feet, the fhield

He

He neither touch'd, nor was he far removed,
Miraculously! Unsupported, framed!
Thus by the skill of sapient Vulcan wrought.
In gold he shone, and from his ancles clipp'd
The golden wings. Depending in a belt,
Which from his nervous shoulders graceful flow'd,
In it's black scabbard hung the brazen sword.
Swift was his flight as Thought.   O'er all his back
Was stretch'd the savage Monster's ample head,
Pernicious Gorgon, in a silver case
Included, wonderful to view ; beneath
Dropp'd it's sustaining thongs of lucid gold.
Around the temples of the King was placed
The helm of Orcus, shaded by the gloom
Of heaviest night.   He, flying as in fear,
Strain'd every limb.   Behind him furious rush'd
Dreadful, ineffable, the Gorgons ; sharp,
With their quick-trampling feet, and loudly, rung
The Buckler's pallid steel.   Their zones embraced
Two Serpents huge, curving aloft their necks,
Licking their teeth, and whetting them with rage,
Horribly glaring.   O'er their ghastly heads,
The mighty Terror of the Gorgon's waved.

This

This fcene above, a Battle met the eye;
Warriors in arms; thefe from their City bounds
And from their Parents, anxious to avert
Ruinous ftorm, thofe eager to deftroy.
On the firm battlements the Matrons ftood;
Shrill lamentations, like the ear-piercing brafs,
They pour'd, and tore their cheeks, as if alive;
So form'd by fkillful Vulcan.   But the Sires
Stooping with age, thick iffued from the gates,
And trembling for their Offspring, Heaven's blefs'd Powers
Invoked with fuppliant hands.   Meanwhile the Sons
Impetuous mix'd in fight; clofe on whofe rear
Hung the black Furies, ftern, and drench'd in gore,
Horrid, infatiable, their white teeth crafh'd,
And fierce they combated for thofe which fell.
For all were thirfty for the dark-red blood,
And whom they firft beheld, failing, or fallen
Recently wounded, on him ftrait they caft
Their mighty talons.   To the realms below,
To Orcus, and to frigid Tartarus,
Swift fled the Soul.   Fill'd with the reeking ftream,
Behind their backs each bloodlefs corfe they threw,

And

And to the tumult and the flaughter rufh'd
With double fpeed.   Clotho and Lachefis
Befide them ftood, and of inferior fize,
Atropos, no Gigantic Goddefs, She,
But Queen confefs'd, and of more antient birth.
All now engaged around one body flain
In bitter fight, with fierce and cruel glance,
And eye-balls red with ire, with their ftrong hands,
And talons fharp, they waged commutual war.

Befide ftood Woe, all-comfortlefs, and drear,
Pale, fhrivell'd, worn with famine to the bone,
Her knees enlarged, and her neglected nails
O'er-grown, her noftrils wet with conftant rheum ;
Upon the ground beneath, her cheeks dropp'd blood,
Inceffantly fhe gnafh'd her quivering teeth,
And on her breaft and fhoulders the thick duft
Was moiften'd with her tears.——Next rofe to view
Another tower'd City. On their pofts
Nicely fufpended, moved feven golden gates.
The jocund Habitants their bofoms cheer'd
With paftimes, and the dance. Some homeward bore

A Bride,

A Bride, confpicuous in her ftately Car,
And frequent Hymeneals fung around ;
While far and wide the blazing torches fhone,
Waved by Miniftrant hands.   In beauty's bloom
Precede fair Dames, the choral Troop purfues ;
And Youths to breathing reeds pour'd dulcet ftrains,
While Echo pleafed, replied : The Virgins trod
Their lovely mazes to the foft-toned harp.
Within the City Square to the fhrill pipe
Sported a Stripling Band, in dance, and fong,
And laughter, all employ'd, yet following ftill
Ths Minftrel's guiding ftep.   In every ftreet
Were feftive Choirs, and joy and pleafure reign'd.

Without the gates, fome, riding, urged their fteeds.
And near them Ploughmen turn'd the fertile glebe,
In decent garbs fuccinct.   A fpacious Field
Adjoin'd, thick-fet with corn ; fome labouring, reap'd,
O'er-weigh'd with copious grain, the bending reed,
As if by Ceres crown'd : While others braced
The yellow fheaves, and caft them on the floor.

With

With knives in hand, here fome unload the Vines,
And in the bafkets place, by others held,
Large clufters, white, and black, from branches wide,
Heavy with leaves, with filver tendrils deck'd.
Again, a different fet their bafkets raifed,
Near ranks of golden Vines, celeftial work !
Whofe light leaves waved, by filver poles fuftain'd :
Each to the merry pipe then danced along,
Loaded with grapes, all of the darkeft hue.
Some prefs'd, and others drank the flowing muft,
While others wreftling ftrove, or with the fift
Dealt mutual blows,—Now Hunters fill'd the fcene,
To chace the winged Hares ; two fharp-fang'd Dogs
Before them ; thefe all-eager to purfue,
And thofe to fly.—Upon the champaign ground
Horfemen appear'd, and ftarting from the goal,
For prizes, fwift contended.   In their Cars
Stood Charioteers, impelling the fleet Steeds,
Loofing their reins.   Bounding the Chariots flew,
The plain reechoed to the fervid wheels.
With ever-during conteft there they ftrove,
On either fide the victory unobtain'd,

Uncertain

Uncertain the event.   Of fize immenfe
A golden Tripod graced the middle courfe,
Their deftined meed, the God's illuftrious work.

   Encompaffing the variegated fhield
The Ocean flow'd, as if with furging waves,
On which loud clang'd Swans of high-foaring wing,
There fwimming numerous on the flood, and Fifh
Of every kind near them exulting play'd ;
E'en to the eye of Heaven's deep-thundring Sire
A Prodigy of Art, by whofe command
Vulcan the Shield thus moulded, vaft, and ftrong,
And duly polifh'd ; by the Son of Jove
Wielded with eafe.

———————————

The SHIELD of ACHILLES.

From HOMER.

INDOMITABLE brafs, tin, precious gold,
And filver, glitter'd on the flaming forge.
Then firft a Plate he fafhion'd, folid, large,
In every part with various artifice
Adorn'd ; it's verge a triple circle bound,
Of dazzling fplendour, and of pureft white,
A filver chain fufpended.   Five ftrong folds
Compofed the broad expanfe.   There, godlike works
Arofe, bright image of the mafter mind.

There he defcribed the Earth, the Heaven, the Sea,
The Sun unwearied, and the full-orb'd Moon.
There, all the ftarry Lamps which gird the fky,
The Pleiads, Hyads, and Orion's might,
The Bear, who ever fixes full on him

Her

Her radiant eye, as duly fhe revolves,
Nor bathes her blazing forehead in the main.

  Two fplendid Cities on the Shield appear'd,
In one was folemn pomp, and feftivals,
And matrimonial rites. The torches fhone,
And thro the City, from their chambers led,
Fair Nymphs proceeded ; frequent was the found
Of Hymenæal fong. Here Striplings danced
In airy circles to the mingled tune
Of pipes and harps. In every portal ftood
The admiring Matrons.——In the Forum fwarm'd
A Band of Citizens, where long debate
Arofe, the caufe of ftrife, a Townfman flain.
One, vehement, appealing to the Croud,
Affirm'd the fum difcharged ; another ftood
Adverfe, the fact impeaching. Both defired
By witneffes adduced the fuit to end.
The Multitude, as favour fway'd their minds
Clamour'd for each. The Heralds ftill'd their cries.
Seated on polifh'd ftones, the Elders form'd
A facred circle, with their hands they touch'd

The

The Heralds' fceptres, and arifing gave
Their fentence each in turn.   Amidft them lay
Two golden Talents, recompence of him
Who beft adjudged the right.——Another part,
Far different profpect, glow'd with fulgid arms.
Two Hofts befieged a City, to deftroy
And raze it to the ground, or feize it's wealth,
And equally divide, between them ftirr'd
Diffention.   But the Inhabitants to treat
Refufing, arm'd for ftratagem deep-veil'd ;
Their tender Offspring, Wives, and aged Sires
Guarded the walls ; they fallied ; at their head
Pallas and Mars, both golden, and in vefts
Of fhining gold, in beauty, armour, fize,
Confpicuous, and as Gods.   The following Train
Humbly proportion'd, and inferior framed.
When at the fpot arrived for ambufh meet,
A ford, where various Cattle flaked their thirft,
Clofe they reclined, all fheathed in dazzling brafs.
From them apart, two Spies infidious couch'd,
Marking if Sheep or Oxen fought the ftream.
Soon they appeared, two Shepherds at their fide,

Playing

Playing on reeds amufive, nought they fear'd
Of lurking guile.   Forth rufh'd the glittering Bands
To feize their plunder ; hurried on the herds,
And fnow-white flocks, and flew the Shepherd Swains.
In council, the Befiegers heard the din,
The lowing oxen, and the bleating flocks,
Then mounted their fleet fteeds, and overtook
The hoftile Throng.   Now, boldly, front to front,
They fought befide the River's verdant banks,
And with their brazen fpears dealt mutual deaths.
Difcord and Tumult in the battle raged ;
There a deftructive Fury in her hands
Grafp'd One with wounds half dead, and One unhurt,
Dragging Another thro the ranks of fight
Deprived of life.   Around her fhoulders hung
A veftment grain'd in blood.   Like living men
Join'd the thick fquadrons, fuch their bitter ftrife ;
Each with alternate victory dragg'd the Dead.

    Next he defign'd a fallow field, thrice-turn'd,
Rich, fpacious, many Ploughers on the glebe
Their yokes directing, labour'd ; when arrived

H h 3   At

At the fields diſtant edge, a goblet crown'd
With ſweeteſt wine to each their Maſter gave.
They ſtrait the plough reverting, eager ſeem'd
To reach again the border.   Black behind,
Like earth new-raiſed the furrow'd field appear'd,
Tho golden ; wondrous power of art divine.

Another field aroſe, thick-ſet with corn,
With their ſharp ſickles bend the ſturdy Hinds,
While frequent from their arms in even ranks
The yellow harveſt falls ; bracing the ſheaves
Three Labourers cloſe attended ; and behind
The Children, who their burthens ſcarcely graſp'd,
And added to the ſtore.   With ſcepter'd hand
The Monarch ſilent and exulting ſtood,
Eyeing his wealth collected ; underneath
An Oak apart, his Herald's buſy toil
Prepared the banquet, a well-fatted Ox
New-ſlain ; the Handmaids near, aſſiduous mix'd
Large ſupper for the Hinds of whiteſt flour.

There

There beauteous, laden with it's grapes, he form'd
A golden Vineyard, rich the clusters hung
Of deepest purple, silver poles sustain'd
Each branch in order'd rows.   Sable the trench,
And firmly fenced around with glittering tin.
One pathway was discern'd, by which alone
The Gatherers past to strip the teeming vines.
Virgins and Boys with innocence of heart
In frails of wicker bore the luscious fruit.
Amid them, on his soft-toned Harp, a Youth
Melodious play'd, and graceful his sweet voice
Answer'd the stricken chord.   Behind with song,
And gentle modulation, all advanced
Beating the ground in unison.—An Herd,
Spotted with gold and tin, he next design'd,
Of Oxen, rearing high their massy horns.
Lowing they rush'd to pasture from their stalls,
Where rapid mid it's numerous reeds a stream
Sonorous flow'd.   Four golden Swains attend,
Follow'd by nine swift Dogs.   While on he moved
Amid the foremost, two fierce Lions seized
A mighty Bull ; deep were his plaintive groans,

And hollow murmurs as they dragg'd him on:
Tearing his skin, the entrails wide they bared,
And drank the fable gore.   The Herdfmen ftrove
In vain, in vain their active Dogs they cheer'd,
Who the grim Monfters fearful to affail,
Yet clofe advancing bay'd, and nimbly fhunn'd.

ο

And now the art of Vulcan leads the eye
Thro beauteous woods, to paftures widely fpread,
Whiten'd with flocks ; and fhepherd huts, and fheds,
And fcatter'd fheep-cotes variegate the fcene.

A figured Dance fucceeds, the curious work
Of fkill divine ; fuch once in Crete's broad Ifle
For Ariadne Dædalus compofed.
There Youths and lovely Virgins hand in hand
Nimbly advanced, the Virgins lightly clad
In fineft linen, and around their brows
Frefh-blooming wreathes ; the Youths in gloffy vefts,
With golden fwords, in belts of filver hung.
Now undiftinguifh'd, and with well-taught feet
They fpeed the flying circle ; fo a wheel

Adapted

Adapted to his hand the Potter tries,

Proving it's fwiftnefs ; now they break the maze,

And form'd on either fide, alternate blend

The long-continued line.   Around them ftand

Spectators numerous, viewing with delight

The graceful Choir.   Two Tumblers bound between,

And bounding fing.   Now, finifhing the Shield,

He pour'd forth Ocean's mighty ftream, to beat

It's utmoft verge, and circumfcribed the Whole.

I fhall conclude with the addition of a few words relative to thofe who believe Hefiod, Homer, and Virgil had an eye to real and material Pictures, or Engravings, in the compofition of their fhields.   A repetition or two of what has been quoted before, will I hope be excufed.

The Original Shields were formed by a God, for the ufe of Demigods.   Of thefe, the Poets, or rather their Mufes, Deities likewife, and converfant with every celeftial work, give a defcription.   Then follow the Painters, or Engravers, who having never feen the firft great defigns, copy from verbal copies. As if a picture of Raphael's being defcribed to him

by

by an acute and enthufiaftic connoiffeur, an artift fhould attempt a painting, and ftile it a faithful tranfmiffion of the ideas of Raphael. The words of his friend, who had beheld and ftudied " the bright image of the mafter mind," we will fuppofe, were ftrongly ex-preffive, glowing, animated and fublime. The fubject is the fame; but we look in vain for the fpirit, the beauty, the grace, and divine air of the original.

Inftead of pluming themfelves on their in-genuity, thefe Engravers of fubjects, which, poetically defcribed, warm and elevate every bofom of fenfibility and tafte, fhould rather apologize with the Chorus of Shakefpeare in his play of Henry the Fifth.

—————   ————— " Pardon Gentles all
The flat, unraifed fpirit, that hath dared
On this unworthy fcaffold to bring forth
So great an object.   Can this Cock-pit hold
The vafty fields of France ?   Or may we cram
Into this wooden O the very cafques
That did affright the air at Agincourt ?
Piece out our imperfections with your thoughts ;
Into a thoufand parts divide one man,
For 'tis your thoughts that now muft deck our Kings."

But Shakefpeare was obliged to make ufe of the ftage and fcenes which he poffeffed ; they
offend

offend without neceffity. In the drama of
Shakefpeare, independent of the ftage, and
the actors

" With four or five moft vile and ragged foils,
Right ill difpofed, in brawl ridiculous,"

We fee

—— " The warlike Harry like himfelf
Affume the port of Mars, and at his heels
Leafh'd in like hounds, Famine, and Sword, and Fire
Crouch for employment."

So turning from imperfect, and inadequate
fketches, and engravings, we find in the language of Hefiod, Homer, and Virgil, the
different objects, reprefented with clearnefs,
energy, and propriety.

The Latin Differtation on Æneas's Shield
in the Tranflation of Virgil by Warton and
Pitt, deferves to be read. It contains many
fenfible remarks, worthy the excellent Critic
who compofed it. In that Differtation, another by Count Caylus, in the twenty-feventh
volume of the Academy of Infcriptions, which
I have not feen, is referred to. In it, as I have
been acquainted in general terms, he decides
in favour of the antiquity of Hefiod's Shield to
that of Homer. He then defcribes the latter
from Boivin's print, and *engraves* and defcribes,

fcribes, thofe of Hefiod and Virgil from the refpective Authors.

In the third volume of Warton and Pitt's Virgil, are Obfervations likewife on the Shield of *Æneas* by Whitehead, with an *Engraving* divided into fixteen compartments. Count Caylus divides his into fifteen. They are both unfortunate in their endeavours ; for the fcenes with which they occupy the whole difk of the Shield, are only a fmall portion of its contents. Virgil himfelf did not pretend to defcribe the various incidents reprefented. He calls it—" Clypei *non enarrabile* textum." For it contained, according to him, " *the Italian Hiftory, the Roman Triumphs, all the Defcendants of Afcanius, and their Battles in order as they were fought.*" He felects only a few circumftances from an immenfe number. The whole would require not only thirty compartments, as I have faid above, but even an hundred would not be too many.

The Three Poets feem to have guarded againft Painters and Engravers. Virgil, as I have juft mentioned; for how fhould he fufpect an Artift would prefume to copy that miraculous Shield, the number and variety of whofe figures, eluded his powers of verfe, and the limits of his Poem ?

In

In Homer, Vulcan before he proceeds to his tafk, declares he will make Achilles fuch arms, that all men in future fhall behold them with aftonifhment. When brought by Thetis, the Myrmidons are ftruck with terror, and dare not look on them. The Hero expreffes himfelf thus—"Thefe arms my Mother! are truly the gift of a God—fuch are the works of Heavenly Powers—*not to be accomplifhed by Mortal Man.*"

Hefiod plainly intimates that feveral parts of his defcription no man could reprefent; that they could be expreffed on a Shield by an Immortal Power alone.

For inftance—"Perfeus flies above the furface, he neither touches it, nor is he far removed—Wonderful to behold! for he refted on nothing." But this was poffible, for fo (he tells us) was he fafhioned by illuftrious Vulcan.

"The women fhriek, and tear their cheeks as if alive"—But this too (he informs us) was the work of Vulcan.

The Shield likewife, he affirms, was not only made by that Deity, but planned by Jupiter, who was himfelf aftonifhed at the execution and completion of it.

Such

Such were the Shields of thefe Poets. Having affumed their fuper-human formation, by a Deity, worfhiped at the time when they wrote, and whofe exiftence and power was undoubted, they could give a latitude to their ideas, and defcribe fcenes (inexpreffible by an Artift) without violating probability. Were any objected to, the anfwer was eafy; fo Vulcan chofe to exprefs them.

Thefe Shields therefore were religious, and poetical, fafhioned by a God, or by no lefs creative Imagination. No Sculptor could reprefent various objects which they contain, they are too complicated for his art; nor could he produce loco-motive figures, endowed with fenfe, and the utterance of founds; fix different and fluctuating images in the fame inftant of time, to one and the fame place—or exhibit fhadowy and indefinable Beings, fuch as " the Mighty Terror of the Gorgons waving over their heads." All this is the province of Poetry, not of Sculpture.

T. V.

ON THE

VALLEY of STONES,

AND THE

COUNTRY near LINTON.

T O thofe who have examined *The Valley of Stones*, it may not be unpleafant to retrace objects, with which they muft have been uncommonly ftruck ; and, to thofe, who never had that pleafure, it may not prove unentertaining to be brought acquainted with a *lufus Naturæ*, which, though extremely romantic, is but little known ; and has never yet, I believe, been defcribed.

The village of Linton is fituated on the northern coaft of the county of Devon, about twenty miles from Barnftaple, and nearly the

fame

fame diftance from Southmolton. Of its general beauties I fhall not fpeak at prefent, but confine myfelf to the *Valley*, which lies about half a mile weftward from it, and belongs to the fame parifh.

The fcenery at this fpot was of a different kind from any I had ever met with. The hills at firft floped on towards the weft, fpotted with loofe detached rocks, which in feveral parts lay fcattered about their bafes. Soon however, the fummits of the fucceeding hills, became more and more rugged, affuming the fhapes of ruined towers, obelifks, and other ftupendous and fantaftic forms. On the left, at the entrance of the Valley, afcended in a fimilar manner the craggy hills. In their commencement indeed from the rifing plain, they were lefs broken in their appearance; and at places, not inacceffible, cultivated in patches. Thefe traces of human induftry, thus obtruding themfelves into the barren valley, accord not with the wildnefs of the fcenery; and violate, as it were, the idea of folitude, which was the firft impreffion the whole fcene offered, and which the mind refigns with reluctance.

Advancing

Advancing into the Valley, the more was
seen of objects to admire. The rocky emi-
nencies impreſſed a reverential kind of awe,
their ſloping ſides often terminating in headlong precipices. I marked the variety of their
ſtupendous rugged forms, and the many fragments, which ſhivered from them through a
ſucceſſion of ages, had rolled into the narrow
plain.—Surrounded by them on all ſides, except towards the ſea at the bottom of the
Valley, (for the entrance was now concealed
by the curvature of the path) I ſeemed as if
ſecluded from ſociety by impaſſable barriers.
Silence heightened the illuſion; at times indeed interrupted by the cries of the kite and
hawk, imparting an additional wildneſs to
the ſcene.

With theſe real objects, and the images
to which they give birth, how delicious is
the tranſitory abſtraction from the cares of
mortality !

" Præſentiorem conſpicimus Deum
Per invias rupes, fera per juga,
Clivoſque præruptos."   GRAY.

At it's lower extremity, where the Valley
was wideſt, about four hundred feet, in the

very

very centre, ftopping up as it were the outlet, arofe a large bulwark, like fome gigantic building in part demolifhed.

More than half of the Valley was fhut up from the fea by it's broad bafe. Leffening by degrees, it rofe to a confiderable height, and terminated in a conical form.

While gazing on this majeftic pile, an ad-ventitious circumftance, refulting from the weather, prefented itfelf, and was productive of the fineft effect; the fky had been dark and lowering, the whole morning, attended by violent gufts of wind; the clouds now broke, and fweeping in a pitchy volume around the lower parts of the rock, terminated about two-thirds upwards, and left the more ele-vated fummit beaming with a bright ftream of funfhine. Nothing in a picturefque light could well exceed this moft beautiful appear-ance. The full force of one of the happieft images that a poet has almoft at any time ufed, at once rofe upon my mind, and I wa not more delighted with its truth, than witl the aptnefs of the comparifon, and the fweet-nefs of expreffion.

> " As fome tall cliff that lifts its awful form
> Swells from the vale, and midway leaves the ftorm,

Though

Though round its breaft the rolling clouds are fpread
Eternal funfhine fettles on its head.''

Deferted Village.

Of this mafs, my defcription will convey
but a faint notion ; for the imagination would
be at a lofs to figure to itfelf a ruder congeries
than was here beheld. Rocks piled on rocks ;
at one time in unequal and rough, layers ;
at another, tranfverfe, and diagonally inclined,
againft each other. In fhort, in every poffible
form that can be conceived ; threatening however every moment to be disjoined, and to
precipitate themfelves either into the Valley,
or beyond it, into the depth of waters.

At this fpot alfo objects were more difcriminated ; and the fcenery, comprifing the
grandeft features, at once charmed and aftonifhed the fpectator. To have juftice done
it would require the pencil of a Salvator ; for
it is in unifon with all that is fublime, and
romantic. It is the fequeftered fpot, which,
in a barbarous clime, would have been a den
for wild beafts, or the retiring place of a
banditti.

On the left fide, one rock only attracted my
notice. This projected boldly from the inclining fteep, and, thrufting itfelf forward,

oppofed

oppofed the Severn fea with its broad, perpendicular front, chequered by ivy, and
tinted with variegated mofs.

The Valley loft itfelf rapidly, on either fide
the conical mountain, in the fea. Beyond,
the cliffs rofe higher, and higher, upright from
the water; and at times being elevated above
the farm lands within, protected them from
the north wind, which, where its blafts had
been unrefifted, appeared to have checked the
harveft, and impeded the progrefs of every
kind of vegetation. The woods fcattered over
thefe parts, intermingled with the corn and
pafture grounds, though feen at a diftance, yet
formed a pleafing and ftriking contraft with
the fcenery on this fide, which had nothing
of the picturefque in it; but comprifed every
thing that was wild and magnificent.

In the central part of the Valley, which in
general was about three hundred feet broad,
were feveral circles of ftone, above forty feet
in diameter. Unlefs thefe are druidical remains, no veftige of that fuperftition is here
to be difcovered.

Without accounting for the origin of the
Valley of Stones, it appears as if a vaft collection of waters, refting on the furface of the
mountainous

mountainous country behind, had burft thro'
all oppofition, and forced it's way into the
fea, carrying with it in it's torrent every
earthy fubftance, and leaving the firmer rocks
in their prefent fhapes, mimicking the remains of antique towers, of caftles fplit
afunder, and mouldering into ruins.

The fcenery in this Valley cannot fail of exciting admiration.. But the feveral portions
of the compofition are fo various, and complicated, that they feem to mock all art, and
preclude imitation : my pencil therefore lay
untouched.

A detached rock, or a particular group
might be fketched ; yet even then, through
the fingular difpofition of the feveral parts of
the piles of ftones, and the fcattered fragments, they would be generally viewed in a
different manner; and in as many hands as
they were painted by, become as many different pictures ; " for though the vale, the
broad cliff, or the fhivered ridge, may be the
fame in all, yet will there be an effential variation where the accidental beauties, and
contingent features, are dependant on a multiplicity of adventitious circumftances, fuch as

light

light and fhade, the clouds, fituation with refpect to objects, and above all the time of
the day."

Thus to the painter—but the effect produced to the contemplative mind, and to the
admirer of the grand and romantic objects of
Nature, will, in every inftance, be the fame.
For the fenfations impreft by a furvey of fuch
retreats from the bufy world, are ever of the
moft pleafing and foothing kind, reading a
better leffon than perhaps any other fchool
can teach.

> " Hail awful fcenes ! that calm the troubled breaft
> And woo the weary to profound repofe !
> Can Paffion's wildeft uproar lay to reft
> And whifper comfort to the Man of Woes ?
> Here Innocence may wander fafe from foes
> And Contemplation foar on Seraph wings.
> O Solitude ! the Man who thee foregoes
> When Lucre lures him, or Ambition ftings,
> Shall never know the fource whence real grandeur
>   fprings."
>
> *Beattie's Minftrel.*

Having done with the Valley of Stones, let
us attend for a moment to the fcenery round
the Village of Linton.

From the Church, which is a plain unornamented building, the road defcends rapid
                                            to

to the Vallies. It is a bad Alpine way, down a mountain, all but perpendicular; making many traverses, so close, that persons advancing in the different windings, appear to be moving in the most opposite directions. From the middle of the declivity, at an angle of turning, the two rivulets, called the East and West Lin, before faintly descried, became conspicuous. They were beneath my feet, and I beheld them hurrying over many an obstructing rock, uniting before they lost themselves in the sea.

On the western side of the East Lin, the mountain descending with a sharp ridge, and declining steep and abrupt on both sides, from the Church of Countisbury, terminated in a point, just above a bridge with two arches. Beyond it, and still more eastward, the cliffs rose from the sea nearly in a perpendicular line to the height of at least three or four hundred feet, and rounding as they rose, appeared verdant and smooth, trending on for some space, till they shut out, by the intervention of a promontory called *Foreland Point*, all further land view.

On the west of these, a picturesque woodland dell appeared, glittering in its dark re-

cesses

cesses with a succession of silver water-falls, whilst a barren bleak mountain frowned above, having a channelled furrow on one of its sides, which was strongly tinted of a reddish colour, the occasional passage of a fretting torrent. The little quay rises on the western side of the rivulets, just below their junction, where are a number of decent houses. Beneath it, is a wear, marked out in the water by parallel lines of long poles, where salmon are caught, and at their particular season, herrings in great abundance.

As I returned from the beach of Linmouth, and the charming little green which borders it, the picturesque arch of a bridge over the West Lin attracted my notice. The river beneath, at one time clear as crystal, at another, foaming, and bounding over every obstacle, is, strictly speaking, a mountain stream, and realizes the faithful portrait of those drawn by the poet,

— — — " Quæ
." Saxosas inter decurrunt flumina valles."

The bridge was of a grey tint, and covered with moss ; the ivy in some parts crept on its surface, at others, hung over the stream. On
either

either fide, young trees, and brufhwood of more than common growth, encroached even on the margin of the river; and beyond (while on the right rofe a thick and beautiful wood) on the oppofite quarter, tower'd the craggy mountain, affording a moft ftriking contraft in its ftunted and fcattered fhrubs, and its ledges of rough and grotefque rock.

A more romantic and pleafingly picturefque fcene will not often be met with. Such an affemblage of unornamented nature far outvies all the laboured works of art. The eye of fimple unperverted tafte would dwell on it without fatiety, and leaving the decorated arch, and the enriched column, gaze with admiration on fuch rough unornamented objects, which the correctly-refined eye would glance over with faftidioufnefs, and which the common incurious obferver would pafs unnoticed.

Reflecting on what had been feen, I had no difficulty in forming the following opinion. That, though the Valley of Stones was a fingularly rude and uncommon fcene, poffeffing a great degree of wildnefs and fublimity, yet, when brought into comparifon with the beautiful, the picturefque, and romantic
fcenery

scenery on the eastern side of the Village of Linton, its attractions lessened; and it would, at least in the eye of the painter, be considered in a secondary light.

N. E.

OBSER-

OBSERVATIONS on LIGHT,

*Particularly on its Combination and Separation as
a chemical Principle.*

— — — — ex fumo dare lucem
Cogitat.   HORAT.

IF in the firft ftep of this enquiry, it be af_
fumed, that Light is a body confifting of
material particles of fingular tenuity, moving
with inconceivable fwiftnefs in ftrait lines, the
principle will receive fufficient fupport from the
arguments of Newton, various aftronomical
obfervations, and Dr. Bradley's very fatisfactory
explanation of the apparent aberation of the
fixed ftars. The oppofite fyftem of Euler
formerly occafioned a controverfy which has
now fubfided, and philofophers have ac_
quiefced, with few exceptions, in the opinion
of his antagonifts. We can admit, that rays

of

of light are interrupted in their progreſs by air, that they mutually impinge on, and change each others direction, for M. M. Bouguer, Sauſſure, and Thompſon, have demonſtrated that nearly one half of the light of the ſun is loſt in paſſing thro' the lower part of the atmoſphere; that its effects are proportionally diminiſhed; and that images, perceived by reflection, are clear and diſtinct, though one-third of the light is loſt by unavoidable imperfections of the mirror. The immediately ſucceſſive impulſe of luminous particles is by no means neceſſary to viſion, ſince the retina for a time retains impreſſions once received; and M. d'Arcy has computed, that the ſenſation is diſtinct, tho' each atom of light be more than 27000 miles diſtant from that which ſucceeds.—In ſhort, " a body whoſe motion we can perceive, whoſe velocity we can calculate, whoſe direction we can change, which we can accumulate and diſperſe, whoſe conſtituent parts we can ſeparate and reunite, which we can combine with, and ſeparate from other bodies, muſt be a ſubſtance peculiar and diſtinct" (Macquer).

Light probably conſiſts of atoms or particles darted from their ſource with different velocities,

cities, for to employ the term, rays, would imply rectilineal bodies, an idea adopted probably from the appearance of light, when seen to pass thro' a small aperture, and fixed in the mind, by the diagrams of optical writers, without adverting to mathematical distinctions. No phænomenon supports this idea; and, if light consisted of fasciculi of any assignable length, the objections of Euler would receive additional force, and the distance, compatible with sensation, between successive particles, must be essentially varied.

Tho' luminous particles are apparently very minute, yet from different experiments, they appear susceptible of attraction, when passing thro' transparent media, and of being diverted from their course, when passing by the edges of thin bodies. Numerous phænomena seem also to require the admission of the hypothesis, that one side of the atom is differently affected by the power of attraction, from the other, so that supposing the particle originally globular, it will be projected, after passing thro' a refracting medium, into a parallelogram, rounded by an imperfectly defined circle. The coloured spectrum in consequence of the refraction of light thro' a prism, is of this shape, and it

leads

leads to a fufpicion, that the luminous globule is xpanded only, and becomes coloured in confequence of attenuation. This fufpicion derives fome ftrength from various other facts : light, for inftance, paffing thro' air, in very minute maffes, appeared, in Sir Ifaac Newton's experiments, to be coloured ; and, when broken and divided by paffing over the edges of thin bodies, it affumes the appearance of a coloured fringe connected with the body. The colours exift only in our minds, for the light, thus divided, has no diftinct effects in its different parts, and appears, in every experiment, to be light only of different intenfities. Phofphoric bodies, when made to fhine by coloured lights, do not affume the different colours to which each is expofed ; and, when they appeared to reflect the peculiar light in Beccaria's firft experiments, it is generally fuppofed that he was deceived by an optical illufion, for no one has fince been able to repeat them, with fuccefs. In the fynthetical experiment of the coloured card, the colours confound each other, but the refult is a brownifh grey, like the atmofpheric glow ; and we are informed by painters that the union of the different primary colours is requifite

quifite to produce an imitation. The imper-
fection of colours will indeed prevent us from
being perfectly fuccefsful in the experiment,
and this argument might be admitted, if other
forcible facts could be adduced in fupport of
white being the refult, when the different colours of the fpectrum are united.

Of thofe colours into which each globule
is apparently divided, blue feems to be
light in its pureft and moft active ftate, for the
light which has formed a component part of
bodies affumes this colour: blue produces the
effect of the undivided light in vegetation, and
in deepening the colour of different woods
more perfectly than light of any other colour;
blue light will fometimes impart its own colour to phofphoric bodies, blacken luna cornea,
and give the peculiar red to the ftalks of the
fpinage;* while Mr. Wilfon's phofphorus, whofe
light was red, could not be made to affume its
diftinguifhing colour by being expofed to red
rays: the more active light of blue was effentially
requifite. In the changes, produced on acids
by the addition of light, the firft portion produces an orange, and only after a longer period, the green and the blue appear: the
progrefs

* Sennebier.

progrefs of the colours is inverted in the oppofite procefs. The blue rays produced a change in the colour of luna cornea in fifteen feconds; the red required twenty minutes; and, even after this period, the change was lefs confiderable.

Light feems to be impelled with different velocities according to its fource, and the rapidity of its feparation. The velocity and impulfe of light, from the fun, has been often calculated: its rapidity repreffes every fainter illumination, for it repreffes the feparation of light from inflammable bodies, and confequently impedes combuftion. There are fome lights vifible only in the dark, becaufe they are not expofed to this counteracting impulfe, and, are only perceived by eyes, for a time difufed to the more violent impreffions; but there are probably inftances of a feparation of light, whofe impulfe is not fufficient to penetrate the cornea, for effects, ufually the confequence of its prefence, are fometimes perceived where no illumination can be obferved. It is enough however to mention the probability of the fact, which muft be admitted with caution, as it is at prefent without any very decifive argument in its favour.

Solar

Solar light feems to dart thro' the air, with
rapidity, and, in no inftance, to combine with
the atmofphere or any other gas. We feem
to perceive light in the air, by no means air
enlightened ; for, in every inftance, illumination requires reflected or feparated light.
The fimpleft example of the latter is the light
imbibed by phofphoric bodies, and feparated
without any change in their texture, or their
chemical nature. After having been expofed to the light, they appear luminous
in the dark, for a time proportioned to
the period of their expofure. This property,
which is very extenfively diffufed, proves not
only that light is a body, but, tho' active in
its nature, compofed of parts mutually repulfive, and generally fo active in thefe repulfions, as to be projected in ftrait lines to
immenfe diftances, it may yet become latent
and quiefcent. The light, imbibed by a diamond brilliantly phofphoric, was preferved
for fix months without any diminution, by
covering it with black wax (Du Fay).

Various facts fhow that light may combine
with, become a component part, and give
new properties to bodies in confequence of a
permanent union. It blackens the oxyds of

K k   filver,

filver, of mercury and bifmuth, whitens the
fulphurated calx of antimony (Senebier);
reduces the calces of filver and of gold* ; gives
the purple colour to the juice of the murex ;
the violet to the decoctions of archil and tre-
foil ; the red fumes to the nitrous acid ; and,
when ftrong or long continued, will even deftroy the phofphorifm of phofphoric bodies.
Light will expel the vital air, from the oxygenated muriatic acid, and, in this operation,
which heat alone will not effect, and which
cold even feems to affift (Sauffure and Scni-
bier), the acid is changed in its properties and
affinities. The experiments of Sauffure, made
on the Col de Geant, with the comparative
trials of his fon at Chamouni, have placed
the conclufion beyond a doubt (Turin Tranfactions); for the expulfion of the air was
more compleat in the exact proportion of
the different intenfities of light ; nor can it
now be objected, that it does not expell vital
air from the oxygenated acid of fulphur,
fince M. Giobert has found that the manganefe is united with the acid, in the procefs,
which immediately abforbs the vital air, as
foon as it is formed (Turin Tranfactions).

In

* Scheele on air and fire.

In other inftances, light expels vital air, and gives colours and properties to the new compound. Animals, confined in obfcurity, become white from the arctic bear to the larvæ of the minuteft infeᴄt; and, when the latter are compelled to bear the light of the fun, they become brown: the tree frog alfo, brought from its dark recefs to a more enlightened habitation, changes from a dirty yellow colour to a dark green. Water, we have feen in a former effay, is not decompofed without the affiftance of light; and whatever violently attraᴄts or expels vital air from water, will produce a decompofition: light in the procefs of vegetation, and liver of fulphur, in a ftill fhorter period (Deiman Paets, &c. dans le Journal de Rozier Tom 42. P. 31), produce the fame effeᴄt.

The effeᴄts of light on plants form a more extenfive fubjeᴄt of confideration; but they will be found confiftent with the other phænomena. The direᴄtion of the flowers and leaves of plants towards the fun is well known to be the effeᴄt of light, and this property is fo univerfally diffufed thro' the whole of the vegetable kingdom, that every plant may be ftiled, with propriety, an heliotrope. The

blanching

blanching of plants is well known to be the effect of feclufion from light ; and the Abbè Teffier, by varying the experiments, has found that the green colour is owing to light acting *on* the vegetable, and its degree to be in proportion to the intenfity of the light (Memoires de l'Academie 1783). Thefe facts, connected with the obfervations of plants expiring vital air, may be thought fufficiently decifive ; but it is neceffary, from more recent experiments, to purfue the enquiry farther.

The moft modern fyftems fuppofe that water abforbed by the roots of a plant, is conveyed to the extremities of its leaves by a power, either vaguely attributed to capillary attraction, or more pointedly referred to irritability, where, by the action of light, it is decompofed. The oxygen of the water is fuppofed to be difcharged as excrementitious, and its inflammable air to be united with the plant. It is not generally known, that every vegetable will not grow in the dark ; that every plant does not breathe vital air ; that the leaves of fome are naturally white ; and that others are green in the darkeft fituations. Thefe apparent exceptions, which feem to deftroy the whole fyftem, will appear, in reality, its beft fupports,

if

if they are found to depend on the fame principle, differently varied, on the fame effects
produced by different agents. Light is indeed
the irritating principle of plants, the means
by which their circulation is carried on, for
their functions are connected more with the
ferenity of the fky, than with the temperature
(Guetard ap. Senebier Mem. Phyfico Chemi-
ques v. 2d); and, while light, by decompofing water, leffens the refiftance above, the
irritability, affumed by M. Girtanner, is as unneceffary for the continuance of the motion of
the fluids, as it is contradicted by the anatomy
of a vegetable, which feems to poffefs no veffels, but the fpiral ones, containing air only.
The change is probably produced in the leaf,
and perfected only at its margin, or its extremity, for, when blanched vegetables are reftored to the light, the green colour firft appears, in thefe parts ; and plants, which have
been for a time confined to obfcurity, contain
water in a proportion, unufually large. This
is the fimpleft view of the œconomy of
vegetables ; and, fo far as it extends, it is
compleat, for the hydrogen of the water, united
to the light, forms the rezinous fubftance,
which exifts in a fmall quantity in plants nou-

K k 3   rifhed

rifhed by water only; and M. Fourcroy alfo
found, that plants yielded oxygen in proportion to their green colour. When plants grow
in the earth, they there find the carbone of the
French chemifts, the bafis of fixed air,* which,
taken up with the water, is conveyed to the
extremities of the leaves, and adds to the
quantity of oil and rezin. The bafis of the
fixed air, uniting with the inflammable air of
the water, produces oil, which, with additional oxygen, forms a rezin (Haffenfratz An.
de Chym. xiii. 318). This new ingredient leffens the apparent quantity of oxygen,
for a part of it fometimes forms fixed air; and,
in gloomy days, when the decompofition of
water is not rapid, and, at nights, when it is
partly checked, the exhalation of vegetables
confifts of fixed air only. From the rezinous
fubftance, thus forméd, the fplendor of the
colours in the flower leaves, and the various
hues of fruits proceed. Spirit of wine fometimes diffolves the rezin, and preferves the
colour, but it is deftroyed by the fun's light,
while

---

* The principle by which different manures fertilize the
ground, is yet obfcure. The fcattered obfervations meet
however in one point; for all manures contain fixed air, or
greedily attract it.

Haffenfratz A. de Chym.

while the coloured aqueous folutions are uninjured, when joined with acids. It is moft
probable therefore, that in thefe inflances alfo,
the oxygen is expelled by light, and the rezinous fubftance deftroyed : the acid preferves
the colour, becaufe it fupplies by its own decompofition the vital air.

If light is chiefly ufeful in feparating vital
air from the decompofed water, other agents
may fometimes fupply its place. Phlogifticated and inflammable air will produce the
fame effect ; and, when we fee various plants
and moffes, particularly the poa annua and
compreffa, the plantago lanceolata, trifolium
arvenfe, cheiranthus cheiri, the lichen verti-
cillatus, and another mofs yet imperfectly defcribed, of a green colour, tho' growing in the
galleries of mines, where a ray of light does not
penetrate, we may reafonably attribute their
verdure to the gaffes, juft mentioned, which
abound in thefe regions, (De Hombolt ap. Rozier). The azote and hydrogen fupply the place,
or increafe the effects of light. In Senebier's
experiments, they fupplied its place, and M.
Ingenhouz found a little inflammable air,
joined with the vital, increafe the green colour,
when growing vegetables were confined in thefe
gaffes. The Count de Morozzo (Turin Tranf-

actions

actions 1786-7) difcovered plants in marfhy
fituations whofe leaves were covered with a
brown powder, which produced fixed and inflammable air; the leaves were of a colour
unufually deep, and thofe of the falix vimi-
nalis, which was particularly examined, were
highly inflammable. In fome inftances, the
oxygen is retained, and, in others, expired in
a new form. It is retained in many pale acid
plants, where, with the carbone, it produces
the acid: in various lichens, in the byffus
lactea, &c. it feems to be retained, and they
are found of a whitifh colour, highly inflammable. Sometimes, joining with the hydrogen, it is expired in the form of an inflammable gas, as in the flowers of the fraxinella,
many of the fungi and byffi; fometimes with
fulphur, in that of an hepatic gas. In the
cedar, the oak, the white beech, &c. the
oxygen feems to be in part retained, for what
is expired appears in the form of fixed air only,
and we find a larger proportion of oxygen in
their rezins and aftringent juices. Phlogifticated air is another form in which the oxygen is fometimes difcharged, but we are unacquainted with its bafis, except as an ingredient in animal fubftances, where it is conftantly

ftantly found, and is their diftinguifhing chemical principle. The mimofa is chiefly diftinguifhed by its phlogifticating the air, and, as it agrees with animals in this principle, fo it agrees with them alfo in poffeffing ir-ritable fibres, and in its affinity to the electric fluid. But we require a more particular know-ledge of the bafis of the azote, to explain its fource in the expiration of the mi-mofa, and a few other plants. Red leaves of plants refemble the leaves of blanched vege-tables : they are ufually the appendages of acid plants, they feem to poffefs no circulation, and afford no air, from the red points. In plants of this kind, the points of the leaves are ufually green.

We find then that, in all the various facts hitherto obferved refpecting the growth of plants, the fame principle pervades the pro-cefs, and the action of light generally feparates the oxygen, which, tho' difguifed, may be ftill traced ; and, when not difcharged, leaves diftinguifhing marks of its being retained, often of the caufe of its retention. The im-pulfe of light however penetrates farther than, at the firft view, may be fufpected. We know that it penetrates the buds of the more brightly

coloured

coloured flowers, which are found fomewhat
varied in their hues, prior to their expanfion.
M. Bonnet has obferved its effects thro' many
folds of paper ; M. Senebier has perceived
its peculiar changes thro' many ribbons, even
thro' the epidermis and bark of trees, and we
fhall find that, as it evidently penetrates the
cornea, fo its influence extends thro' the cuticle and fkin of the human body. It is remarked by the Abbe Teffier (Memoires de
l'Academe pour 1783), that potatoes, when
guarded carefully from every ray of light, mix
their roots and young branches indifcrimi-
nately ; and M. Fougeroux de Bondaroy perceived the fame confufion among the fhoots
and branches of the Indian chefnut, in a fimilar fituation. In forefts, the fuckers often pafs
laterally thro' the earth, till they reach the
open air, and feel the effects of the fun, at the
edges of the plantation, and light feemed alfo to
M. Senebier peculiarly requifite to the early
vegetation of French beans, for, when tranfmitted thro' coloured glafs, their appearance
was confiderably retarded. It is highly probable therefore, that the influence of light
reaches beyond the furface of the earth ; and,
tho' this element in its active ftate muft foon
be

be loft, yet the chemical changes which it produces, may influence the inferior ftrata. If the electrical fluid is only a more active form, or a peculiar modification of light, an eafy communication is opened for this fubtle fluid to any depth, at which water from the atmofphere can penetrate. We fee the effects of light on a fertile foil, in many inftances : the earth from deep cellars is unfit for vegetation ; the good effects of fallowing proceed in a great meafure from expofure to light ; and we fhall probably find, that this element contributes effentially to the formation of nitre. We know alfo that light is capable of combining with one of the ingredients of every rich earth, viz. aerated lime. The phofphorifm of this fubftance has been illuftrated by many chemifts in the Annales de Chymie and particularly by by M. Dolomieu (Journal de Rozier Anneé 1792): a fingular inftance of its containing light, as a component part, was obferved by M. Sennebier, who found both the calcareous earth and magnefia capable of blackening luna cornea, a property confined exclufively to inflammable fubftances and light. Nor is this circumftance peculiar to our planet, for the illumination, that remains on the moon in a

total

total eclipfe, cannot, in Mr. Herfchell's opinion, be wholly afcribed to the light, which
may reach it from the refraction of the earth's
atmofphere ; and the faint illumination of the
unenlightened part of Venus, as it does not
arife from a fatellite, according to the fame
author, is probably owing to fome phofphoric
quality of the planet, or fome luminous de-
compofitions in its atmofphere.

In thefe inftances of its combination with
the earth, there is no evidence of its expelling
vital air ; yet, in every fertile foil, this principle is fcarcely perceptible, except in the very
fmall proportion of manganefe or of lead, in
a calciform ftate, which it may contain, and,
from neither of thefe ingredients, is the earth
fuppofed to derive any advantage. From the
effects of light in another way, the foil may
be benefited, tho' probably in no very confiderable degree. It has been found by M.
M. Lavoifier, Petit, Chaptal and Dorthes, to
affift the procefs of chryftallization, and to be
effentially neceffary to that beautiful form of
chryftal, which many falts affume called af-
borefcence, from the varied ramifications. The
force, with which the minuter molecules of
falts fhoot into chryftals, is well known, often
to

to break the chemifts glaffes (Vauquelin An. de Chym. xiv. 292), and we frequently fee the fame effects from water chryftallizing into ice. The effects of froft on the ground from this caufe, have been known from the earlieft ages,* and fimilar benefit may probably refult from the chryftallization of falts in more ge-nial feafons.

Light, in decompofing water during the procefs of vegetation, becomes the falutary agent whofe influence we feel fenfibly, during the day, in our renewed fpirits and activity; the animating principle of life and health, the caufe of colour in living animals, the fource of heat from producing changes in bodies of almoft every kind. On the human frame, its effects are by no means peculiar, or un-known, tho' not yet traced with accuracy. The infant negro and native American are, we know, of a fairer hue, than their parents, and become darker, as they advance in age. Dr. Bancroft attributes this change, with great propriety, to the combination of light with their

---

" * Gelidus canis cun montibus humor
" Liquitur, et Zephyro putris fe Gleba refolvit."

GEORG. I. 44.

their reticular membrane : we have already
seen, that light can penetrate, and produce its
peculiar effects, thro' thicker coverings, than
the cuticle and skin. The distinguishing principle of animal nature, in a chemical view, is,
we have said, the azote or basis of phlogisti-
cated air, and, with inflammable air, the
azote forms volatile alkali, which exists in
every animal matter, combined with phosphoric acid. Light seems to be an ingredient
in volatile alkali, visible only on its decomposition, and phosphorus appears to contain
light in a considerable proportion, for it affords no heat when decompounded in vacuo,
and is scarcely luminous, in its acid state, when
combined with vital air. As light therefore
appears to be a component part of the two
substances peculiar to animals, we may conclude that it has a more important effect than
darkening the skin, or blackening the hair ;
and we shall immediately perceive why the
fluids of the fœtus have no phosphoric or ammoniacal salts (An. de Chym vii. 165). All
animal substances are highly phosphoric, and,
with gold and silver form exceptions to the
general rule that the best conductors of electricity do not absorb light or obstinately retain
it,

it, for metals in general, water and mineral
acids never become phofphoric (Beccaria
Comment. Bonon. 11. 96). The yolk of an
egg, when dry, is an excellent phofphórus;
the white can fcarcely, by any management,
be rendered phofphoric. The Pholades (luminous fifh) will not illuminate water, but
render milk very brilliant; and the light of
the fea, when not owing to minute infects, is
feemingly produced by the fpawn of fifh, or
putrid animal fubftances. It is obferved only,
when the water is glutinous and agitated, confequently forms no exception to the fact juft
mentioned, the difficulty of rendering water
phofphoric. The fuperior utility of ifinglafs
to every other varnifh, in preferving the brilliancy of water colours, ufually injured by the
light, may be owing to the fame property,
derived from its animal nature. Light then
feems to be an important agent in the animal
œconomy; and, when we perceive the fallow
complexions, the languid circulation, and the
cold extremities of thofe confined, where
little light enters, or none is reflected, we may
perhaps conclude, that changes, ufually attributed to confinement and want of exercife,
may in part be owing to a defect of this animating

mating principle. Girtanner found white animals and white plants, peculiarly weak and irritable.

If light however be the cause of colour in living bodies, it has a very different and opposite effect on dead animals, and on some vegetable substances. The doctrine of colours is still very obscure; and we can enlarge no farther on the subject than to connect it, with the principal position which pervades this essay, that light and oxygen mutually separate each other. In the operation of bleaching cloths, this mutual repulsion is rather between the adventitious substances, than the vegetable fibres to be whitened; for the acids employed, whether, as in the original process, it be sour milk, or in subsequent more improved methods, oil of vitriol, and oxygenated spirit of salt, differ only in the facility with which oxygen is separated from them by light. The vital air of acids is combined with the colouring matter of vegetable fibres and the compound, which is transparent, leaves their white basis unclouded. That such is the foundation of the process is evident from many circumstances, connected with its success; and we find that inflammable air, which cloth in

this

this ftate greedily attracts, deftroys the brilliancy: even foap, in frequent wafhings, is
decompounded, and the hydrogen of the alkali reftores to the flax its original hue.
All bleachers know, that the two fummer
months are more ferviceable than any other
period; and the bleachers of Beauvois have
particularly obferved, that the moft drying
winds, with a cloudy fky, are of little utility.
Indigo, without any combination, is a fugitive
colour; and experiments fhow, that its change
is owing to a feparation of oxygen: the colour
of ink depends alfo on oxygen, for its bafis
oxygenates the muriatic acid, and becomes
tranfparent; but it is not deftroyed by light,
being combined with a metallic oxyd, which
fupplies the lofs. In various experiments of
M. Senebier, on the colours of vegetable fubftances, it has been found, that when the bafis
contained a body capable of fupplying oxygen,
its hue was changed, but not deftroyed:
the brilliancy of carmine depends alfo on light,
and fo peculiarly delicate is its colour, that
a fingle cloud is fatal to the preparation. The
colour of woods is equally connected with
light, for the woods of the tropical regions are
generally dark, and their fhades are confider-

L l   ably

ably more deep, after having been expofed to an unclouded fun. (Senebier).

In animal fubftances, there is by no means fo ftriking a connection between the effects of light and the feparation of oxygen. Wax, which is an inflammable body, is certainly bleached in confequence of the feparation of part of its vital air ; and light is the principal, and, in reality, the only agent (Anali di Chimica di Brugnatelli). Wool and filk partake of the ufual principles of animal matter, azote and hydrogen : neither is particularly affected by light, except when whitened by volatile vitriolic acid. Light will then deftroy the brilliancy of thefe fubftances, by feparating the oxygen that had contributed to it, and which they had derived from the oxygenated acid. The apparent effects of light on dead animal fubftances, on colours originally derived from the fun's rays, probably depend rather on general decay, than any particular effect of light, as a chemical principle.

Light and oxygen feem in thefe various inftances, to repel each other ; but oxygen owes its elaftic form to the matter of heat, and appears to be heat, (the caloric of the French chymifts) in its leaft compounded ftate. If

therefore

therefore light feparates oxygen, in the form of vital air, it muft feparate caloric alfo ; and heat and light which have been generally confidered as the fame principle, or different modifications of one fimple element, will appear to be two diftinct and mutually repulfive fluids. Various facts fupport this opinion, and it requires no profound fagacity to difcover that the fimultaneous appearance of caloric and light, in confequence of the decompofition of bodies which contain them, is as compatible with two mutually repulfive bodies, as with the fame element in two different ftates.

Heat is diftinguifhed from light by various properties. Light paffes thro' glafs, while heat is excluded : it penetrates bodies of a peculiar ftructure, and is reflected by thofe of a different nature ; but heat unites with every fubftance, and foon attains a perfect equilibrium. The progrefs of reflected or refracted light is rapid and uniform ; that of heat variable in different media without any inflection, frequently without being reflected.* Heat, in

L l 2   every

* M. M. Lambert (Pyrometrie §. 378, &c.) and Pictet (Effai fur le Feu §. 49, &c.) found, that heat, independent of light, might be reflected and concentred in a focus ; yet they

in every inftance, promotes the liquefaction of bodies, light contributes to their affuming folid forms ; and fo diftant are the effects of light and heat, that light paffes with unimpaired power thro' plates of ice (Senebier 11. 346), and the growth of vegetables is affifted as by the fun, without any interpofition. Water checks the progrefs and feparation of heat, but neither impedes light, nor prevents the fplendor of phofphoric bodies. Heat combines with air of every kind, and forms an effential ingredient in each ; but light does not unite with atmofpheric air, and probably with no other gas.

Light, which combines with neither air hor water, when accumulated in the focus of a fpeculum, produces no heat in either. Bodies, which fuffer the light to pafs thro' their fubftance, are uninjured ; and the focus of Trudaine's large fpeculum, which would fcorify any opaque body in an inftant, had no effect on a thin tranfparent piece of glafs (Macquer). A glafs mirror, which reflects light with little lofs,

they acknowledge that the heat, accumulated, is greater if joined with light, even when the temperature of the body affording it, is lefs. On comparing however the experiments of M. Pictet §. 49 and §. 54, there is reafon to fufpect, that light, tho' not vifible, had a fhare in the event.

lofs, and heat lefs perfectly, foon grows warm, while a concave fpeculum, which reflects both equally, continues for a long time cool. Heat, when applied to manganefe and other metallic calces, feparates the phlogifticated air only; but, when combined with light, in a red heat, feparates their vital air (Berthollet and Fourcroy A. de Chym. 1. 50. 81). M. Wedgwood, junr. (Phil. Tranf. 1792) found that a blackened cylinder began to grow red in the fire in two-thirds of the time a polifhed cylinder required, fo that the reflected light leffened the heat produced; and, inverfely, the blackened cylinder ceafed to fhine proportionally fooner. Gold, filver, copper, and iron, when blackened, became luminous in the fame order, in the *inverfe* ratio of their fpecific heats.

Dr. Higgins, a chemift of confiderable reputation, confiders light and heat as the fame principle; heat as *luminous,* when thrown off with a rapid projectile motion, and *hot,* when this motion is checked or ftopped (Philofophical Converfations p. 302). Facts however fcarcely fupport his opinion, for light is retarded and arrefted in its motion, when combined with phofphoric bodies, but does not

L l 3   produce

produce heat; and, when heat is the confequence, it appears to have been feparated
from the body, inftead of having been brought
by the light, for after inflammation is begun, the exciting principle is no longer required. He obferves alfo, that, in burning
bodies, light appears, cæteris paribus, proportional to the velocity, with which the
caloric is emitted, and when emitted flowly
or where its projection is impeded, no light is
obfervable. Yet in the phofphorifm of tal-
low* and phofphorus, the combuftion is flow,
and the light is unattended by heat. He admits the laft to be a true oxygenation, and
allows, that the light, in the moft dreadfully
violent explofion of argentum fulminans,
where the projectile force muft be rapid, is
only a momentary gleam, "without any adequate effect of heat." The light, as he al-
ledges, *may* be brighteft in fubftances, from
whofe combuftion, no gas is produced for a
reafon very different from that he has affigned. If
light and heat repel each other, the light muft
be greateft when the heat is moft active; but,
in the formation of gas, heat is immediately
abforbed,

---

* The beft method of obferving the phofphorifm of tal-
low is by melting a candle over a warm coal, juft as the red
heat has difappeared.

abforbed, and its repulfive power will be lefs confpicuous. The experiment, adduced by Dr. Higgins in fupport of his pofition, where pyrophyrus which kindled in the neck of a mattrafs, filled with nitrous vapour, was not luminous in the acid below, is ftill lefs conclufive, fince conductors of electricity, among the moft powerful of which are mineral acids, do not admit of the feparation of light. To which may be added, that the pieces which fell into the acid were " of a coarfer grain and a clofer texture" than thofe which kindled in the vapour; and it is well known, that the goodnefs of the pyrophyrus which he employed, is in proportion to its lightnefs and fponginefs.

While light and heat therefore ufually appear to be antagonizing principles, they feem to be combined in inflammable bodies, by a peculiar power of attraction, and their mutual repulfion becomes only confpicuous, from decompounding the fubftance. In fome inftances, additional light feems to operate by fetting heat at liberty; in others, heat feparates light. Thus, for inftance, light only will not kindle inflammable air, and many mines are enlightened by fparks from flints

and

and fteel, which we fhall find to be in themfelves luminous only : the greateft heat without light will not inflame a mixture of vital
and inflammable air (Gadolin An de Chym.
xvii. 107); and heat only will not inflame
gunpowder, fpirit of wine, camphor, oils,
rezins, &c. In various inftances, where light
would have occafioned decompofition, the
power of attraction muft be weakened by heat,
before inflammation can begin. The violence
of the feparation feems to depend in part on
the proportion of thefe principles, and in part
on the force of attraction between them and
the other *ingredients.*

Many bodies are phofphoric in a double
fenfe : they emit light, which they have imbibed, and that which formed a component
part of the body may be alfo feparated by a
degree of heat below what is neceffary for their
inflammation. Light from decompofition is
blue, from ignition red ; the procefs in the
former inftance is flow, in the latter rapid
(Fordyce Phil. Tranf. lxvi. 506). Mr. Wedgwood, junr. in the volume formerly quoted,
hath examined the light produced by bodies
not ignited, and from bodies raifed to a red
heat by attrition. The luminous appearance of
bodies not ignited might be repeated ; but the
repetition

repetition was limited. Subftances thus rendered luminous by heat, are flowly decompofed; and this diftinction reconciles the opinions of Mr. Wilfon and Mr. Morgan. The former calls the illumination of phofphorus a flow combuftion, which is true only of thofe phofphoric bodies, which are rendered fo by heat: thefe were firft defcribed by Margraaf (Berlin Tranf. An. 1749. p. 70). Phofphoric phænomena, produced by attrition, are not of the fame kind, for, in different experiments, the fame bodies were phofphoric in different degrees. All the appearances of light, from attrition, appear to be truly phofphoric, and the heat, occafionally produced, to be a fecondary effect, for a flafh of light ufually pervades the whole fubftance (Macquer), and the light is equally obfervable under water. M. Pictet found a brilliant pyramid of fparks, ftruck from fteel by flints, had no effect on a nice thermometer: when ftruck in an exhaufted receiver, light alone is vifible, and the fteel is not fufed. When two hard fubftances were rubbed together, no heat appeared; and it was only fenfible, on attrition of hard and foft wood, when the latter was in part deftroyed, and its

caloric

caloric confequently liberated. The neceffary prefence of a body, which can afford the heat, may perhaps contribute to illuftrate a fact, obferved by Count Rumford (Phil. Tranf. An. 1781). He remarked, that a cannon was much more heated when fired with powder only, than when a ball was added. In reality, the refiftance of the ball admits of a very fmall proportion of air, till it efcapes from the gun, while the loofer wadding is diffipated with the deflagration of the firft portion of the powder fired. The air, from which the heat proceeds, is admitted in the latter inftance, before the whole charge explodes, and the heat is confequently more fenfible : in the former the little heat feparated, is immediately combined with the gaffes produced.

In a common fire, heat and light efcape at the fame time, with little violence, and feldom with any detonation. Bodies, placed within their influence imbibe both, and lofe each at different periods, without any chemical change, unlefs they contain heat or light in their compofition, or are capable of attracting them fo as to form a new compound. In the inftances of metallic oxyds and lime, heat is attracted ; in that of the common pyrophorus,

rophorus, light. Both are feparated, from inflammable fubftances in general, flowly and
without violence; but with rapidity and an
explofive impulfe, when each ingredient is at
once liberated, in an active form, with its mutually repulfive power. Gunpowder, when
heated flowly to a degree fufficient only to inflame the fulphur, without melting the nitre,
is as innocent, as the flame of a common
match; and phofphorus, when warmed fo
carefully as not to feparate its heat, allows the
light to pafs off in innocent corufcations. The
violence of each, when their heat and light are
at once liberated, is well known.

To eftablifh more fully the pofition juft
ftated, that explofions are chiefly owing to the
fimultaneous feparation and mutual repulfion
of heat and light, it is neceffary to trace light,
as a chemical principle, in various compounds, where its prefence has not been often
fufpected. The facts have been in part anticipated, for the illuftrations formerly adduced
have been felected, with a view to this conclufion.

The pneumatic chemifts have analyzed
nitre, with particular accuracy; and the gaffes,
of which it is compofed, are known to float in
every

every region, among the atmofpheric fluids. Yet nitre is the production chiefly of unclouded fkies, where the folar light can combine with it, unimpaired. We have feen that light unites with every fertile foil, and particularly with one of the fubftances preferred for the extraction of this falt, viz. the rubbifh of old houfes. The manufacturer, not contented with expofing his materials to the air, turns them often, that they may imbibe, perhaps, light more copioufly, for, in this refpect only, the plains of Languedoc and Indoftan differ from thofe of Britain. We find the light on decompofition, in the brilliant fparks which nitre produces when combined with any in-flammable body, but the light feems to be retained with obftinacy, and without an ex-citing caufe to pafs off flowly, fince the falt may be melted in a red heat, without defla-gration. The addition of inflammable matter however, gives activity to the luminous prin-ciple, and both efcape with violence. If the heat be gradually applied, without any ad-dition, it is combined with the acid, the refult of their union, and does not exert a repulfive power; but the acid is feparated in the red fuming ftate, which it acquires by being ex-posed pofed to light, and which the white acid will affume, even from the flame of a candle (Scheele ap. Crells Journal Eng. Tranf. iii. 198).

We have feen light combining with vegetable fubftances, and we may again expect it from their decompofition. Farinaceous feeds, particularly the feeds of plants, called antifcorbutic, make both phofphorus and pyrophorus (Chaptal) ; and the finer particles of meal, when forcing their way thro' an aperture from an upper chamber, exploded with great violence, in confequence of a light fixed againft the wall, at fome diftance (Count Morozzo Turin Tranf. 1786-7). When vegetable fubftances are charred, an operation in which the heat and light are partly fet at liberty, and forced again to combine, in a flighter union, with the coal, we fee them feparate, on the addition of an inferior degree of heat, with fparkling detonations ; and charred farina, with allum, forms an excellent pyrophorus. In this inftance, perhaps, the allum furnifhes the heat from the decompofition of its acid, and the clay contributes to keep the mafs from agglutinating, fince the excellence of fuch pyrophorus depends on its light, fpungy, texture.

texture. Of this kind was the pyrophorus of
Dr. Higgins.

Animal fubftances equally imbibe light and
heat, and the appearances which attend the
decompofition of their diftinguifhing principles, phofphorus and volatile alkali, contribute to illuftrate a prior union. In fome inftances, light is feparated by the animal
functions, as in fire flies and glow worms. In
the glow worm, and probably alfo in the fly,
it is feparated by a kind of excretion, and, except folar light is probably the fimpleft form
of that element (Beckerheim An. de Ch. iv.
19), for the glow worm does not injure the
airs in which it has lived. Yet this light, when
joined with inflammable air, in which heat is
in a ftill larger proportion than in vital air,
will form an explofive compound, on the addition of external heat, tho' the inflammable
air will not explode alone. Oyfter and egg-
fhells, (probably from their animal nature)
as well as calcareous earths in every other
form, contain light, which they occafionally
emit, and in fome inftances, as in Can-
ton's and Baldwin's Phofphori are capable of
exploding (Phil. Tranf. lviii. 337. Mem de
l'Acad. An. 1693). When calcareous earth is
calcined,

calcined, it is combined with heat, and the light is feparated; for, in no inftance can I difcover any phofphoric or explofive qualities in lime, except where light is alfo a part of the compofition. In Homberg's ammoniacal phofphorus (Mem. de l'Academie An. 1693), the light is afforded by the volatile alkali. This falt is difcovered to contain light, by becoming intenfely luminous in a heated crucible, and by the copious red flafhes obfervable, when it is added to the marine acid vapour. Sulphur alfo contains light, tho' in a lefs proportion, and a weak degree: it is feemingly derived from the fun, for the pyrites grow hot in the open air, previous to the fublimation of fulphur, or from the red heat, to which they are fubjected in the procefs.

Thefe are the principal ingredients in fulminating powders; and, when the fource of the light which they difplay is inveftigated, many proofs of the mutual repulfion of light and heat have occurred. But it is neceffary to examine the compofition of the different fubftances, and to trace the caufe of their explofions more particularly.

The ingredients of gunpowder are well known; and its excellence depends on their minute

minute and intimate union. The light, from
a fpark of fteel, will inflame the fulphur which
will explode with the nitre, fetting at liberty
light and heat with a violent explofion, in
each fucceffive grain of the mafs. This
explanation is by no means hypothetical, for
we know that, in the largeft charge, grains
of gunpowder explode in fucceffion, and that
light or a red heat is neceffary to the effect :
when charcoal falls into melted nitre, or
nitre into flaming fulphur, the confequence is
fimilar. The compofition only increafes the
explofion, and the intimate union of the particles admits of its beginning in the moft
minute mafs. Dr. Higgins reluctantly con-
feffes (l. c. p. 315), that charcoal does not
deflagrate in melted nitre, unlefs one of the
ingredients be red hot, however near the temperature may be to a red heat; and, in explaining ignition from a fpark (p. 319), allows that its caloric is much lefs than can be
imparted by heat.

Pulvis fulminans refembles gunpowder in its
nature and properties; the falt of tartar, a
vegetable fubftance, which feems to contain
light, fupplying the place of charcoal. It
differs in the ingredients not being intimately
united,

united, and confequently the compound muft be melted, in fome quantity, before the explofion will take place; for, if heated fuddenly, the ingredients will deflagrate feparately. In this cafe, as well as in the explofion of fulminating gold, Dr. Higgins allows, that a particle of luminous charcoal will fupply the place of more intenfe heat.

The union of oxygenated acids with alkalis, or calcareous earths, as containing both heat and light, ought, if the preceding obfervations be juft, to increafe the lift of explofive compounds. The oxygenated muriat of potafh (fixed alkali, united with oxygenated muriatic acid) will explode; oxygenated nitrat of potafh with greater certainty (Carradon An. de Chym), for the light is more copious in the latter than in the former. The French chemifts in the compofition of gunpowder, have endeavoured to fubftitute, on this account, the oxygenated falts for nitre, but as thefe falts explode in confequence of attrition, many fatal accidents, particularly that at Effone, have prevented their adopting more generally this plan. It is probable, that thefe fubftances fulminate lefs certainly from heat alone, becaufe they do not contain a large proportion of

light,

light, for M. de Sage difcovered a violently fulminating falt, in a fchorl from Vefuvius, which on examination appeared to be a cal-careous oxygenated fal ammoniac, in which the volatile alkali probably fupplied additional light.

Oxygenated muriat of potafh fulminates violently, when put into the fulphuric acid ; the explofion is repeated with a brilliant flafh, on every new agitation, and again on the application of the flame of a candle : the falt thrown out is luminous and crackles for many feconds. The explofion of nitre, when made with oxygenated acid, *is ftill more violent ;* and, on the fame principles, the *fuming* fpirit of nitre, a quality which it derives from the fun's light, explodes with effential oils. A candle, in oxygenated marine acid air, burns with an enlarged flame ; and phofphorus, as well as every other inflammable fubftance, explodes in the fame air, facts which have occafioned fome controverfy, but feem to be now well eftablifhed (Crells Annals Englifh Tranf. 1. 144. 11. 157). A mixture of phofphoric acid air and oxygen, when joined with nitrous gas, exploded with great violence (Pelletier An. de Chym).

Fulminating

Fulminating gold is known to be an oxyd of that metal, combined with volatile alkali (Scheele on air and fire 137-140), confequently containing heat and light in a confiderable proportion. But the light, which the volatile alkali contains, is greedily attracted by the gold ; and the oxygen of the calx contributes to the gafeous form of its ingredients. When therefore, the attraction of the volatile alkali for its light, is, in any degree, weakened, the latter will be attracted by the gold. The heat, thus feparated, contributes to form the gaffes, which explode with violence. This is certainly the reafon of its fulminating, for the alkali is loft, and gold reftored with its metallic fplendor. The event is inexplicable, except on the foundation explained, affifted with Scheele's remark, that a calx of gold may be reduced by light alone. The explanation, ufually given, refts on the formation of gaffes ; that, which is now offered, proceeds one ftep farther, and attempts to explain the caufe of their recovering an elaftic and active form. Sulphuric æther, which contains light in a large proportion, produces the fame effect, as the volatile alkali (Gottling Annales de Chymie xii. 106).

The

The heat, in the explosion of aurum fulminans, is inconsiderable, for it is almost immediately abforbed by the bafis of the gaffes:
in the explosion of argentum fulminans, it is
fcarcely obfervable. The latter, an oxyd of
filver, precipitated by lime water, poffeffes an
unufual proportion of caloric; but is afterwards digefted with the pureft volatile alkali
for three days in a ftrong folar light. The fulminating fubftance is therefore charged with
heat and light in confiderable proportions;
and the flighteft attrition will occafion a feparation: the explosion is dreadfully violent. In
argentum fulminans, light feems to predomi-
nate, and to be the chief agent, for attrition is
neceffary to produce the effect, to which the
heat of boiling water is unequal. Attrition,
we have feen, feparates light, that had been an
ingredient in compounds; and it will feparate
this principle from almoft every fubftance which
contains it in a large proportion, from aurum
fulminans, oxygenated muriat of potafh, and
the calcareous phofphat of Eftremadura (An.
de Chym. vii. 81).

A doubt has lately arifen, from fome ingenious experiments of Mrs. Fulhame, whether
light alone will reduce filver and gold: fhe
thinks

thinks the hydrogen of decompofed water alfo
neceffary, and feems to have fupported its
utility by ftrong facts. The additional agent
will make no effential change in the above
conclufions, and I have mentioned the obfervation only to introduce a fact from Morveau
(An. de Chym. ix. 4 and 6), which feems decifive in oppofition to her doctrine. Nitrat of
filver was reduced in *white* glafs tubes, herme-
tically fealed, when expofed to a red heat, but
remained unaltered in tubes of *green* glafs.

A lefs violent explofion, in which light
feems to have the chief fhare, occurred to Dr.
Pearfon. A combination of quick lime and
phofphorus contains both heat and light; and
the union is fo flight, that this liver of phofphorus, as he ftyles it, will explode even with
the warmth of the tongue.

Prince Rupert's Drops, Lacrymæ Batavicæ,
vel Borufficæ, for they are known by all thefe
appellations, are formed by dropping fome
green or black glafs, while melted, into cold
water. The form, which the drop of glafs
affumes, is that of a retort; and breaking the
flighteft portion of the neck, burfts the whole
in fmall pieces: when broken in vacuo, it explodes in a powder. The phænomenon re-

fembles

fembles the cracking of glafs, not annealed ;
and many of the drops will not even fuſtain
the contact of cold air. A gleam of light only,
without heat, attends the explofion. In the
formation of thefe drops, heat is certainly carried off, but the light is confined : it cannot
permeate the black glafs ; it cannot be conveyed
away by the water. This element is however
reſtored to activity by deſtroying the continuity
of the cruſt, formed by the external portion
of the glafs which is hardened by the cold
water, and its efcape feems to fcatter the
whole, in the moſt minute particles. The falt
of glafs, the fcum which rifes on the furface,
when the marine barilla is employed, if taken
from the melted metal, explodes in the air,
and is an inſtance of fulmination fimilar to
that of Prince Rupert's Drops. The alkali is
made from a marine fucus, which on diſtil-
lation affords a volatile alkali and other animal
products, confequently contains light in a large
proportion. By the continuance of heat it
might be gradually decompounded ; but when
its light is confined by the cooling of the furface, the whole mafs burſts with violence.*

The paffage of the electric fluid, from one
conductor to another, feems to be an explofion
of

* Repertory of Arts and Sciences, v. 4, p. 420.

of light only. Dr. Latham has lately fuggefted (Higgins Phil. Converf.), that it is
owing to the inflammation of the air, through
which the electricity paffes; but a fact recorded by Mr. Morgan (Phil. Tranf. lxxv.
203), feems decifively to controvert this opinion. He found the electrical fluid, in vacuo,
darting, between two contiguous wires, with
the fame brilliancy as in open air. This
fluid never appears to us, but in the form of
light, and its affinities, or its effects, are in
no inftance, thofe of heat, except when the
caloric is furnifhed by bodies decompofed or
deftroyed by the charge. Thus it fufes iron
without inflaming the fubftance around, and
deftroys animal life without expanding the
fluids or rupturing the veffels. In rarefied air,
it efcapes in harmlefs corufcations, like the
phofphoric light, and is feemingly loft in the
brilliancy; in other air, it appears alfo to
efcape in light leaving the gas it paffed thro',
inflammable. In chemical changes, it acts as
light only, kindling fubftances, which heat
alone cannot raife into a flame, and failing to
kindle thofe which light will not affect. When
refifted, it becomes luminous, and paffes thro'
bodies which, in its former, probably more

M m 4   denfe

denfe or more compounded ftate, refifted its progrefs ; and is repelled by bodies which it cannot penetrate or decompofe. Like light, the electric fluid renders phofphoric bodies luminous, and fubftances become fo in the inverfe ratio of their conducting powers (Morgan l. c.) : like light from the decompofition of bodies, it is blue, before it becomes red and white ; and is affected by the prifm, as folar light (Morgan). The electricity of the tourmalin is excited by warmth, and not repelled by water ; a circumftance, in which it agrees with the luminous appearance afforded by many bodies, which contain light. Electrical atmofpheres feem, like light, to feparate heat, for they convey or excite heat more readily and intenfely than a vacuum (Pictet § 108): probably the electric fluid itfelf may develope heat from the air, or its light may produce the fame effect. In fhort, various facts feem to fhow, that light is a copious ingredient in the compofition of electricity, perhaps the caufe of its activity, influencing very ftrongly its affinities.

If the ignis fatuus be the electrical light, or the air of marfhes illuminated by electricity, we can eafily explain why it appears to fly from the

the perfon, who attempts to purfue it, and, in one fingular inftance, recorded by Dr. Prieft-ley, feemed to follow a perfon, who came from a clofe room, where electrical experiments had been made. In the evening of a warm day, when this meteor appears, the electricity of the air is pofitive, and of the fame kind as the human body : they therefore repel each other; but the electricity of the air of a crouded room is negative (Read Phil. Tranf. 1794), oppofite to that of the body, and confequently attracted by it.

The facts, thus accumulated, appear clearly to prove the mutual repulfions, the antago-nizing powers of heat and light, and to eluci-date, often very ftrikingly, many chemical facts, many natural phænomena. Here then the proofs muft for a time reft; but I fhall beg leave to enforce them by fome meteorological phænomena and the aftronomical obfervations of Mr. Herfchel.

The heat, we feem to feel from the fun, is moft probably feparated from the earth, or from our bodies, in confequence of the in-fluence of its light; and, when feparated from ourfelves and the objects around, the warmth is equable and pleafing. But, when the fun

fhines

shines after a shower, and the heat elicited from the earth, becomes a part of the air newly formed, we then feel its influence only on ourselves, and we complain of an unpleasing heat, as from the partial warmth of a fire. Tho' the earth is cooled by evaporation, we do not feel this partial influence in the cloudy weather of summer. The vesicular vapour is warmed, and communicates the heat more gradually. On high mountains, the air is extremely cold, and the heat scorching, for no reflected heat is felt, and no vesicular vapour communicates it equably. The observations of M. Pictet materially illustrate this subject. He found a thermometer, at five feet from the earth's surface, coincide in its changes with one at seventy-five feet, only in a cloudy day, when the warmth was communicated by the vesicular vapour: they coincided too, when the thermometer near the earth was shaded from the immediate influence of the sun. The coldest part of the night was always immediately before sun-rise. These facts are only explicable on the system originally suggested by M. de Luc, that the sun is a luminous body, and the remote, not the immediate cause of heat.

These

These facts will contribute to support the opinion, which Mr. Herschel has derived from his observations, and we may safely conclude, that the sun is a luminous body, or rather opake in its substance, and luminous in consequence of an atmosphere of light. From the same source, we may probably conclude also, that light is transparent, and inelastic, for the body of the sun is visible, when the mass of surrounding light is diminished, and the spots appear to be excavations with shelving sides. Thus, even the light within our power, is transparent, and seemingly inelastic, for the flame of a candle, impelled by a blow pipe, is at its extremity transparent, and the light of the sun, collected in a focus, and thrown into the middle of an exhausted receiver, is invisible; nor can we find, in any experiment, light capable of compression, and of consequent expansion.

I may be allowed, perhaps, to suggest an opinion, not essentially different from those of M. M. De Luc. Scheele and Herschel, but more comprehensive and probably more strictly chemical. The sun we know to be a body of considerable magnitude, and of a density inconsistent with its being a mass of actual fire or light.

May

May we not fuppofe it then to be a folid, in which light is a copious ingredient, and de-compofed on the furface where it is unre-fifted, and where only the accumulation of a luminous atmofphere fets limits to a farther decompofition. This atmofphere,* from its repulfive energy, and from the centrifugal force will be conftantly paffing away, and other parts of the vaft mafs will, in turn, affume its luminous activity : an idea which will relieve the mind of the gloomy fpeculator, who fears, that the fun may decay, and the regularity of the planetary motions be difturbed. Dr. Horfley has already fhown, that, as probably fome reflected light may return, and, as it is not neceffary on the grounds ftated in the firft part of this effay, that the difcharge of light fhould be unremitted, the fun will not lofe $\frac{1}{71132}$ part of his diameter in more than one
hundred

---

* Tho' I fpeak of an atmofphere only, yet it is the atmo-fphere of a mafs, exceeding 800,000 miles in diameter, in no part probably lefs than 334 miles in depth, while in the faculæ, which may be called the fpring tides of the folar at-mofphere, it rifes more than 2000 miles (the mean of 1843 and 2765 miles, the extremes of Mr. Herchel's obferva-tions). On the contrary, two contiguous fpots vifible in 1779 to the naked eye, but not leffening the brilliancy of the folar light were together equal in length to more than 50,000 miles more than twice the circumference of the earth (Herchell).

hundred and thirty-five millions of years. Tho'
the admiffions juft mentioned be not allowed,
yet, the apprehenfion will perhaps continue
equally groundlefs. The particles, which iffue
from an inch of phofphorus, converted into
light, are too numerous for calculation; and,
if we fuppofe the fun luminous in no greater
degree, myriads of ages will pafs away, before
its diameter can be effentially leffened: in other
words, it will laft with unimpaired luftre
till that moment, when, by the Almighty
FIAT, every thing will have an end.

C. A.

ODE.

O D E.

The GENIUS of DANMONIUM.

———

WHERE reftlefs Teign, with many a furge
  Foams to his facred Logan's height,
The rockftone, at the wood's dark verge,
  Shook to the moon, array'd in light ;
When, as a cloud far off, difparting, flew,
A fhadowy form appear'd, majeftic to my view.

" Child of the duft (the Genius cried)
  To thee (no trivial boaft) 'tis giv'n,
To hear, with emulative pride,
  How Concord links the infpir'd of Heaven
Not with the Mufe's filken ties alone,
But in that Harmony which Friendfhip deems her own.

" 'Twas

" Twas Concord bade the Bards of old
    To Infpiration's numbers ftring
Their fweet-ton'd harps of burnifht gold
    By funny mount, or moffy fpring—
Bad them, where Echo loves the fylvan dell,
The Druids myftic pomp, the Hero's prowefs tell.

" The foul-fubduing ftrain was high !
    Still, ftill, it vibrates in mine ear !
I catch the holy minftrelfy
    To Devon's faery vallies dear !—
Though central oaks no more, in foreft deep,
Around the grey-ftone cirque their twilight umbrage fweep.

" Snatcht from the altars of the eaft
    I fee the fires of Danmon rife !
To mark the new-moon's folemn feaft,
    Behold, they lighten to the fkies :
And, as affembled clans in filence gaze,
The diftant Karnes draw near, and kindle to the blaze ఏ

" Faft

" Faſt by yon chaſmed hill that frowns
  Cleft by an elemental ſhock,
As aſhen foliage light embrowns
  Its rude ſide ribb'd with maſſy rock ;
Lo, on the pillar'd way the white-robe'd bands
In long proceſſion move, where proud the Cromlech ſtands.

" But ſee, where breaking thro' the gloom,
  Danmonium's warrior-genius ſpeeds
That ſcythed car, the dread of Rome !
  See, fiercer than the lightning, ſteeds
Trampling the dead, their hoofs with carnage ſtain,
Ruſh thro' the ſpear-ſtrown field, and ſnort o'er heaps of
      ſlain.

" Such was the heart-inſpiring theme
  Of bards who ſung each recent deed ;
Whether amid the mailed gleam
  Of war, they ſaw the hero bleed ;
Or, whether, in the Druid's circling fane,
They hymn'd to dreadful rites, the deep myſterious ſtrain.

" No

" No more to boast a spotless green,
  E'er long their garlands deck'd the dead;
As, fading from the sight, the scene
  Of oriental glory fled!
Then written verse for oral numbers came—
And lays of little worth were confecrate to fame,

" Then Saxon poets swept their lyres,
  But harsh was their untutor'd song:
Then Norman minstrels vaunted fires
  That ill to Phœbus' train belong—
Not that the Bard of Isca's elder'd vale
Told to the sparkling stream, an inharmonious tale.*

" Nor idly wrapt in fairy trance
  While each plume'd Edward fill'd the throne;
The daring offspring of romance
  Gave to the glens a thrilling tone;
Chaunting the wizards spell in ruin'd halls,
Castles with ivy cloath'd, and mouldering abbey-walls:

* Josephus Iscanus.

N n

" And

" And o'er the dreary waſte of years
   Devonia mark'd ſome ſcatter'd rhymes:
But ſtill, her eye ſuffuſe'd with tears,
   Wiſtful, ſhe look'd to ancient times—
Ah! few, monaſtic Tavy's banks beſide,
Few were the BROWNES that trace'd the ſilver-winding
      tide.

" And tho' of fancy and of taſte
   A *Rowe*, the firſt-begotten child,
By dark romantic woods embrace'd,
   Warbled his native carols wild,
'Twas from the lonely copſe that high o'erflung
The Tamar's haunted wave his ditty ſweet he ſung!

" Tho Gay attune'd his Dorian oat,
   Such as beſeems a ſimple ſwain,
He only pipe'd a ruſtic note
   To cheer the ſolitary plain—
Where, ſince the Bards have ſlept, hath Genius wove
His many-colour'd wreath, to grace the Muſe's grove?

                                     " Where

" Where, as in Danmon's myrtle bowers
   The race of Iran caught the flame,
Exerting their congenial powers,
   Not envious of a rival's name ;
Where now, in clofe fraternal union meet,
Spirits that court the Mufe by friendfhip doubly fweet.

" Ev'n now they live ! Ev'n here they hail
   Their reddening cliffs, in ftrains fublime ;
Embofom'd in the vermil dale,
   Nurft by the rofy-breathing clime !
Here many a letter'd minftrel, more refine'd
Than Bards of other times, difplays the ingenuous mind.

" Behold, where lingering Ifca laves
   The turrets on her floping banks,
While, far reflected by the waves
   Rife her rich elms in tufted ranks,
The wreaths of Genius and of Tafte adorn
Thofe, whom with partial fmile I greet in Devon born.

       " What

" What tho' the Bards fhall harp no more
   To wondering ears their magic lays ;
Yet fhall my chofen Tribe reftore
   The long-loft fame of other days—
Rapt with diviner energies, afpire
Ev'n to empyreal worlds and catch the feraphs fire."

He ceafe'd : And to the faultering found
   The Spirit of the Rock replied—
The old oaks bending *kifs'd* the ground
   Then wave'd their boughs with confcious pride,
While, borne on his tranflucent fhell, hoar Teign
Joy'd that ‡ two fons were his, to rival Ifca's reign.

‡ Alluding to two literary gentlemen refident near that river.

THREE

THREE SONNETS.

I. *SONNET.*

O SLEEP! and haſt thou deign'd once more around
My temples, thy refreſhing wreathe to twine,
Moiſten'd with fragrant balm, and grateful dews,
Each anxious thought in ſilken ſlumbers bound;
So oft of late dragg'd to my painful bed
By force of opiate ſpell ?—Thy gift renews
O condeſcending Power! my vigour loſt;
I ſee with joy the face of morning ſhine:
Swift in their paths again the ideas tread,
Impriſon'd long, and fetter'd as in froſt.
Hail gentle Sleep!—But I in time forbear
Thy tranquil ſoul to ruffle with my ſtrain:
Still thy ſpontaneous favours let me ſhare,
And not compell thee to my couch again.

II. SONNET.

II. SONNET.

SWEET Star of Morn! who, beaming health and joy,
And newly rifen from thy orient bed,
View'ft the calm fea of life, without alloy,
Thy foft and trembling radiance o'er it fpread
Well-pleafed, and with a bland and crifped fmile
Reflecting from its liquid face; to thee
Still unpolluted by the clouds of guile,
From envy, and tumultuous uproar free,
May its pure waves their cheerful luftre yield!
And, oh! fweet Star! ftill beaming health and joy,
May no malignant influence e'er annoy
Thy mild unfpotted rays: but through the field
Of yonder azure fky thy courfe purfue,
And bathe thy forehead in ambrofial dew.

III. SONNET.

III. SONNET.

DEEP in a gulph of liquid radiance bright
Sinks Heaven's prime Orb; and now a level flood
Of mellow gold along the horizon flows,
Skirting whose sides the vivid crimson glows,
Or where above, its scattered spots instud
The subject azure, sheds a milder light:
While high o'er all sublime, embattled rise
The dark grey clouds, and frown across the skies.
Soothed by the solemn pleasing vision, wide
My mind dilates: oh! take me by the hand,
And in yon gloomy wood, celestial Maid!
Pensive, yet calm Reflection! let me stray;
Or sit enrapt mid thy ideal Band,
Whose magic power creates internal day.

A. Y.

AN

An APOLOGY

for the

Character and Conduct of SHYLOCK.

—— Vir bonus eſt quis ?
Qui conſulta patrum, qui leges juraque ſervat.
Horat.

THE vindication of injured innocence is commonly reckoned among the ſuperior order of virtues ; and to defend a *blemiſhed character* in thoſe points where it has ſuffered unjuſt cenſure, or even to extenuate its imputed errors, muſt deſerve ſome praiſe. Juſtice would authoriſe, and humanity applaud us for reſcuing a culprit from the gallows, who merely deſerved a whipping.

Impreſſed with this idea, I lately ſtepped forward in defence of the injured Iago ; and

N n 3 impelled

impelled by the fame fentiments, will now undertake the caufe of Shylock, who has likewife met with much unmerited ill treatment; being commonly looked upon, in fubordination perhaps to Iago alone, with the moft unqualified averfion entertained for any character in Shakfpeare's Dramas—poffibly for any at this time exhibited on the Britifh ftage.

To form an impartial idea of his character and conduct, we fhould diveft ourfelves of that prejudice we have contracted againft him on account of his being a Jew—a prejudice equally unjuft and illiberal. How far it may be a misfortune to be born a Jew, is a fubject on which I am neither inclined to treat, nor competent to decide—moft affuredly it cannot be a fault. As however it is no eafy matter to lay afide prepoffeffions, that we may judge with more candour, let us reverfe the cafe; and fuppofe that Shylock, a wealthy burgefs of fome jewifh republic, had treated Antonio, an alien, a chriftian merchant, in the fame manner; had

—— " Called him mifbeliever, cut-throat dog,
And fpit upon his chriftian veft"——

Had

Had

____ " voided his rheum upon his beard,
And footed him, as you'd fpurn a ftranger cur
Over his threfhold ;"

Would Antonio, had he inftantaneoufly avenged himfelf for fuch grofs infults, have incurred any feverity of cenfure? Yet that precept of forbearance, which few Chriftians in a fimilar fituation would have complied with, is here exemplified by a Jew.

" Still have I borne it with a patient fhrug,
For fufferance is the badge of all our tribe."

It muft be allowed that *this forbearance is to be confidered* rather as political than moral. Yet, had a fimilar fentiment been uttered by the follower of the gofpel in the fame fituation, fuch as

Humbly to fuffer is a Chriftian's part,
So wills the law divine, and 1 obey—

And had his infulting enemy replied like the merchant in the play,

" I am as like to call thee dog again,
To fpit on thee again, to fpurn thee too"—

Whofe

Whofe bofom would not have melted with
compaffion for the former character, and burnt
with indignation againft his infolent oppreffor?

It may be afferted in return, that if a
Chriftian were an ufurer, as rapacious as Shylock, he would have merited the fame treatment. This argument, however, is by no
means conclufive. We ought not to try Shylock by our laws, but by thofe of the community to which he belonged. To determine
on the propriety or impropriety of his behaviour in this refpect, we muft place ourfelves
in his fituation. Ufury is generally confidered
by Chriftians as a difgraceful traffick, but not
fo by the Jews. Having been long debarred
from every other mode of improving their
temporal property, ufury has been their hereditary profeffion from the capture of Jerufalem
to the prefent time; and the *defence Shylock
makes in its favor, however inconclufive it
may appear to a chriftian moralift, will, I
doubt not, in the opinion of thofe, to whom
Stock is *terra firma*, and quarterly intereft and
dividends (" a breed from barren metal") its
living

* Act 1. Scene 3.

living produce, be unanfwerable : they will ad—
mit the full force of his obfervation, that
" thrift is bleffing, if men fteal it not." Nay
farther, the Divine permiffion to " take ufury
of a ‡ftranger," has in latter times been pretty
generally underftood by the Jews as an injunc—
tion to do fo. Men's inclinations are com—
monly admirable cafuifts in their own favor ;
and that they fhould ftrain a precept to over—
reach thofe who cruelly oppreffed them, can—
not be thought highly criminal by the moft
rigid moralift : for at the time when the moft
enlightened nations of Europe were putting
jews, infidels, and heretics to the fword, for the
glory of God, the more tolerant difciples of
Mofes

‡ Deut : xxiii. 20. Dr. Patrick, in his notes on this paffage, obferves that, " fome of the Jews would have this to
be an affirmative precept, *obliging* them to make the ufury
of a Gentile, if they lent him any money." Munfter likewife fays, " Colligunt ex hoc loco perfidi judæi argumen-
tum, quod licitè exercere poffint ufuras erga alienos. Atque
in Germania inveniuntur quam plures qui fupra modum
prætextu hujus privilegii ditefcunt." (Crit : Sac : vol. 1.
1296.) In the fame work Fagius remarks, " mirum eft
quantum hodie triumphent ac glorientur judæi, quòd ipfis
etiamnum hodie licet exercere ufuram in gentes . . . . . .
perfuafiffimi funt fibi licere quocunque modo, etiam injuf-
tiffimis rationibus, pecuniam a nobis Chriftianis extor-
quere," &c. (p. 1299) I proceed no farther ; for in the
fubfequent part of his annotation, the learned Divine exhibits much more zeal than charity.

Mofes were content to pillage the purfe, without taking the lives of thofe whom they conceived to be mifbelievers.——It is in fact no lefs
abfurd to condemn a Jew for ufury, than a
Mohammedan for polygamy.

It may be alledged likewife that Shylock
was vindictive and cruel. But thofe who condemn him for his ftern unforgiving difpofition, do not confider that he had fuffered the
moft intolerable injuries from Anthonio——that
he had been publicly infulted, been fpurned
and fpit upon by him, been deprived by his
means " of his well-won thrift," and been
robbed of his daughter and property by one
of his affociates. Who can reflect on this, and
not make great allowance for his meditating
fo fevere a retaliation! Befides, in this inftance alfo, he ought not to be tried by the
mild precepts of Chriftianity, but by the lefs
perfect laws of Mofes. " An eye for an eye,
and a tooth for a tooth," was, with his fol-
lowers, legal reparation and found morality.
This accorded with their ideas of retributive
juftice: they had a right to expect it, and
for that right could plead divine prefcription.

The

The account which Solarino gives of Shylock's diftrefs on his daughter's elopement
with Lorenzo, always excites, as was intended,
laughter. But to place this circumftance in a
fair point of view, to confider it impartially,
let us again reverfe the cafe; let us fuppofe
that a diffipated young Ifraelite ftole an only
child from a Chriftian parent, with a confiderable treafure, either acquired by his own
induftry, or derived to him through the frugality of his anceftors, together with fome
valuable memorials of former love or friendfhip. Let us fuppofe fuch a character introduced on the ftage, bewailing, in broken fen-
tences and pathetic exclamations, his lofs of
fortune, his daughter's ingratitude, and his
own defolated ftate.——" Quis talia fando tem-
peret a lachrymis?" Can we entertain the
leaft doubt, but that our hearts would fympathife with the injured father, and fecretly wifh
that fome fignal punifhment might be inflicted on the unnatural daughter, and her
abandoned feducer? The fame ideas as thofe
which Shakfpeare attributes to Shylock, and
he certainly did not mean to intereft us in his
favour, with little alteration, with a few tender
expreffions,

expreffions interfperfed, would in all probability have that effect. It is incredible how much the manner of a difcourfe affects us more than the matter; and how much lefs things depend on themfelves, than on the mode in which they are related! Of this I fhall endeavour to produce an inftance, and it is not irrelevant to the fubject, by giving in other words, the fcene betwixt Shylock and Tubal; a fcene, that never fails in the reprefentation to excite a mixture of mirth and indignation, at the expence of thefe unpopular characters.

Let us however, if poffible, drop the idea of Shylock and Tubal, and imagine that we are looking over a domeftic tragedy, in which a parfimonious, fevere, but affectionate parent, is deprived of his daughter in the fame manner. Let us read the fcene, as it might have been written, if not ludicroufly intended—I do not prefume to fay as Shakfpeare would have written it. One or two of the original ideas have received a little variation, but none are fuppreffed, nor any addition but of the flighteft kind made, except the two lines marked with inverted commas : they are taken from a fpeech of Shylock's to Antonio in the

firft

firſt act, who does not diſavow, but rather
*exults in the charge.—For obvious reaſons, let
us now for a while expunge theſe characters
from our memory, and ſuppoſe the interlo-
cutors to be two*reſpectable Venetian merchants, Alberto and Spinoſa.

Al. ‡Spinoſa here! what news from Genoa?
Say, haſt thou found my daughter?

Spi. —— —— Oft I came
Where Rumour ſpoke of her; but ſhe eluded
My ſtrict purſuit.

Al. —— —— Oh wretched that I am!
(Reduced in hoary age to indigence)
The precious caſket that ſhe bore away
Contained unvalued wealth—one ſingle gem
Coſt her fond father full two thouſand ducats.
Surely till now our frugal race hath lived
Exempt from heavenly wrath! on me alone
Lights every ill—Oh, were ſhe at my foot
Dead, and the glittering miſchief in her hearſe!
My wealth, by painful induſtry acquired
Is loſt, the thief who riots in my ſpoils

Unfound,

* Act 1. Scene 3.   ‡ Act 3. Scene 1.

Unfound, and added fums vainly expended
In fearch of thofe the traitors bore away.
No gleam of comfort to confole my heart!
No vengeance to appeafe my wounded fpirit!
On me, on me alone Misfortune pours
The cup of woe—I figh, I weep alone!

Spi. Deem not that mifery is thine alone.
Grimaldi, as I heard in Genoa,

Al. Ha, fay'ft thou friend! has he, has he too fuffered?

Spi. A fhip of his, with all its precious ftores,
Was lately whelmed beneath the furging main.

Al. For this I thank thee, heaven! " the haughty foe,
Who in the wanton infolence of power,
Would fpurn me like a dog, and fpit upon me,
Feels Fortune's fad reverfe"—I thank thee, heaven!
But art thou fure?

Spi. —— —— Some failors, who efcaped
The wreck, informed me of it.

Al. —— —— Thanks, my friend!
This is a cheering cordial to my foul—
In Genoa heard'ft thou this?

Spi.

Spi. —— —— E'en there, in Genoa:
Where thy falfe daughter, fuch was the report,
Lavifh as falfe, expended of thy ftores,
Within a fingle night one hundred ducats.

Al. Thou plant'ft a dagger in my breaft—Alas,
Within how fhort a time the hard-earned thrift
Of years, to be reftored no more, is fled !

Spi. Have comfort—many of Grimaldi's creditors
Embarked with me at Genoa, and are now
In Venice, all convinced that thy proud foe
Is bankrupt in his fortunes.

Al. —— —— My grieved foul
Revives, and gladdens at the hopes of vengeance.

Spi. One fhewed me a bright fapphire : by your daughter
Moft idly bartered for an Indian bird
Of gorgeous plumage.

Al. —— —— How thou riveft my foul
With torture ! Oh ! ungrateful child ! that gem
Was once Æmilia's : in my youthful days,
When firft fhe liftned to my vows, a pledge
Of her affection. I would not have parted

                                    With

With that dear monument for all the birds
Of splendid plume that India's groves contain.

Spi. Despond not ; for the wretch thy soul abhors
Is now more fallen than thou art.

Al. —— —— True, my friend !
If he fulfill not his engagement with me,
My high-wrought rage shall tear the bleeding heart
From his perfidious breast.   Away, Spinosa !
And bid the officers of justice seize him,
Soon as his bond is forfeit :—thro' his means
Oft have my dues, my equitable claims,
Been shamefully evaded.   He no more,——
Fortune again may crown my industry.
Away, and execute thy friend's request,
Then meet me in the square.—Away, Spinosa !

Notwithstanding the homeliness of the garb
in which the father's sentiments are cloathed,
I do not conceive that any reader, impressed
with the idea of his being a Christian and a
man of integrity, would smile at his intempe-
rate passion, or allow that his wrongs did not
greatly palliate the severity of his intended

vengeance.

vengeance. And yet many arguments that might be urged in favor of the Jew, ftrongly militate againft the Chriftian. The former, under the idea of ftrict retribution, acts in conformity to the Mofaic law, the other violates one of the'moft pofitive precepts of the gofpel. Shylock's feelings are certainly neither laudable, nor confonant to the purity of *our* religion; yet they are not unnatural to any one in *his* fituation. He does not appear, knowingly, to violate any divine or human law, but boldly avows, in confcious integrity, before a Court of Judicature, that " he dreads no judgment doing no wrong."

We are in general fufficiently candid with regard to the civil or religious prejudices of dramatic characters. When a Cato or a Brutus ftabs himfelf, we allow for the manners and opinions of the times; for the imperfect ftate of morality when they exifted : we even applaud their unwarrantable conduct; we fympathife with *their* diftreffes, and yet we exult over thofe of Shylock. But if we reafoned impartially, we fhould no more condemn a Jew for ufury and revenge, than a Greek or a Roman for fuicide, a crime, according to Chriftian precepts, of a much deeper dye.

We

We commiſerate Cato in ſpite of his ſtoic pride and invincible obſtinacy. We love Brutus notwithſtanding his ingratitude. But in Shylock, the inſulted and injured old man, the deceived and plundered father make not the leaſt impreſſion on us. Nay, ſo engroſſed are our minds with the deteſtation of him, that no one who peruſes, or ſees the " Mer-chant of Venice" repreſented, ever conceives an unfavourable opinion of the undutiful Jeſ-ſica, or the prodigal Lorenzo.—And why? be-cauſe the perſon whom he robs of his wealth, and of his daughter, is a JEW. A moſt ex-quiſite reaſon! on the ſame admirable prin-ciple he is ſuppoſed to have been perſecuted by Antonio, who " diſgraced him, hindered him of half a million, laught at his loſſes, mocked his gains, ſcorned his nation, thwarted his bargains, cooled his friends, heated his enemies, and for what reaſon? becauſe *he was a Jew*. But hath not a Jew eyes? hath not a Jew hands, organs, dimenſions, ſenſes, affec-tions, paſſions? Is he not fed with the ſame food, hurt with the ſame weapons, ſubject to the ſame diſeaſes, healed by the ſame means,

warmed

warmed and cooled by the same summer and winter as a Christian* is?"

Were any of Shylock's countrymen poets, I am convinced they would represent him in a very different light, and indeed a much fairer one, than that in which he appears to us. They would most probably convert his story into a deep tragedy, and by giving it a different catastrophe, softning some harsh expressions, and introducing others of a pathetic kind, interest every sentimental and tender-hearted descendant of Abraham in his favor.

Let us, and the supposition will cost nothing, conceive the Jews to be again settled in their former territories, or any where else you please; dramatic entertainments to be a fashionable amusement, and the story of Shylock brought forward on their theatre. In such a case it might be easily imagined that some Jewish stage-enamoured critic, a correspondent of the Jebusite Morning Post, or the Jerusalem Daily Advertiser, would communicate his opinion in terms not unlike the following.

" On the fourth day of the first week in the month Nisan was represented the tragedy of " Shylock," written by Nathan Ben Boaz. The

---

* Act 3. Scene 1.

The plot is borrowed from an old Britifh bard,
who flourifhed about the beginning of the
17th century of their æra; and who compofed it under the influence of the fpirit of
inveterate malice againft our nation, for which,
in that and many preceding ages, the Europeans were notorious. The fcene is laid in
Venice. Shylock, the hero of the drama, is
reprefented as an exemplary follower of the
law, and as having acquired a confiderable
property by adhering to that precept, which
enjoins lending to the ftranger upon ufury. He
excites, a cafe too common in thofe days, the
envy and hatred of the Chriftians among
whom he dwells. He is more particularly injured and infulted by a Merchant, named
Antonio, and meditates a plan of retaliation,
which he purfues with addrefs, perfeverance,
and refolution. He carries, indeed, his refentment fo far, that fome perfons of weak
minds and tender difpofitions, particularly feveral of the fair fex, who did not properly reflect on his various and complicated fufferings,
looked upon him at firft as rather too violent
and obdurate. Thofe, however, who poffeffed a ftronger underftanding, and liftned
with deep attention to the ftory, neither won-

dered

dered at his warmth, nor cenfured his inflexibility, for he is not only grievoufly wronged by the Merchant, but his only child, the daughter of his bofom, whom he moft dearly loved, is ftolen from him, together with an immenfe treafure, by a young profligate companion of the Merchant, and, like him, a fcoffer at our law and our religion. When Shylock complains of this double robbery, he is * ridiculed by his other libertine affociates, and derided by the city at large. Thefe fcenes, in which the father's different fenfations are delineated, his rage, grief, paternal tendernefs and indignation, are peculiarly interefting, and produced repeated plaudits from the audience. We muft conclude that he would have funk under thofe diftreffes, but for the confolation he received from Antonio's having forfeited his bond; which was, to repay Shylock 3000 ducats within a limited time, or to allow him, in cafe of failure, to cut off a pound of flefh neareft his heart. The money not being repaid at the time appointed, Shylock expects to obtain a fignal and glorious revenge on his own and his people's enemy; to fhew the world an example, that a

son

---

* Vide Act 2. Scene 9. and Act 3. Scene 1.

son of Abraham was not to be wronged and trampled on with impunity. His firmness and patriotic sentiments on this occasion deserve the higheſt commendation. His reſent-ment, though ſevere, is juſt : he had endured irreparable wrongs, and had a right to expect the moſt exemplary vengeance for their atonement. The law, however, on which he founds his claim, is evaded by ſhameful ſophiſtry. Shylock is permitted to take the pound of fleſh, but is warned at the ſame time, that if he ſheds " one drop of Chriſtian blood in cutting it, his lands and goods are confiſcate to the ſtate, by the laws of * Venice." But how can we ſuppoſe its legiſlators could have foreſeen and obviated the fulfilling of ſo ſingular a contract as that between the Merchant and Shylock ? that, in their great wiſdom, they ſhould enact a decree, by which a man is allowed to take his creditor's forfeiture, yet puniſhed for not performing an impoſſibility in taking it ? can we imagine that Shylock's notary could have drawn, or himſelf have ſigned a bond, that *fairly* admitted ſuch an interpretation, or incurred ſuch a penalty ?

yet

* Act 4. Scene 1.

yet on this abſurd, perverted, conſtruction of
a plain contract is Shylock condemned!

" Another quibble of equal weight is urged
againſt him ; that having a right to cut from
the merchant's breaſt a pound of fleſh, and a
pound *only*, if he took more or leſs than that—
even the minuteſt particle—he ſhould ſuffer
death ; as if the ſpirit of the bond did not
clearly imply that he was limited to take no
more than a pound! Shylock is found
guilty of death by this curious expoſition of
the Venetian laws ; but Antonio, not ſatisfied
unleſs inſult was added to injuſtice, requeſts
the Duke that his life might be ſpared, if
he would make *over his* remaining fortune to
his unnatural daughter and profligate ſon-
in-law, now reduced to penury by their extravagance ; with this trifling addition, that he
renounce his faith, and embrace Chriſtianity.
Theſe conditions he complies with in the
Britiſh drama ; but at the inhuman propoſal
mentioned above, not an eye was to be ſeen
unmoiſtened with tears in our theatre. The
ſenſations of the audience correſponded with
thoſe of Shylock, which were indeed ſuch as
could only have juſtice done them by the maſ-
terly pen of Nathan Ben Boaz."

It

" It may not be unworthy notice that fuch a character as Shylock's, in the fame fituation as here reprefented, from the addrefs of the Chriftian poet, and the prepoffeffion of the audience, never appeared on the Englifh ftage but as an object of abhorrence, inftead of that commiferation which was fo generally excited by this performance. It appears, likewife, on examining Shakfpeare's numerous commentators, and other records of the times, that no cenfure was ever caft, no unfavorable fentiment entertained of the unjuft judge, the injurious merchant, the undutiful daughter, and prodigal lover. Nay, 'tis recorded that the following profligate fpeech of the latter has not unfrequently been received with applaufe, never with difapprobation, on the Britifh ftage.

> —— " She hath directed,
> How I fhall take her from her father's houfe;
> What gold and jewels fhe is furnifhed with;
> What Page's fuit fhe hath in readinefs.
> If e'er the Jew her father come to heaven,
> It will be for his gentle daughter's fake :
> And never dare misfortune crofs her feet,
> Unlefs fhe doth it under this excufe,——
> That fhe is iffue to a faithlefs * Jew."

" By

* Act 2. Scene 4.

" By this extraordinary declaration we are first to underſtand, that robbery, ingratitude, and a want of filial affection towards a Jewiſh parent, are ſuch ſupererogatóry virtues in a daughter, as will not only atone for her own faults, but moſt probably for his alſo, and en‐ title him to a happy immortality. In the ſe‐ cond place we learn, that the ſame *meritorious demerits* (if I may ſo denominate them) will even preſerve her from the common calami‐ ties and caſualties of life, unleſs the untoward circumſtance of her *faithleſs father's* being de‐ ſcended from ' the father of the faithful' ſhould counteract their effect. What an idea does this give of the Engliſh nation when ſuch ſentiments could be applauded ! What a ſtri‐ king inſtance does it afford of the lax ſtate of morality, and the dominion of religious pre‐ judices in the darker ages !

" The ſudden yet natural death of the ma‐ levolent merchant, is well imagined. The turbulent frenzy of the judge, brought on by the recollection of his corrupt deciſion, and the tender melancholy of the daughter, who bewails her miſconduct too late, are equally affecting and demonſtrate the author's perfect knowledge of the human heart. The moral
fenſe

fenfe may be awhile fuppreffed or perverted, but confcience fome time or other, will refume its dominion, and feverely punifh the violators of her laws."

T. O.

F I N I S.

E R R A T A.

Page 81, line 14, *for* iflands *read* ifland.—96, l. 6, *f.* Ægyphus *r.* Ægyptus}—99, l. 4, and paffim *f.* Cadonim *r.* Cadmonim.—120, l. 24, f. μϣ r. μοι.—ib. l. 26, f. αιγ r. αιμ.—ib. ib. f. ϲο r. ϲοι.—141, l. 16, *f.* Fueberville *r.* Tuberville.—156, l. 15, f. Γιγεται r. Γινται.—ib. 18, *f.* fhare *r.* fhun.—163, l. 13, *f.* no *r.* one.—202, l. 17, *f.* ; that the Iris *r.* , the Iris.—212, l. 13, *f.* the Dog *r.* a Dog.—214, l. 4, *f.* is *r.* are.—249, l. 5, *f.* irradicates *r.* irradiates.—288, l. 18, *f.* diftinguifhing *r.* difguifing. —306, l. 8, f. εϲι τανουτων r. εϲτι θανουτων.—310, l. lait, *f.* any *r.* only.—315, l. 10, *f.* recapitulation *r.* reciprocation.—316, l. 4, *f.* of *r.* to.—329, l. 19, *f.* inclinations *r.* intimations.—353, l. 24, *f.* obvious *r.* fpecious.—385, l. 12, after attraction, dele the comma.—415, l. 19, *f.* rigour *r.* vigour.—410, l. 7, *f.* judical *r.* judicial.—434, l. 7 and 19, in fome copies, dele 9. - 437, l. 6, f. ϲπιιχες r. ϲπιιιχες.—438, l. 7, &c. place " Homer" before " Virgil;" " Æfchylus" before " Sophocles." 439 l. 4. in fome copies dele 9.—493, l. 8, *f.* fafculi *r.* fafciculi.—546, l. 12, *f.* overflung *r.* overhung.

WS - #0019 - 310523 - C0 - 229/152/34 - PB - 9780371794272 - Gloss Lamination